Justice for Atrocities

This book examines how national and international regional courts in Europe and Latin America address justice for serious human rights violations, comparing approaches across these distinct regions. It analyzes judicial responses to gross violations of international human rights law and humanitarian law—including genocide, crimes against humanity, and war crimes—through the lens of regional institutional frameworks.

The comparative analysis explores decades of significant case law addressing atrocities such as murder, torture, sexual offenses, and enforced disappearances in both conflict and peacetime settings. The book contrasts Europe's experience with mass atrocities during the World Wars, Balkan conflicts of the 1990s, and recent violations in the Caucasus and Ukraine, against Latin America's widespread abuses under dictatorial regimes and internal armed conflicts in countries like Argentina, Brazil, Chile, Colombia, Guatemala, and Peru during the latter decades of the 20th century.

This volume is essential reading for legal scholars, human rights practitioners, judges, prosecutors, defense attorneys, and policymakers working in international criminal justice. It also serves as a valuable resource for graduate students and researchers in law, political science, international relations, and peace and conflict studies who focus on accountability mechanisms for serious human rights violations across different regional contexts.

The chapters in this book were originally published as a special issue of *The International Journal of Human Rights.*

Marco Longobardo is Reader in International Law at the University of Westminster, UK. He undertook his doctoral studies at the Sapienza University of Rome, Italy. He is the author of *The Use of Armed Force in Occupied Territory* (2018), for which he was awarded the 2021 Paul Reuter Prize. For his scholarship on general international law, the law of occupation, peace and security, and the protection of community interests, he has received prizes from the American Society of International Law, the Asian Society of International Law, and the Italian Society of International and EU Law. He is the Reviews Editor of the *Journal of International Humanitarian Legal Studies* and a member of the advisory boards of the *International Community Law Review* and the *Journal du Droit Transnational.*

Juan-Pablo Perez-Leon-Acevedo is currently pursuing a second doctoral degree of DPhil in Law at the University of Oxford, UK. He is also a tutor in international law and tort law at the University of Oxford as well as a tutor in the Stanford in Oxford program. He holds a PhD from Abo Akademi University, Finland, an LLM from Columbia University, USA, and an LLB from the Pontifical Catholic University of Peru. He has also served in different capacities at, inter alia, the International Criminal Court, the International Criminal Tribunal for the Former Yugoslavia, the United Nations, the University of Oslo, etc.

Justice for Atrocities

Dialogues and Encounters between Latin America and Europe

Edited by
Marco Longobardo and Juan-Pablo Perez-Leon-Acevedo

Routledge
Taylor & Francis Group
LONDON AND NEW YORK

First published 2026
by Routledge
4 Park Square, Milton Park, Abingdon, Oxon OX14 4RN

and by Routledge
605 Third Avenue, New York, NY 10158

Routledge is an imprint of the Taylor & Francis Group, an informa business

British Library Cataloguing in Publication Data
A catalogue record for this book is available from the British Library

ISBN13: 978-1-041-15237-8 (hbk)
ISBN13: 978-1-041-15239-2 (pbk)
ISBN13: 978-1-003-67843-4 (ebk)

DOI: 10.4324/9781003678434

Typeset in Minion Pro
by Newgen Publishing UK

Publisher's Note
The publisher accepts responsibility for any inconsistencies that may have arisen during the conversion of this book from journal articles to book chapters, namely the inclusion of journal terminology.

Contents

Citation Information

The chapters in this book were originally published in *The International Journal of Human Rights*, volume 29, issues 4 (2025). When citing this material, please use the original page numbering for each article, as follows:

Introduction

Justice for atrocities: dialogues and encounters between Latin America and Europe. Introduction to the special issue
Marco Longobardo and Juan-Pablo Perez-Leon-Acevedo
The International Journal of Human Rights, volume 29, issue 4 (2025), pp. 625–631

Chapter 1

Leadership responsibility in non-state criminal organisations. The rediscovery of indirect perpetration through an organisation by Latin American courts and the ICC
Harmen van der Wilt
The International Journal of Human Rights, volume 29, issue 4 (2025), pp. 632–649

Chapter 2

The role of Criminal Justice in dealing with past atrocities in the Spanish and Argentine transitions: common grounds, but different pathways
Elena Maculan
The International Journal of Human Rights, volume 29, issue 4 (2025), pp. 650–671

Chapter 3

The ping-pong strategy: confronting atrocities from the exile
Valeria Vegh Weis
The International Journal of Human Rights, volume 29, issue 4 (2025), pp. 672–690

Chapter 4

Impunity in cases of serious human rights violations: three relevant aspects of contention in the jurisprudence of the Inter-American Court of Human Rights
Harold Bertot Triana and Elena C. Díaz Galán
The International Journal of Human Rights, volume 29, issue 4 (2025), pp. 691–712

Chapter 5

Access to justice for atrocities in the comparison of land-mark cases on state immunity in Brazil and Italy
Marco Longobardo and Federica Violi
The International Journal of Human Rights, volume 29, issue 4 (2025), pp. 713–735

Chapter 6

Comparing universal jurisdiction in Europe and in Latin America: a vehicle for international justice or for colonial reckoning?
Alexandra Fowler
The International Journal of Human Rights, volume 29, issue 4 (2025), pp. 736–757

Chapter 7

The intercontinental dialogue on enforced disappearances: the case of massive disappearances during hostilities
Ioanna Pervou
The International Journal of Human Rights, volume 29, issue 4 (2025), pp. 758–771

Notes on Contributors

Harold Bertot Triana, Professor of Public International Law and Director of the International Relations Degree, Universidad Internacional de la Empresa (UNIE), Madrid, Spain. He holds a PhD in International Law. He completed postgraduate studies in diplomacy and international relations and in constitutional law.

Elena C. Díaz Galán, Professor of Public International Law and International Relations. Coordinator of the International Relations Degree, University Rey Juan Carlos, Madrid, Spain. She holds a PhD in International Law. Her research focuses on the sustainable development, international organizations and institutions, human rights and international peace and security.

Alexandra Fowler obtained her Doctorate in Juridical Science from the University of Sydney, Australia, in 2018. She is a specialist in international humanitarian law, international criminal law and human rights law, and teaches and researches in these fields. Before academia, she served as an Australian diplomatic officer with several postings overseas including to United Nations specialist missions.

Marco Longobardo is a Reader in International Law at the University of Westminster, London, UK. He undertook his doctoral studies at the Sapienza University of Rome, Italy. He is the author of *The Use of Armed Force in Occupied Territory* (2018), for which he was awarded the 2021 Paul Reuter Prize. For his scholarship on general international law, the law of occupation, peace and security, and the protection of community interests, he has received prizes from the American Society of International Law, the Asian Society of International Law, and the Italian Society of International and EU Law. He is the Reviews Editor of the *Journal of International Humanitarian Legal Studies* and a member of the advisory boards of the *International Community Law Review* and the *Journal du Droit Transnational*.

Elena Maculan, Professor (Profesora Titular de Universidad) of Criminal Law at UNED, Madrid, Spain. Previously, she was Post-doc Research Fellow at the same university and Lecturer at the University of Trento, Italy. She holds a PhD in Comparative and European Legal Studies from the University of Trento and in Peace and International Security from UNED under a co-tutelage regime with the label of Doctor Europaeus and the Extraordinary Prize for PhD fellows of both universities. She has published extensively in her main research fields, which are international criminal law, transitional justice, restorative justice, terrorism and comparative criminal law.

Juan-Pablo Perez-Leon-Acevedo is currently pursuing a second doctoral degree: the DPhil in Law at the University of Oxford, UK. He is also a tutor in international law and tort law at the University of Oxford as well as a tutor in the Stanford in Oxford program. He holds a PhD from Åbo Akademi University, Finland, an LLM from Columbia University, USA, and an LLB from the Pontifical Catholic University of Peru. He also served in different capacities at, inter alia, the International Criminal Court, the International Criminal Tribunal for the Former Yugoslavia, the United Nations, Oslo University, Norway, and Jyvaskyla University, Finland.

Ioanna Pervou is Assistant Professor (elected) in Public International Law at the Law Faculty of Democritus University of Thrace, Greece. She was also nominated by the Hellenic Branch of the International Law Association as a representative to the ILA Committee on Global Health Law and appointed as a Visiting Fellow at LSE Health with a specialization in Health Law (2023–2025).

Harmen van der Wilt is Former Chair of International Criminal Law, University of Amsterdam, the Netherlands, and Emeritus Professor since 2022.

Valeria Vegh Weis, LLM, PhD, is a senior researcher at the University of Konstanz, Germany, where she studies the role of human rights and victims' organizations in combating state crimes. In her native Argentina, Dr. Vegh Weis is an associate professor at the University Law School of Madres de Plaza de Mayo and a faculty member at the University Law School of Buenos Aires (UBA). She holds a PhD in Law and an LLM in Criminal Law from UBA and an LLM in International Legal Studies from New York University. She has received several grants from prestigious institutions, including the Fulbright Commission and the Alexander von Humboldt Foundation. Her first book, *Marxism and Criminology: A History of Criminal Selectivity* (2017, 2018, republished in Spanish, 2024) was awarded the Choice Award by the American Library Association and the Outstanding Book Award by the Academy of Criminal Justice Sciences. She is also co-author of *Lawfare: The Criminalisation of Democratic Politics in the Global South* with Raúl Zaffaroni and Cristina Caamaño (2020, Portuguese 2021, English 2023) and book editor of *Criminalisation of Activism* (Routledge, 2021). She has published dozens of peer-reviewed articles and book chapters on the critical examination of power dynamics within criminal justice systems, with a focus on crimes of the powerful, green criminology and bottom-up resistance strategies, in the fields of state crime criminology, green criminology, transitional justice and criminal law. She has fifteen years of experience working in criminal courts and international organizations and is the winner of the American Society of Criminology DCCSJ Critical Criminology of the Year Award (2021).

Federica Violi is Associate Professor in International Law at Erasmus School of Law, Erasmus University Rotterdam, the Netherlands. Dr. Violi received her PhD in international law from the University of Milan La Statale, Italy, with a thesis on land grabbing and permanent sovereignty over natural resources. She has been a visiting researcher at the Max Planck Institute for Comparative Public Law and International Law in Heidelberg, Germany, and at the Columbia Center on Sustainable Investment in New York, USA. Her research focuses mostly in the areas of international economic law, sovereignty over natural resources, investment contracts, international investment agreements and due diligence. Dr. Violi actively lends her expertise to inform institutional practice and NGOs' activities and has recently appeared as an expert before the Italian and German Parliament.

Introduction – Justice for atrocities: Dialogues and encounters between Latin America and Europe

Marco Longobardo and Juan-Pablo Perez-Leon-Acevedo

In an interconnected and globalised word such as the international society in the twenty-first century, it is commonplace that transnational issues are presented before domestic or international courts. As a consequence, it is not a novelty the fact that these courts usually take into consideration, in their decisions, the case-law of different national or international courts, in what is usually referred to as 'judicial dialogue' (See, among many others and in different contexts, Burgorgue-Larsen, 2013; De Vergottini, 2010; Ferrer Mac-Gregor, 2017; Giacco, 2022; Martins de Araujo & Vauthier Borges De Macedo, 2015; Terris et al., 2008; Tzanakopoulos, 2016). Scholarly analysis has focused on this judicial dialogue mainly in its 'vertical' dimension: for instance, numerous studies explore how national courts in Europe have engaged in judicial dialogue with international regional courts such as the European Court of Human Rights (ECtHR) and the Court of Justice of the European Union and vice versa (See, e.g. Jaremba & Kappé, 2024; López Guerra, 2018; Mengozzi, 2015; Ridolfi, 2016; Tridimas, 2015), or on how national courts in Latin America have conducted a judicial dialogue with the Inter-American Court of Human Rights (IACtHR) and vice versa (See, e.g. Contesse, 2017; Gonzalez-Ocantos & Sandholtz, 2021; Neves, 2014; Nogueira Alcalá, 2013a; Nogueira Alcalá, 2013b). Less explored – although not totally novel – is the 'horizontal' judicial dialogue between national courts in different continents, or between different international regional courts (For some exceptions, see Ansuátegui Roig, 2016; Corte Interamericana de Derechos Humanos, 2020; Di Stasi, 2014; Masol & Perez-Leon-Acevedo, 2024).

The articles in this special issue focus on such a horizontal judicial dialogue, narrowing down its scope both in relation to its geographical dimension and its subject matter. Indeed, it is impossible to address in one special issue only the entirety of the horizontal judicial dialogue that occurs between national courts and between regional international courts around the word. Accordingly, first, the papers collected here explore only horizontal judicial dialogue between Latin America and Europe, leaving to future projects the exploration of such a dialogue in relation to different areas of the world, in particular the African continent, where a sophisticated international regional human rights machinery is in place (See more comprehensive works such as *Towards Convergence in International Human Rights Law: Approaches of Regional and International Systems*, Buckley et al.,

2017; Burgorgue-Larsen, 2020). Second, the papers in this special issue address only horizontal dialogue pertaining to justice for atrocities, rather than a similar dialogue in relation to different matters.

The special issue aims at analysing whether national and international regional courts in Europe and Latin America address issues pertaining to justice for serious violations of human rights in similar or different ways. The focus is on how gross violations of international human rights law and international humanitarian law, which are constitutive of international crimes (genocide, crimes against humanity, and war crimes), are addressed by national and international regional institutions in Europe and Latin America. National jurisdiction and international regional jurisdiction in Latin America and Europe have dealt for decades with these atrocities, as demonstrated by the significant case law on human rights violations such as murder, torture, sexual offences, and enforced disappearances, both in armed conflict and peacetime.

Among the several factors that influenced the choice of focusing on Europe and Latin America, the strongest one is related to historical considerations. For over five centuries, Latin America and Europe have had a strong and intense relationship throughout different historical stages: from the conquest/colonial times, to the decolonisation process, to connections as sovereign states and, more recently, increasing integration within the globalisation process, the two continents have developed an intense exchange in many areas. Unfortunately, the commission of atrocities consisting of serious violations of human rights and humanitarian law (which may constitute international crimes) have tragically been present on a large scale in both regions during the XX century and their consequences are still on-going today. This is reflected in some ongoing investigations and prosecutions of these crimes at national and international regional levels. While Europe suffered mass atrocities during the two World Wars and in the Balkan wars during the 90s, as well as, more recently, serious violations of human rights/humanitarian law in the Caucasus and Ukraine, Latin-American countries such as Argentina, Brazil, Chile, Colombia, Guatemala, and Peru, endured widespread and systematic abuses committed by dictatorial regimes and/or during internal armed conflicts, particularly over the last decades of the XX century. In order to protect the fundamental rights of persons under the jurisdiction of Latin-American and European states from similar atrocities, strong international regional human rights systems, namely, the Inter-American and the European human rights systems, were established and have developed robust practice. In turn, national judicial authorities in both sides of the Atlantic have been active in investigating and prosecuting individuals who committed atrocities and sought impunity as powerfully illustrated in the Military Junta trial in Argentina, the Pinochet case before British courts during the late 90s (See, for an original account, Sands, 2025), the trial of the former President Fujimori in Peru, and recent cases related to the so-called Operation Condor (Plan Cóndor) before Italian courts (See, recently, Lessa, 2022).

This special issue aims at leading the debate between researchers and practitioners from Europe and Latin America in relation to the dialogue or lack of dialogue between Latin America and Europe in in the field of justice for atrocities at national and supranational levels. To this end, the special issue brings together scholars from different disciplines (e.g. human rights, international law, criminal law, and criminology). The articles collected here tests the applicability of Latin-American legal solutions in the European contest, and of European solutions in the Latin-American contexts. These solutions pertain issues such as the possibility to get reparations for historical wrongs, barriers to justice posed by amnesties and immunities, as well as hurdles generated by the need to coordinate different legal criminal systems when transboundary (and transcontinental) crimes occur. It is our hope that the papers in this special issue will foster the circulation of Latin-American legal solutions in the European legal debate, overcoming geographical, cultural, and language barriers.

With regard to the articles that constitute the present special issue, the following can be said very briefly. Harmen van der Wilt in his article 'Leadership responsibility in non-state criminal organisations. The rediscovery of indirect perpetration through an organisation by Latin American courts and the ICC' examines the interaction between the Latin American domestic courts and the International Criminal Court via the adaptation and expansion of the concept of indirect perpetration through an organisation (*Organisationsherrschaft*) in order to accommodate the individual criminal responsibility of leaders of non-state armed groups. Nevertheless, Van der Wilt remarks that such a process has been challenging. This is because the *Organisationsherrschaft* doctrine was initially designed by Claus Roxin as a legal device to sustain the criminal responsibility of the kingpins who operate within tightly hierarchical structures. The Eichmann case and the related Nazi structure constitute the paradigm of such situation. Yet, the author concludes that domestic and international courts have successfully shown that the *Organisationsherrschaft* doctrine can be tailored to less rigidly structured organisations. Van der Wilt notices that those courts have achieved it by drawing attention to the essence of the doctrine: to connect the leader's capacity to guarantee (quasi)-automatic compliance with orders through his/her dominance over an organisation. Indeed, the concept of indirect perpetration via an organisation demonstrates that mutual interaction/influence between Latin American national courts and international courts like the International Criminal Court (ICC) can be meaningful in international/national criminal law.

Elena Maculan through her article 'The role of Criminal Justice in dealing with past atrocities in the Spanish and Argentine transitions: common grounds, but different pathways' employs a comparative methodology of relevant Argentinian and Spanish law and case law to offer a good picture of the debate surrounding the role and limits of criminal law in scenarios of transitional justice. Maculan sustains that an analysis of the two above-mentioned experiences and of the different choices they have taken is useful to point out some controversial elements. First, the clashes between, on the one hand, legislative choices that frequently imply amnesties or similar measures and, on the other one, judicial decisions that may attempt to amend the former. Second, the concerns related to such creative jurisprudential developments concerning compatibility with the principles of legality and non-retroactivity as well as the prohibition of arbitrariness. Third, the extent of the obligations to prosecute and punish gross violations of human rights vis-à-vis the limits of criminal justice. Thus, Maculan recommends that, in extraordinary transitional scenarios, criminal justice can and should be combined with other complementary mechanisms that seek to provide truth, justice, reparations, and the construction of a shared memory.

In her article 'The ping-pong strategy: confronting atrocities from the exile', Valeria Vegh Weis focuses on what she considers a still marginal matter of atrocity crimes. By building upon Southern studies, she exposes how global power inequalities have led to the presentation of knowledge from a small number of Northern societies as universal, timeless and placeless, but also disregarding valuable knowledge and experiences from the South. Additionally, Vegh Weis also challenges the 'static' approach in atrocity scholarship that has largely focused on either national or global issues, but without paying enough attention to the dialogues, connections normative transfers, and shared practices between the South and the North. In arguing all of this, the article focuses on a disregarded specific actor: individuals in exile and their role in the confrontation of the atrocities back home. This article goes beyond the European-centred and static approaches. Instead, it considers points of dialogue and encounters between Europe and Latin America and the role of the diaspora/exile as a legal and dynamic protagonist in fighting against atrocities. More specifically, the article explores the Argentinian activists' role in Europe and their struggle against the dictatorship that governed Argentina (1976–1983) plus their activism against impunity laws upon the re-establishment of democracy.

In their article 'Impunity in cases of serious human rights violations: three relevant aspects of contention in the jurisprudence of the Inter-American Court of Human Rights', Harold Bertot Triana and Elena C. Díaz Galán acknowledge that the IACtHR pioneered international human rights law by construing important jurisprudence against impunity. The authors remind us that Latin America has been prone to political and policymaking processes to provide impunity for those responsible for serious violations of human rights since the 1970s. The authors remark that such impunity has sought to render amnesty and self-amnesty laws or implement procedural mechanisms (e.g. *ne bis in idem* principle) in order to block the investigation and punishment of perpetrators of gross human rights abuses. In this context, the authors analyse the IACtHR's jurisprudence to identify some key argumentative lines aimed at combating impunity in cases of serious human rights violations. Thus, the authors focus on the specificities of the duty to investigate established by the IACtHR, the development of *jus cogens* vis-à-vis these serious situations, and the scope of reparations. Comparatively speaking, the article points to the need for other international courts like the ECtHR to follow these jurisprudential approaches to fight impunity in cases of serious violations.

Marco Longobardo and Federica Violi in 'Access to justice for atrocities in the comparison of land-mark cases on state immunity in Brazil and Italy', from a comparative perspective, examines the differences and similarities in the approaches of Italian and Brazilian national courts to the topic of access to justice for atrocities and the role of state immunity. The article draws particular attention to the limited and select dialogue between the two judiciaries and discusses the potential for further developments of the customary international law rule on state immunity. In doing so, the authors first examine the rule on state immunity and overview the articulated Italian case law on why state immunity cannot bar access to justice for atrocities, regarding post-2004 judicial developments. Then, the authors describe the 2021 decision of the Brazilian Supremo Tribunal Federal, when the Brazilian judiciary seemingly joined the Italian trend against state immunity when atrocities are perpetrated. These two different judicial trends are subsequently compared and examined, discussing the limited explicit reference to Italian decisions by the Supremo Tribunal Federal. Finally, the authors describe the likely impact of the above-mentioned judicial trends on future developments in the relationship between access to justice for atrocities and state immunity.

In 'Comparing universal jurisdiction in Europe and in Latin America: a vehicle for international justice or for colonial reckoning?', Alexandra Fowler notices that the limited options for prosecutions of persons responsible for atrocities in States not amenable to ICC jurisdiction have been a particular concern in recent times. The article considers that: (i) the need for accountability for atrocities builds on long histories of human rights and humanitarian law practice (treaty-based and customary), driven also by the work of the ECtHR and the IACtHR; and, (ii) nationally, since the Pinochet decision, universal jurisdiction (UJ) has been considered a promising manner to fill the lacuna. Fowler highlights that some commentators have noticed a resurgence in the use of UJ in recent times, which is illustrated by a number of trials of former ISIS and Syrian regime members in European national courts. Nevertheless, as exercised, the UJ has presented serious limitations. The author sustains that, although there are exceptions, many European states are transforming UJ into the application of extraterritorial jurisdiction under active or passive personality, particularly regarding their former colonies. Fowler also considers that, in Latin America, while there have been some recent examples of 'pure' UJ, most jurisdiction has been exercised in furtherance of extraditions, specifically at the behest of former colonial powers. Thus, the article: (i) compares the recent uptick in European and Latin American usages of UJ; (ii) concludes that both regions have so far shown little appetite for pursuing 'pure' UJ; and (iii) cautions against colonialist pressures in both regions that threaten to limit this key international justice mechanism.

Finally, Ioanna Pervou in her article 'The intercontinental dialogue on enforced disappearances: the case of massive disappearances during hostilities' examines the intercontinental judicial dialogue on enforced disappearances. First, it discusses the concept of enforced disappearances and chronologically examines how practice shaped the course of the two regions, exploring pivotal elements of the case law of the IACtHR and ECtHR and remarking differences between these regional courts. Then, it deepens the analysis of the dialogue between the two courts and how this is evolving concerning massive disappearance in hostilities. It fleshes out the functional term 'massacre' and discusses its relationship with other legal terms such as extrajudicial executions. The article highlights the legal obstacles when characterising the widespread conduct of enforced disappearances of persons as a crime against humanity and it suggests how the non-legal term 'massacre' has assisted in the punishment of the crimes. Finally, it examines how justice is rendered in such cases and whether the legal responses are sufficient.

The articles collected in this special issue are a product of a project launched in December 2021, with a call for papers that invited submissions for three workshops that was held at the University of Westminster, London, and online on 6 and 7 December 2022. All the articles in this special issue where originally presented there. We are extremely grateful to the authors for having worked with us all these years to improve their papers, patiently and collaboratively. More papers than those collected here were presented at the workshops. They are not included in this special issue because of the commitments of their authors. Yet, we want to express gratitude to those colleagues who have enriched our discussion even if they decided not to submit a final article. They are Pablo del Hierro and Lucas Lixinski, Tamás Hoffmann, Dilek Kurban, Nikolas Kyriacou, and Sergii Masol (presenting with one of us, Juan-Pablo Perez-Leon-Acevedo). Particular thanks also to our keynote speakers and commentators, which have enriched the workshops, and the articles published here, with their observations: Kai Ambos, Fabricio Guariglia, Philippe Sands, Hélène Tigroudja, Paula Wojcikiewicz Almeida.

Disclosure statement

No potential conflict of interest was reported by the author(s).

References

Ansuátegui Roig, F. J. (2016, June). Human rights and judicial dialogue between America and Europe: Toward a new model of law? *The Age of Human Rights Journal*, *6*(6), 24. https://doi.org/10.17561/tahrj.v0i6.2928

Buckley, C. M., Donald, A., & Leach, P. (Eds.). (2017). The Hague: Brill | Nijhoff.

Burgorgue-Larsen, L. (2013). *El diálogo judicial: máximo desafío de los tiempos jurídicos modernos*. Porrúa.

Burgorgue-Larsen, L. (2020). *Les Trois Cours Régionales des Droits de l'Homme in Context: La justice qui n'allait pas de soi*. Pedone.

Contesse, J. (2017). The final word? Constitutional dialogue and the Inter-American Court of Human Rights. *International Journal of Constitutional Law*, *15*(2), 414. https://doi.org/10.1093/icon/mox034

Corte Interamericana de Derechos Humanos. (2020). *Diálogo entre Cortes Regionales de Derechos Humanos*. Corte IDH.

De Vergottini, G. (2010). *Oltre il dialogo tra le Corti: Giudici, diritto straniero, comparazione*. il Mulino.

Di Stasi, A. (2014). The Inter-American Court of Human Rights and the European Court of Human Rights: Towards a "Cross fertilization"? *Ordine Internazionale e Diritti Umani*, *1*(1), 97.

Ferrer Mac-Gregor, E. (2017). What do we mean when we talk about judicial dialogue: Reflections of a judge of the Inter-American Court of Human Rights. *Harvard Human Rights Journal*, *30*(1), 89.

Giacco, L. L. (2022). *Judicial decisions in international law: Argumentation between entrapment and creativity*. Hart.

Gonzalez-Ocantos, E., & Sandholtz, W. (2021). Constructing a regional human rights legal order: The Inter-American Court, National Courts, and Judicial Dialogue, 1988 – 2014. *International Journal of Constitutional Law*, *19*(5), 1559. https://doi.org/10.1093/icon/moab094

Jaremba, U., & Kappé, M. (2024). The unfolding story of judicial dialogue in the EU: The coercive and persuasive motives behind the participation of Belgian Highest Courts in the preliminary ruling procedure. *German Law Journal*, *25*(5), 690. https://doi.org/10.1017/glj.2024.9

Lessa, F. (2022). *The condor trials: Transnational repression and human rights in South America*. Yale University Press.

López Guerra, L. (2018). Dialogues between the Strasbourg Court and National Courts. In A. Müller (Ed.), *Judicial Dialogue and Human Rights* (pp. 401). Cambridge University Press.

Martins de Araujo, L. C., & Vauthier Borges De Macedo, P. E. (2015). O Diálogo Institucional Entre Cortes Constitucionais: A Jurisdição Constitucional Justificada Pelos Diálogos Transnacionais. In P. R. Barbosa Ramos & M. Mont'alverne (Eds.), *Teoria Constitucional* (pp. 328). Barreto Lima.

Masol, S., & Perez-Leon-Acevedo, J.-P. (2024). Lessons to learn? Using the Inter-American Court of Human Rights' Jurisprudence on Amnesties and Pardons in the Context of the Russo-Ukrainian War. *Leiden Journal of International Law*, 1–27. [advance version]. https://doi.org/10.1017/S0922156524000335

Mengozzi, P. (2015). A European partnership of courts. Judicial dialogue between the EU Court of Justice and National Constitutional Courts. *Il Diritto dell'Unione Europea*, *20*(3), 701.

Neves, M. (2014). Do diálogo entre as cortes supremas e a Corte Interamericana de Direitos Humanos ao transconstitucionalismo na América Latina. *Revista de Informação Legislativa, 51*(1), 193.

Nogueira Alcalá, H. (2013a). Diálogo interjurisdiccional y control de convencionalidad entre los tribunales nacionales y la Corte Interamericana de Derechos Humanos en Chile. *Anuario de Derecho Constitucional Latinoamericano, 19*(1), 511.

Nogueira Alcalá, H. (2013b). El control de convencionalidad y el diálogo interjurisdiccional entre tribunales nacionales y Corte Interamericana de Derechos Humanos. *Revista de Derecho Constitucional Europeo, 19*(1), 221.

Ridolfi, A. (2016). Giurisdizione costituzionale, corti sovranazionali e giudici comuni: considerazioni a proposito del dialogo tra corti. *Rivista AIC, 3*(1), 1. www.rivistaaic.it/images/rivista/pdf/3_2016_Ridolfi.pdf.

Sands, P. (2025). *38 Londres Street: On Impunity, Pinochet in England and a Nazi in Patagonia.* W&N.

Terris, D., Romano, C. P. R., & Swigart, L. (2008). Toward a Community of International Judges. *Loyola of Los Angeles International and Comparative Law Review, 30*(3), 419.

Tridimas, T. (2015). The ECJ and the national courts: Dialogue, cooperation, and instability. In D. Chalmers & A. Arnull (Eds.), *The Oxford handbook of European Union Law* (pp. 403). Oxford University Press.

Tzanakopoulos, A. (2016). Judicial dialogue as a means of interpretation. In H. P. Aust & G. Nolte (Eds.), *The interpretation of international law by domestic courts: Uniformity, diversity, convergence*, 72–95. Oxford University Press.

OPEN ACCESS

Leadership responsibility in non- state criminal organisations: The rediscovery of indirect perpetration through an organisation by Latin American courts and the ICC

Harmen van der Wilt

ABSTRACT

This article addresses the interaction between Latin American courts and the International Criminal Court in adapting and expanding the concept of indirect perpetration through an organisation (*Organisationsherrschaft*), in order to accommodate the criminal responsibility of leaders of non-state armed groups. This project has turned out to be a challenge, because *Organisationsherrschaft* was initially designed by it's inventor, Claus Roxin, as a legal device to sustain the criminal responsibility of the kingpins, operating within tightly structured, hierarchical structures, Eichmann being the paradigmatical case. Nonetheless, the author concludes that national and international courts have succeeded in demonstrating that the doctrine of *Organisationsherrschaft* can be tailored to less rigidly structured organisations. They have accomplished this by keeping a close eye on the essence of the doctrine, to wit the leader's capacity to assure (quasi) automatic compliance with orders through his dominance over an organisation. The development of the concept of indirect perpetration through an organisation proves that interaction between and mutual inspiration of national and international courts can chart new waters in (international) criminal law.

1. Introduction

In international criminal law discourse the issue of how to link political and military leaders to atrocity crimes is widely discussed. The reason for this scholarly and judicial interest is not hard to grasp. People who occupy positions at the top of criminal organisations or corporations do not – or only rarely – physically commit crimes, but outsource the dirty work to their subordinates. If one harbours a narrow, physical conception of 'perpetration', the principals who stay aloof from the crime scene cannot incur criminal responsibility under that label. However, as precisely these individuals concoct heinous crimes and can therefore be rightly considered as the *autores intelectuales* (masterminds) such an outcome does not satisfy one's sense of justice. Several solutions have been probed to resolve this conundrum, each of them displaying advantages and disadvantages. For one thing, leaders who prompt others to commit crimes might be qualified as participants, under the heading of well-known modes of criminal liability like 'aiding and abetting' or ' instigation/ inducement'. After all, typical of these secondary forms of criminal responsibility is that they do not require the culprit to have physically committed the crime. However, the very depiction of their being 'secondary' to the main perpetrator downplays their prominence in the criminal event.

In the famous doctrine of superior or command responsibility this hierarchical order between superiors and subordinates is at least clearly acknowledged. Here we stumble on another problem. The responsibility of a military or civilian superior is engrafted on an *omission* to control his/her subordinates and can therefore not be easily reconciled with active furtherance of crimes.

Some concepts of criminal responsibility emphasise the collective nature of international crimes and appear to be less interested in the specific division of labour between leaders and executioners. As is well known, the ICTY and ICTR, SCSL and ECCC have amply applied the concept of Joint Criminal Enterprise (JCE) in order to prosecute and punish all those individuals that embark on a common criminal objective and in some way contribute to the accomplishment of that purpose. All the members of the JCE incur criminal responsibility for the crimes that are committed by (an)other member (s) in pursuit of realising the common purpose, provided that they knew that such crimes (s) would be committed or that it was at least foreseeable that (an)other member(s) would engage in such crime. While the JCE-doctrine therefore adequately captures the collective dimension by pointing out that all members are 'in it together', it fails to differentiate as to the nature and weight of respective contributions. Indeed, the very element 'some contribution' is questionably vague in view of the *lex certa* principle.[1] Moreover, in the case law of the ad hoc tribunals, the agreement of the members to engage in a criminal venture is often taken for granted or conveniently glossed over, as they need not even mutually be aware of their existence. This is rather remarkable, in view of the fact that an agreement or common understanding is the gist of the doctrine and the justification for expansive criminal responsibility.[2]

In an attempt to remedy the shortcomings of JCE-doctrine, the International Criminal Court (ICC) has largely repudiated the concept and has, instead of this, concentrated on the substantive contribution and the guilt of individual culprits. In the *Lubanga* case, the Trial Chamber elaborated on the concept of 'co-perpetration', explaining that each perpetrator would have to provide an 'essential contribution' and would thus have 'control over the crime', in that his/her absconding would thwart the completion of the crime.[3] In such an understanding of co-perpetration the equality of the 'partners in crime', in terms of capacity, resources and psychological influence, is conspicuous. Such parity is absent in a configuration in which leaders and superiors have clear ascendancy over their subordinates. That situation would rather be covered by 'indirect perpetration', a mode of criminal responsibility that was newly introduced in the Rome Statute and that counts as a primary form of criminal responsibility, on the same par as 'perpetration' and 'co-perpetration'.[4] The immediate perpetrator that is used as an instrument by the person in charge need not be a passive, inert tool that is absolved from responsibility, on account of his/her having succumbed to unbearable threats or force, being deceived, or lacking responsibility as a minor or due to insanity. In this sense, the final part of art.

25, 3 sub a of the Rome Statute – 'regardless of whether that other person is criminally responsible' – introduced a novelty, deviating from national criminal law *Dogmatik*. The innovation encouraged the ICC to chart new waters, by introducing a new mode of liability – *Organisationsherrschaft* –, following in the footsteps of the inventor of the concept, the famous German lawyer Claus Roxin.[5] The empirical and normative finding that the executioners of heinous crimes in concentration camps or of summary executions of civilians on behest of the Nazi regime were fully responsible had prompted Roxin to the conclusion that the original interpretation of 'indirect perpetration' had been too narrow. The 'perpetrator behind the desk' (*Schreibtishmörder*) could be entirely confident that his intentions would be carried out, if he dominated the organisation, in a similar vein as if he were to exert control over a single irresponsible human being.[6] Roxin postulated three requirements for criminal responsibility of masterminds on the basis of their wielding full control over an organisation (*Organisationsherrschaft*). First, the organisation must have a tight hierarchical structure. Secondly, the head of the organisation must be assured that his orders are complied with, even if a particular subordinate were to refuse or disobey. It meant that the subordinate members of the organisation were 'interchangeable', in the sense that the vacant place would be automatically filled in by a willing executioner. Roxin himself used the expression *Fungibilität* (fungibility). And finally, the organisation must at least partially operate outside the realm of the law.[7] In his discussion of Roxin's original ideas, Thomas Weigend provides a very lucid explanation of this last requirement. If an organisation were to operate within the confines of the law, the head of that organisation who would order his subordinates to engage in unlawful action would never be certain of their unfaltering obedience, because they could always opt for law-abiding behaviour.[8]

In the *Katanga* case, the Pre-Trial Chamber employed Roxin's theory to sustain the accused's criminal responsibility, leaving the final element in abeyance.[9] The Pre-Trial Chamber took an even bolder step by lumping two modes of criminal liability, to wit co-perpetration and indirect perpetration, together. The resulting concept of 'Indirect Co-perpetration by Means of an Organization' enabled the Trial Chamber to hold Katanga and Ngudjolo Chui not only responsible for the crimes that had been committed by their own subordinates, but also – on a mutual basis – for the atrocities committed by the foot-soldiers under the command of their partner in crime.[10]

The arduous efforts to find legal constructions that adequately and fairly reflect the involvement of leaders in system criminality have been extensively discussed in legal literature and we need not rehash this further.[11] This contribution focusses on the question whether the doctrine of *Organisationsherrschaft* can also be applied in respect of leaders of organisations that do not display the rigid structures which Roxin envisaged when he invented the concept. The topic seems to be fitting for the purpose of this conference. In the call for papers, the organisers welcomed discourses on the interaction between Latin American and European courts that subsequently informed the case law of the ICC. They thus hinted at a triangular exchange of legal deliberations between domestic courts and the ICC. References to the case law of Latin American and German courts by the ICC and – vice versa – to the judgments of the ICC in the legal decisions of national courts indeed suggest that all these courts have been influenced by their colleagues. *Grosso modo,* the chronology of the process developed as follows. While the ICC has been credited with both procuring the renaissance of

Organisationsherrschaft and expanding its application to more loosely structured organisations, these initiatives have been preceded by case law in Latin American countries, in particular in Argentina and Peru, that paved the way for such developments in international criminal law. In their turn, the Latin American courts were inspired by the findings of the German Federal Court of Appeals (*Bundesgerichtshof*) that applied Roxin's insights in the Berlin Wall Shootings cases.[12] In sum, the search for an adequate concept to hold leaders of organisations criminally responsible has been conducive of a vivid interaction between international and national courts and between domestic courts *inter se*.

The essay is structured as follows. In a slightly reversed chronological order, section 2 addresses the ICC's expansive interpretation of the concept of *Organisationsherrschaft* and the opinions on such developments in legal literature. In section 3 the attention is turned to the Latin American case law in which leaders of non-state groups were convicted on the basis of the concept. Section 4 intends to offer some very tentative observations on the question whether the amendment of the doctrine was primarily triggered by factual – social/political – realities or was also to a certain extent inherent to the legal culture that constituted the background of that development. Section 5 rounds off with some final conclusions and reflections.

2. *Organisationsherrschaft* as a proper device to convict leaders of non-state groups? The case law of the ICC

The issue whether the concept of *Organisationsherrschaft* can be expanded to cover the criminal responsibility of leaders of less tightly organised non-state groups is a matter of controversy. As a prelude to the analysis of the case law of the ICC, this section in a nutshell presents some positions in legal literature. A profound theoretical discourse is not envisaged, because that would exceed the limited scope of this contribution. Some doctrinal reflections will be revisited in the subsequent section on Latin American case law, but only to the extent that they feature in the judgments themselves. In short, the emphasis in this article is on case law of international and national courts and the question whether and how they have mutually inspired each other's findings. The brief theoretical excursus starts with an exposition of the opinions on the topic of the spiritual father on the matter, Claus Roxin.

To be sure, Roxin did not exclude the applicability of the concept beyond the context of criminal state bureaucracies. He explicitly acknowledged the feasibility of indirect perpetration through an organisation in respect of 'acts committed as part of underground movements, secret organisations, gangs and similar associations'.[13] Roxin even considered it to be conceivable that his doctrine might serve useful purposes in case of 'purely criminal gangs', engaging in property crimes and extortion.[14] However, he immediately added a note of caution, warning that 'we must be careful in assuming organizational control in such domestic groups'.[15] Decisive seems to be whether there is a power structure (*Machtapparat*) that functions irrespective of the persons that are deployed and that can be fully controlled by the man at the top. Roxin qualified Al Capone's infamous *Murder Inc.* as an example in kind.[16] According to Roxin, then, the applicability of the doctrine of *Organisationsherrschaft* does not depend on the organisation being embedded in a state apparatus, but rather on the nature of the organisational structure.

Nonetheless, these two aspects have often been confounded in later commentaries. Mark Osiel, for instance, gives a particularly strict interpretation of Roxin's ideas, asserting that

> Roxin's analysis assumes the existence of a rigidly formal bureaucracy of the sort contemplated by Weber's famous ideal-type, developed from his understanding of the authoritarian Prussian army, which in the organizational chart perfectly mirrors the behavior of the people occupying positions within it.[17]

Kai Ambos has explicitly criticised this interpretation as being too stringent, where he holds that 'the theory – of indirect perpetration by virtue of a hierarchical apparatus – is not only applicable to rigidly formal state bureaucracies but also to less formalized non-state groups'.[18] At first sight, Ambos appears to disregard Roxin's careful differentiation between the political allegiance of the group (state versus non-state) and its power structure. However, his references, in support of his opinion, to the Peruvian judgment against the founder and highest leader of the Peruvian Communist Party-Shining Path, Abimael Guzmán and other senior leaders of this terrorist organisation, as well as the decision of the Pre-Trial Chamber in the Katanga-case shed a different light on his contention. Not only did these cases concern leaders of non-state – terrorist or paramilitary – groups, but the ICC and the Peruvian courts seemed also to harbour a more lenient interpretation of hierarchical relations within the group. In other words, Ambos' suggestion that the application of the concept of indirect perpetration by means of an organisation to non-State groups requires some concession to the rigidity of it's hierarchical structure is not far-fetched. The case against Guzman and the Shinning Path's leadership will be discussed in more detail in the next section. We will first take a closer look at the approach of the ICC.

In the confirmation of charges decision in the case of Katanga and Chui, the Pre Trial Chamber(PTC) took the lead.[19] The PTC invoked three reasons for relying on 'control over the organisation' as an appropriate basis for criminal responsibility in the case under scrutiny. First of all, the concept had been incorporated in the Rome Statute. After all, so the PTC argued, 'the most serious crimes of concern to the international community as a whole are paradigmatically committed by organized collectives. Any attempt of suppressing such crimes by legal means would involve the prosecution and trial of those controlling such organizations'.[20] Secondly, the notion of 'control over an organization' had been embraced by 'numerous national jurisdictions'.[21] And finally, the concept had been addressed in the case law of international tribunals.[22] With the exception of the first element, the arguments were not particularly convincing. The Pre-Trial Chamber only referred to two European countries (Germany and Spain) and three Latin American countries (Argentina, Chile and Peru) in which the concept of control over an organisation had sustained the criminal responsibility of leaders. Moreover, the PTC admitted that the ICTY Trial Chamber's conviction of Milomir Stakić by virtue of his wielding control over the Prijedor municipality had been overturned on appeal, but reasoned that this did not obviate the validity of the concept under the Rome Statute.[23] After all, as the PTC reasoned, in the hierarchy of applicable legal sources the Statute prevails. And as the Statute explicitly provides for ' joint commission through another person, the fact that it was not recognised under customary international law was immaterial, in view of the secondary position of customary international law in Article 21 of the Statute.[24] The argument is slightly spurious and contradictory: if a court seeks to find the support of another court in order to buttress its interpretation of the law, it is not very helpful to emphasise the latter's deviating approach or opinion.

For the purpose of our topic, it is particularly relevant that the Pre-Trial Chamber considered the potential application of the concept of 'control over an organization' in the context of a para-military, non-state group that lacked the structural rigour of the Nazi bureaucracy for which the concept had initially been developed. Profusely quoting the work of Roxin, the PTC held that the control over the crime, justifying the qualification of a leader as a principal, rather than as an accessory, followed from his/her control over an organisation. While thus paying homage to the concept's founding father, the PTC subtly amended the doctrine, by subordinating one of its central tenets – to wit, the fungibility of executioners – to the overhauling question whether the leader could count on automatic compliance with his orders via his control over the apparatus.[25] For sure, replaceability of subordinates would be a highly effective tool, but such automatic compliance could also be accomplished by means of 'intensive, strict and violent training regimes'.[26] Obviously alluding to the situation under scrutiny, the PTC provided the example of '(…) abducting minors and subjecting them to punishing training regimens in which they are taught to shoot, pillage, rape and kill', qualifying these as 'an effective means for ensuring automatic compliance with leaders' orders to commit such acts'.[27]

The Trial Chamber reached a different conclusion.[28] In the absence of a centralised and effective chain of command, the Ngiti militia that was headed by Katanga and had allegedly engaged in atrocities could not be qualified as an organised apparatus of power and Katanga could therefore not have wielded complete control over his subordinates, as suggested by the Pre Trial Chamber.[29] Nonetheless, the Trial Chamber largely concurred with the PTC's legal analysis of the concept of *Organisationsherrschaft* and in particular shared the latter's opinion that the (semi) automatic compliance with orders was its crucial element. That could be achieved, according to the Trial Chamber, quoting Roxin with approval, if the organisation enjoyed 'an autonomous existence and its existence and survival did not depend on personal relations'.[30] Such features, however, were not confined to bureaucracies akin to those of the Third Reich in Germany for which the doctrine was initially designed, but could also be displayed in the 'very varied manifestations of modern-day group criminality'.[31] The Chamber acknowledged, however, that any court of law would have a hard time in disentangling the lines of authority and decision-making in modern criminal organisations, in order to answer the question whether the organisation would meet this demanding standard: 'The Chamber recognizes that the modalities of control over persons can be increasingly varied and sophisticated and that it is particularly difficult to conceive of and grasp the nature and internal dynamics of contemporary criminal organizations'. [32]

The re-invention of the doctrine of *Organisationsherrschaft* by the ICC has elicited mixed reactions in legal literature. While the norm-expressive force of the concept has been praised, it's bold application by the Pre-Trial Chamber in the Katanga case, diluting – if not de-naturalizing – Roxin's stringent framework, has met with criticism. Weigend, for instance, comments that

> The (Pre-Trial) Chamber may have sensed that Roxin's original model was not conceived for an African environment and attempted to make up for the lack of stringent institutional organization of the militias in question by adding new elements it found in the facts of the particular case.[33]

Others have expressed a slightly more positive opinion, by pointing out the necessity of adapting Roxin's doctrine to new configurations: 'Such a flexible approach, geared to the specific circumstances, may prove the versality of the concept and its resilience against the wear and tear of time'.[34]

In between the Decision of the Pre Trial Chamber and the Judgment of the Trial Chamber in the Katanga case, the doctrine has been mentioned as a potential basis for criminal responsibility in several cases.[35] All these cases concerned political leaders wielding power over a state apparatus, rather than leaders of non-state groups or criminal gangs. Moreover, these decisions did not offer new insights, so they need not further detain us here.

In recent judgments Trial Chambers have occasionally referred to the notion of control over an organisation without *explicitly* predicating criminal responsibility on this basis. In the Ntaganda-case, for instance, the Trial Chamber acknowledged that the armed group UPC/FPLC had served the accused as a vehicle to make his subordinates commit crimes against humanity and war crimes. The Chamber held that the UPC/FPLC was a well-organised armed group with a formal military structure.[36] The accused could rely on the organisation and obedience was assured by means of severe punishments in case of insubordination, including beatings, rape and deprivation of food.[37] The Trial Chamber concluded that '*taking also into account the number of persons within the UPC/FPLC military structure at the relevant time*, (...) the will of an individual soldier was irrelevant for the execution of a given order', adding that 'the UPC/FPLC as a whole functioned as a tool in the hands of the co-perpetrators'.[38] It is pretty obvious that the Chamber fully endorsed the possibility of indirect perpetration by means of an organisation and considered it applicable to the situation. There is a hardly veiled allusion to the crucial element of automatic compliance, in view of the abundance of recruits, *id est* the fungibility of the direct perpetrator. The only difference with the outcome in the confirmation of charges decision of the PTC in *Katanga* is that the Trial Chamber did not specifically qualify the mode of liability as 'indirect perpetration by means of an organization', but rather suggested that such control over an organisation could serve as an instrument to accomplish quasi absolute powers over subordinates.

It is a matter of conjecture whether the ICC will persevere in considering 'control over an organization' as an appropriate mode of liability for attributing responsibility to leaders of non-state groups. The Trial Chamber in the Katanga case has recoiled from doing so, perhaps startled by some critical reactions in legal literature, and has opted for the safer solution of group responsibility on the basis of a common criminal purpose. A more mundane explanation would be that the Chamber simply did not consider the organisation to have possessed the requisite features. On the other hand, clear references to the doctrine of *Organisationsherrschaft* as an extension of indirect perpetration keep surfacing in the case law, as we have noticed in the Ntaganda-case. Apart from the question whether the Rome-Statute allows for such an expansion – which is of course institution-specific –, the survival of the doctrine depends basically on two factors. First, the question arises whether the doctrine is really needed, in view of existing alternative modes of liability to hold the leaders of non-state groups criminally responsible for the crimes of their subordinates. Secondly – and related to this – we should further explore the boundaries of the applicability of the doctrine in case of non-state armed groups. In other words, we have to ascertain what structural features the organisation should have and which position the accused must occupy within the group to be confident of automatic compliance of his orders.

It is at this point – which is the central topic of this contribution – that case law of Latin American courts can provide useful guidance.

3. Latin American courts' application and interpretation of the concept of *Organisationsherrschaft*

It is probably no coincidence that courts in Latin American countries have been in the vanguard of further developing the notion of 'control of an organisation' as basis for imputing criminal responsibility to leaders. Both political and legal elements have prompted that development. Embedded in the civil law tradition, Hispanic legal systems are traditionally familiar with the differentiation model that distinguishes between principals and accessories and within the former category comprises the notion of 'indirect perpetration' (perpetration by means of another person).[39] It is not surprising that courts have been favourably disposed to adoption of 'control by means of an organization', although some legal systems inhibited such expansion, because they required the non-responsibility of the direct perpetrator.[40] Politically, Latin American countries had to deal with the representatives of bloody dictatorships that had quenched the opposition by violent means.[41]

The first Latin American court that applied the concept of indirect perpetration through an organisation was the Buenos Aires Federal Courts of Appeal in the case against the Military Commanders of the successive Juntas that had governed Argentina during the 'dirty war' (*guerra sucia*).[42] The accused had designed a plan to get rid of subversive elements by means of secret abductions, torture and killings and could be fully confident that the policy was executed by physical perpetrators who operated as mere cogs within a machine. The fact that the commanders could stop the disappearances at will – which they did when the operations did no longer serve their purposes – reflected their absolute power over the organisation. As Muñoz-Conde and Olásolo put it succinctly 'For the Federal Court of Appeals, this was a case in which the instrument operated by the man behind the scene was the system itself, which he manipulates at his discretion, a system of interchangeable men'.[43] However, the judgment of the Federal Courts of Appeal did not stand. In a divided vote, the Majority of the Argentinean Supreme Court reasoned that the qualification of 'principal' should be confined to those who actually performed the elements of the crime. It revised the outcome of the Federal Court by changing the role of the members of the Military Juntas into 'necessary participants', a change that had no impact on the punishment.[44]

Because of the somewhat convoluted interpretation of the concept of control over an organisation by Argentinean courts,, the Peruvian case against Alberto Fujimori emerged as the landmark decision on the topic in Latin America. After having been extradited by Chile, the former president of Peru stood trial and was ultimately convicted in April 2009 by the Peruvian Supreme Court (ratified on appeals later that year) on charges of multiple aggravated homicides, serious bodily injuries and aggravated kidnapping that the Court found to also constitute crimes against humanity under international criminal law. Extra-judicial executions and forced disappearances had taken place in Barrios Altos and La Cantuta, in the context of counter-terrorist operations against civilians who were suspected of supporting Shining Path (*Sendero Luminoso*). The Supreme Court found Fujimori to have orchestrated the events by means of the secret Colina-group which had been integrated in the Peruvian armed forces.[45] Probing the requirements as developed by Roxin, the Supreme Court confirmed that Fujimori could indeed be qualified as an indirect perpetrator by virtue of an organised power structure, adding that the systematic nature of the atrocities warranted their depiction as 'crimes against humanity'. In fact, the Supreme Court's judgment reveals a couple of specific features that may point at an effort to adapt the doctrine to the Latin American context. On the one hand, the Court harboured a broad interpretation of *Organisationsherrschaft* – in line with Roxin's teachings-, by acknowledging the possibility that mid-level perpetrators could also incur criminal responsibility on the basis of the doctrine.[46] The temptation to resort to such a wide reading of the doctrine correlates perhaps with the increasing structural complexities of modern organisations and corporations. We will revisit this jurisprudential development in the next section.[47] On the other hand, the Supreme Court constrained the ambit of the applicability of the doctrine by adding a fifth element, to wit, the 'favourable disposition' of the direct perpetrator to engage in the crime.[48] Interestingly, the Court borrowed this element from a preceding Peruvian judgment in the case of the leader of the guerrilla movement Shining Path (Sendero Luminoso), Abimael Guzmán. For a better understanding of this requirement, in search of an answer to the question whether its inclusion was prompted by the Latin American court's confrontation with the prosecution of leaders of non-state groups, we will turn now to a discussion of this case.

Abimael Guzmán, the founder and leader of Shining Path, alongside other members of the leadership of this terrorist organisation, stood trial on *inter alia* the charge of having master-minded the massacre at Lucanamarca during which more than 80 campesinos were randomly killed with the mere purpose of demonstrating the Peruvian state the movement's capacity to create havoc. Shining Path exhibited a rigid hierarchical structure, with Guzmán presiding over both the Permanent Direction Committee and the Central Committee that had the authority to choose particular geographical targets and issue detailed instructions to intermediate committees when and against whom attacks had to be performed.[49] Against this factual background, it came as no surprise that the Peruvian courts invoked the notion of indirect perpetration by means of an organisation to sustain the criminal responsibility of Guzman and the other leaders of Shining Path.[50] Counsel for the Defence addressed the (non-) applicability of the concept of control over an organisation in case of non-state armed groups head-on, asserting that Shining Path's members, *because* it was not a state organisation, were not obliged to comply with the orders of its leaders. In essence, the defence turned one of Roxin's requirements on its head. The courts were quick to divulge the disingenuousness of the argument by pointing out that Roxin had precisely developed his theory in respect of organisations that acted outside the legal order. Of more substance was the second part of the Defence's claim that purported to contrast Shining Path Luminoso with state organisations in respect of the former's lack of members that could perform specialised tasks. This implied that the organisation could never meet the crucial 'fungibility' criterion of the doctrine. To be sure, the response of the Peruvian courts to this objection was rather confusing. In 2006, the National Criminal Chamber rejected the 'fungibility' element as an exclusive method to obtain automatic compliance of orders to commit crimes within an organisation like Shining Path and held that the 'favourable attitude' of its members to the ideological goals would be an equally suitable condition to achieve the result. It is not immediately clear how this 'ideological zeal' could compensate for the alleged dearth of skills amongst the members to execute the crimes envisaged. In 2007, the Peruvian Supreme Court partially reversed the findings of the National Criminal Chamber by restoring the fungibility element. However, the Court harboured a watered-down version of the requirement by pointing out that a refusal or failure by one member to commit a crime did not need to be followed immediately by a successful performance by another member. It sufficed that the criminal objective would ultimately be achieved. Guzmán (and the other members of Shining Path's leadership) could be virtually certain of the end-result, as he could draw upon a vast reservoir of volunteers. Implicitly, therefore, the Supreme Court shared the Criminal Chamber's opinion that ideological fervour was an important tool to accomplish automatic compliance, but it put it under the label of 'successive interchangeability'.[51]

Whatever the (de)merits of this approach – I will address them in a bit more detail in the next section – it has been corroborated and followed by national courts in other Latin American countries, especially in Colombia. One of the most interesting decisions on the applicability of 'control by means of an organization' in respect of non-state armed groups has been taken by the quasi-judicial Chamber for the Recognition of the Truth, Responsibility and Determination of the Facts and Conduct of the Special Jurisdiction for Peace (hereafter: SRVR).[52] The case concerned the policy, practiced by the guerrilla movement FARC-EP, of widespread kidnappings of civilians and prisoners of war, in order to put pressure on the Colombian government and obtain ransom. Once having determined that these abductions (potentially) constituted war crimes and crimes against humanity, in view of their connection – respectively – with a (non) international armed conflict and their widespread or systematic character,[53] the SRVR turned to the criminal responsibility of the 8 arraigned persons who all occupied leadership positions within the organisation. The SRVR characterised the FARC-EP as an organisation with a 'military hierarchical structure, of the bureaucratic type, directed and dominated by it's *comandantes*'.[54] The Chamber emphasised the pivotal role of the *Secretariado* that *de facto* took strategic decisions and also coordinated the Bloques (local departments of the FARC) which were entrusted with the execution of the kidnappings and other crimes. One of the accused had been a permanent member of the *Secretariado*, while the others were comandantes of the Bloques. In addressing the question whether 'control over an organization' would serve as an appropriate concept to hold the accused criminally responsible, the Chamber identified the well-known requirements that had been adopted by the Supreme Court of Colombia, on the authority of Roxin.[55] Moreover, and especially interesting, the Chamber quoted the case law of the ICC, in particular the Confirmation of the charges Decision of the Pre-Trial Chamber in Katanga as an important precedent.[56] The FARC was an armed group, hierarchically structured and of an illegal character; the accused had wielded domination over the organisation, by cooperating in the collective organs; the direct perpetrators were exchangeable and could therefore not impede the commission of the crimes and they were 'favourably disposed' towards the commission of the crimes. The discussion focused on the fungibility of the direct perpetrators, as the FARC had been structured along entities that were assigned specific tasks, corresponding with the skills of their members. The capture of civilians was outsourced to specific units (*comisiones de cuido*) which only counted a limited number of guerrilleros who could not be easily replaced if someone of them deflected. As we may recall, the issue also surfaced in the case against Abimael Guzmán and the Shining Path's leadership. As helpfully explained by Ambos, it depends on the question whether exchangeability should be understood *in concreto* as the power to replace someone 'on the spot', or rather in a more general (abstract) sense that the organisation could rely on sufficient competent persons. The Chamber opted for the latter, by holding that the accused had the authority to select the most competent persons for a specific mission, which practically precluded the failure of the venture.[57]

The limited scope of this essay allows for the discussion of only a couple of cases, but the concept of indirect perpetration through organised structures of power has been often applied by other Latin American courts, especially in Colombia.[58] The case law demonstrates that courts acknowledge the fitness of the doctrine as an instrument to sustain the criminal responsibility of leaders, also – or perhaps in particular – of those in charge of para-military groups and guerrilla movements. Obviously, the application of the concept to this specific social and political context requires a shift of focus by taking account of particular organisational structures and interaction between leadership and rank-and-file. We have identified two elements in particular that are absent in Roxin's pristine presentation. For one thing, the fungibility of the direct perpetrators is considered to be predicated on bonds of ideological allegiance. Secondly, the exchangeability of executioners may be jeopardised by the scarcity of skilful executioners. Both aspects are presumably emblematic for non-state groups that lack the infinite resources of a state and cannot count on unquestioned obedience. The crucial question is whether the concept allows for such amendments.

4. Control over an organisation in non-state groups: a realistic option?

In spite of its strong intuitive appeal, the concept of *Organisationsherrshaft* suffers from a number of internal contradictions that make it sometimes difficult to apply. The cracks in the wall were perhaps already visible when Roxin designed the notion with the paradigmatic case of the Nazi regime in mind, but the renewed interest of – international and domestic – courts and legal doctrine has further revealed its weak spots. The concept has been challenged in two configurations that are – to a certain extent – each other's mirror image. First, the increasing complexities of modern bureaucratic organisations, in terms of decision making power and competences, raises the question who wields actually full control over the organisation. Secondly, in less rigidly structured non-state groups that depend on loyalty to the member's ideological cause and specific skills, their 'fungibility' may not always be taken for granted. While the emphasis in this contribution is on the second element, the first configuration deserves a brief discussion, because it puts the predicaments of applying the concept of control over an organisation to non-state groups in proper perspective.

Inherent to the concept of *Organisationsherrschaft* (literally 'domination over the organisation') is the assumption that the leader wields absolute control over the apparatus. Ambos has pointed out that this stringent requirement complicates the application of the notion to mid-level perpetrators, because their decisions can always be revoked by the person at the apex of the hierarchy.[59] The observation undoubtedly makes sense, but modern bureaucracies with diversification of competence and delegation of authority also present the reverse possibility of depriving the (wo)man at the top of the knowledge of the organisation's machinations and activities. One could certainly not expect the president of such an organisation to 'oversee the preparation of crimes at different hierarchical levels, and control its performance and execution'.[60] Such potential vulnerabilities have been partially remedied by ingenious constructions, like the suggestion that the mid-level perpetrator would incur responsibility if he/she has at least control over and uses part of the apparatus,[61] and that the leaders at different levels could act in concert and be qualified as co-perpetrators of indirect perpetration.[62] However, such amendments undermine the normative power of the concept. If one takes the notion of 'complete control over the organization' seriously, the concept may turn out to be inapplicable to both the board of directors and the (mid-level) executive management, because of the prior's lack of knowledge and the latter's want of power. Following a number of German court decisions, the possibility of applying the doctrine to business corporations has recently been discussed in legal scholarship.[63] A discussion of this interesting idea that probably emerges from the German reluctance to acknowledge criminal liability of corporations, is beyond the scope of this essay. While I do not completely rule out that Roxin's doctrine can be adapted to accommodate the criminal responsibility of business leaders, it would be prudent to warn against de-naturalization, as it affects the doctrine's fair-labelling quality.

The phenomenon of complex and opaque organisational structures that potentially impedes a straightforward conclusion who wields full domination over an apparatus and warrants a finding of *Organisationsherrschaft* as basis for criminal responsibility, is generally not an issue in non-state groups. In this configuration, hierarchical structures are relatively simple and lines of communication considerably shorter. An example in kind are the para-military rebel groups that operate in African countries and challenge regimes in power. Joseph Kony's Lord's Resistance Army and Hitler's regime could hardly be further apart in terms of technical prowess and organisational sophistication. However, Kony succeeded in creating an army, predominantly comprising child soldiers, by means of a devious mixture of strict discipline, threats of severe punishment, intoxication and instilment of awe and veneration for his supra-national powers. He could count on their unquestioned obedience in performing atrocities that required relatively few skills and even if one of them absconded, he could rely on his reserve of 'willing' executioners that the job was done. It is telling that the Pre-Trial Chamber in the Katanga-case precisely referred to the example of abducted child soldiers, adding that 'the highest authority (...) through his control over the organisation, essentially decides *whether* and *how* the crime would be committed'.[64] From a dogmatic point of view, the African situation of para-military groups (ab)using child soldiers can be seamlessly reconciled with the exigencies of those who favour a more stern interpretation of concepts of criminal responsibility. After all, the diminished responsibility of child soldiers corresponds with the original understanding of 'indirect interpretation' implying that the *Hintermann* uses the innocent direct perpetrator as a tool.

The situation becomes more blurry when child soldiers emancipate from their erstwhile subdued status, develop their own ideas and skills and rise in the ranks of the organisation. Dominic Ongwen could no longer be easily replaced by another willing volunteer if he were to refuse service, because he possessed special skills in the realm of combat and organisation. The tables were turned, as he himself could now select from an abundant pool of available persons relying on their obedience in compliance with his orders and confident that the crimes would be committed because of their fungibility.[65] By acquiring this position, Ongwen had the power to frustrate the commission of the crimes, which made him a key figure in the accomplishment of Kony's plans.[66] The Trial Chamber predicated Ongwen's criminal responsibility on the concept of 'indirect co-perpetration', as he had acted jointly with other kingpins of the LRA, wielding full control over the army of dispensable child soldiers and ordering them to commit the crimes. Like some other African cases that were addressed by the ICC, the Ongwen judgment reflects groups dynamics that are probably inherent to more loosely structured non-state organisations. Changing patterns of social interaction and career mobility give an impression of volatility, casting doubt on the certainty of performance that is the hallmark of *Organisationsherrschaft*. However, the case law of the ICC demonstrates that the application of control over an organisation need not be confined to static bureaucracies. Automatic compliance with orders is the core element of the concept and whoever wields full control over a group of replaceable direct perpetrators qualifies as an indirect perpetrator through an organisation. The means by which such domination is acquired are of secondary importance.

The case law of Latin American courts that have assessed the criminal responsibility of leaders of guerrilla movements reveals yet another social-political context in which 'control over an organization' might be a suitable construct to sustain criminal responsibility. Like state organisations, these non-state groups are tightly structured, along hierarchical lines, although they generally lack the former's division of labour and abundance of professional manpower. This shortcoming in terms of automatic compliance and replaceability is compensated by the members' 'positive attitude' to engage in crimes, in name of their shared ideology. As we noticed before, this element is somewhat equivocal. At first sight, the introduction of ideological affiliation appears to erode the very foundation of the doctrine, because it values personal preferences of direct perpetrators, thus emphasising their freedom to choose. On the other hand, however, one might reason that commitment to an abstract political goal, rather than personal attachment to a charismatic leader, reinforces the uniformity amongst the members and thereby makes their performance more predictable. Arguably, the Latin American situation hovers between the paradigmatic case of a state apparatus with a pool of anonymous 'cogs in the machine' and more loosely structured African paramilitary groups in which strict obedience is enforced by means of harsh discipline and indoctrination. Latin American courts have acknowledged that the leaders of guerrilla groups had to resort to other mechanisms in order to secure automatic compliance with their orders, in view of the limited resources (compared to state organisations) and their dealings with relatively autonomous direct perpetrators (compared to African military groups). The sober conclusion that they succeeded in mobilising their members to commit international crimes on a massive scale prima vista proves that they wielded control over their organisation. Whether the doctrine allows for such an extension of its original scope depends (also) on the availability of alternatives to sustain the criminal responsibility of leaders of organisations. In the context of the Latin American situation and case law, 'co-perpetration' between leadership and direct perpetrators would be an inappropriate qualification, because the latter lacked the power to frustrate the commission of the crimes. Neither would the common purpose doctrine be an adequate label to portray the interaction between leaders and rank-and-file, as it ignores the former's predominance in designing and directing the operations. Superior responsibility could serve as fall back option when there is insufficient proof that the accused could blindly trust that his orders were executed, *id est* without him giving further directions. While the concept of 'perpetration through an organization' admittedly is not always a perfect fit, compared with alternatives it adequately reflects the position and responsibility of leaders of Latin American rebel groups, engaging in international crimes.

5. Final reflections

Latin America courts and the ICC have contributed to the revival of the doctrine of indirect perpetration through an organisation (*Organisationsherrschaft*), in particular in respect of non-state groups. Acknowledging that such groups lack the complex hierarchical structures and surplus of professional manpower of state organisations, they have identified other methods, like strict discipline, indoctrination and ideological affinities, at the disposal of leaders to assure compliance with their orders. National and international courts have thus demonstrated that the doctrine is not a relict of the past that served to capture the working of a delinquent state bureaucracy in factual and normative terms, but can be tailored to less rigidly structured organisations.

The interplay between domestic courts and the ICC which appears from the references to each others' findings enabled them to discover commonalities and differences in the situations they were seized to address, thus assisting them in further exploring the contours of the doctrine. Indeed, application of the concept by Latin American courts that drew inspiration from Roxin's original writings and German case law, have preceded the concept's high profile ' breakthrough' in the jurisprudence of the ICC. In their turn, domestic courts, especially in Colombia have benefited from the insights of (Pre-)Trial Chambers of the ICC. It is submitted that all these courts, by keeping a close eye on the essence of the doctrine, to wit the leader's capacity to assure (quasi) automatic compliance with orders through his dominance over an organisation, have not exceeded the boundaries of the doctrine, as initially intended by Roxin. Moreover, these legal findings have increased our understanding of the mechanisms and functioning of organisations as vehicles to commit international crimes.

Notes

1. See for criticism in particular: A.M. Danner and J.S. Martinez, 'Guilty Associations: Joint Criminal Enterprise, Command Responsibility, and the Development of International Criminal Law', *California Law Review* 93, no. 1 (2005): 75–169. On the failure of JCE-

doctrine to distinguish between senior leaders and the rank-and-file, see Juan Pablo Pérez-León-Acevedo, 'Bringing the Bosses to International Criminal Trials: The Problems with Joint Criminal Enterprise and the "Control over the Crime" Approach As a Better Alternative', *Pace Int'l L. Rev.* 32 (Winter 2019): 15-28.

2. Harmen van der Wilt, 'Joint Criminal Enterprise: Possibilities and Limitations', *Journal of International Criminal Justice* 5 (2007): 91–108.
3. *Prosecutor v. Thomas Lubanga Dyilo*, Trial Judgement, ICC-01/01-01/06, 14 March 2012. For a profound discussion, see Jens David Ohlin, Elies van Sliedregt & Thomas Weigend, 'Assessing the Control Theory', *Leiden Journal of International Law* 26, no.3 (2013): 725-746.
4. Article 25,3, sub a of the Rome Statute reads as follows: 'In accordance with this Statute, a person shall be criminally responsible and liable for punishment for a crime within the jurisdiction of the Court if that person (a) Commits such a crime, whether as an individual, jointly with another or *through another person, regardless of whether that other person is criminally responsible'* (italics added).
5. On the reception of *Organisationsherrschaft* by the International Criminal Court see the article of Thomas Weigend, 'Perpetration through an Organization; The Unexpected Career of a German Legal Concept', *Journal of International Criminal Justice* 9 (2011): 91–111.
6. Roxin had based his theory to a large degree on the paradigmatic case of Eichmann.
7. C. Roxin, 'Organisationsherrschaft und Tatentschlossenheit', *Zeitschrift für internationale Strafrechtsdogmatik* 7 (2006): 293.
8. Weigend, 'Perpetration through an Organization', 97.
9. *Prosecutor v. Germain Katanga and Mathieu Ngudjolo Chui,* Decision on the confirmation of charges, ICC-01/04-01/07, 2008: §§ 515-517; *Prosecutor v. Germain Katanga*, Trial Judgment, ICC-01/04-01/07, 2014: § 1403.
10. Katanga, Confirmation of Charges, note 9: § 484. Judge Van den Wyngaert criticized the outcome of the decision, because the normative elements were not borne out by the evidence. *Prosecutor v. Mathieu Ngudjolo Chui*, Trial Judgment, ICC-01/04-02/12, 2012, Separate Opinion of Judge Christine Van den Wyngaert: § 62/63.
11. Apart from the contributions already mentioned, I would like to refer to Kai Ambos, 'Command Responsibility and Organisationsherrschaft: Ways of Attributing International Crimes to "the Most Responsible"', in *System Criminality in International Criminal Law*, ed. André Nollkaemper and Harmen van der Wilt (Cambridge: Cambridge University Press, 2009), 127–57; Hector Olásolo, *The Criminal Responsibility of Senior Political and Military Leaders as Principals in International Crimes* (Portland, Oregon: Hart, 2009); Mark Osiel, *Making Sense of Mass Atrocity* (Cambridge: Cambridge University Press, 2009); Cassandra Steer, *Translating Guilt; Identifying Leadership Liability for Mass Atrocity Crimes* (The Hague: TMC Asser Press, 2017); Elies Van Sliedregt, *Individual Criminal Responsibility in International Law*, (Oxford: Oxford University Press, 2012).
12. Bundesgerichtshof, Judgment of 26 July 1994, *Entscheidungen des Bundesgerichtshof in Strafsachen* 40 (1994): 228–40.
13. I rely here and in the following passages heavily on a segment of Claus Roxin's 'Crimes as Part of Organized Power Structures', originally published in *Goltdammer's Archiv für Strafrecht*, 1963: 193–207 and published in *Journal of International Criminal Justice*, 9 (2011): 193–205, with an introduction of Gerhard Werle and Boris Burghardt.
14. Roxin, 'Crimes as Part of Organized Power Structures', 204.
15. Ibid.
16. Ibid.
17. Osiel, *Making Sense of Mass Atrocity*, 100.
18. Kai Ambos, 'The *Fujimori* Judgment; A President's Responsibility for Crimes Against Humanity as Indirect Perpetrator by Virtue of an Organized Power Apparatus', *Journal of International Criminal Justice* 9 (2011): 150.
19. Katanga, Confirmation of Charges, note 9: §§ 500–19.

20. Ibid, 501.
21. Ibid, 502. Interestingly, the PTC referred to three Latin American cases, respectively hailing from Peru, Argentina and Chile: Supreme Court of Peru, Case No. 5383-200, 14 December 2007; Federal Appeals Chamber of Argentina (The Juntas Trial), Case No. 13/84, Chapter 7/5; Supreme Court of Chile, Fallos de Mes, año XXXV, noviembre de 1993, 12 November 1993.
22. Ibid, 500, 506–8.
23. Ibid, 506–7.
24. The conclusion that 'control over an organization' had not solidified in customary international law was the reason for the ICTY Appeals Chamber to overturn the judgment of the Trial Chamber; ICTY, *Prosecutor v. Milomir Stakić*, Appeals Judgment, Case No. IT-97-24-A: § 62.
25. Katanga, Confirmation of Charges, note 9: § 518.
26. Ibid.
27. Ibid.
28. Katanga, Trial Chamber Judgment, note 9.
29. Ibid, 1420. Ultimately, the Chamber convicted Katanga on the basis of Article 25 (3), sub d of the Rome Statute (contribution to a group acting with a common purpose to commit international crimes).
30. Ibid, 1410.
31. Ibid.
32. Katanga, Trial Chamber Judgment, note 9: § 1410.
33. Weigend, 'Perpetration through an Organization', 107. Pérez Léon Acevedo, note 1: 54, is equally aware of the problem where he writes that 'Certain concerns may be raised about how a theory originally framed for a very rigid state apparatus with a high level of hierarchical control (Nazi Germany) can work in contexts such as non-international armed conflicts in Africa with non-state actors where such "mechanization" seems to be weaker and the structures of power are more informal.'
34. H. G. van der Wilt, 'The Continuous Quest for Proper Modes of Criminal Responsibility', *Journal of International Criminal Justice* 7 (2009): 312.
35. See, inter alia, *Prosecutor v. Omar Hassan Al Bashir*, Decision on the Prosecution's Application for a Warrant of Arrest against Al-Bashir, Pre-Trial Chamber I, ICC-02/05-01/09, 4 March 2009: §§ 213-216; *Prosecutor v. Francis Kirimi Muthaura, Uhuru Mulgai Kenyatta and Mohammed Hussein Ali*, Decision on the Confirmation of Charges, Pre Trial Chamber, ICC-01/09-02/11-Red.., 23 January 2012: § 292; *Situation in the Libyan Arab Jamahirya*, Decision on the Prosecutor's Application pursuant to Article 58 as to Muammar Mohammed Aby Minyar Gaddaffi, Saif Al-Islam Gaddafi and Abdullah Al-Senussi, Pre Trial Chamber I, ICC -01/11-01/11-1, 27 June 2011: §§ 69–85. For a useful discussion of some of these cases, see Giulia Lanza, *Indirect Perpetration and Organisationsherrshaftslehre; An Analysis of Art. 25(3) of the Rome Statute in Light of the German Differentiated and Italian Unitarian Models of Participation in Crime* (Berlin: Duncker & Humblot, 2021), 96–107.
36. *Prosecutor v. Ntaganda*, Judgment, Trial Chamber, No. ICC-01/04-02/06, 8 July 2019: § 813.
37. Ntaganda, note 36: § 816.
38. Ibid, 819, italics added.
39. J.M. Rodriguez Devesa and A. Serrano Gomez, *Derecho Penal Espanol, Parte General*, (Madrid: Dykinson, 1994), 800 : '(La autoría mediata) es autor el que se vale de otra persona como mero instrumento para executar el hecho'.
40. In the famous Chilean case of the killing of Salvador Allende's minister of foreign affairs, Orlando Letelier, the responsibility of General Contreras who had masterminded the assault, could not be directly predicated on his prominent position in the Chilean secret service DINA, using that organization as a tool, because the immediate perpetrator was fully responsible himself. The Chilean Penal Code of 1874 (article 15) only acknowledged indirect perpetration when the direct perpetrator had been exposed to duress. Compare Kai Ambos, *Treatise on International Criminal Law, Volume I: Foundations and General Part* (Oxford:

Oxford University Press, 2013), 116; Francisco Muñoz-Conde and Héctor Olásolo, 'The Application of the Notion of Indirect Perpetration through Organized Structures of Power in Latin America and Spain', *Journal of International Criminal Justice* 9 (2011): 121/122.

41. A classic scholarly work on the nature and motives of these regimes is: G. O'Donnell, *Modernization and Bureaucratic Authoritarianism: Studies in South American Politics*, (Berkeley, C.A.: Institute for International Studies, 1973).
42. See Muñoz-Conde and Olásolo, 'The Application of the Notion of Indirect Perpetration', 116/117 and, in more detail, Olásolo, *The Criminal Responsibility of Senior Political and Military Leaders*, 128/129.
43. Muñoz-Conde and Olásolo, 'The Application of the Notion of Indirect Perpetration', 117.
44. Muñoz-Conde and Olásolo, 'The Application of the Notion of Indirect Perpetration', 117/118 with other examples of later practice in which courts kept struggling with the concept of indirect perpetration through organized structures of power. As a matter of fact, Muñoz-Conde and Olásolo give an abbreviated and slightly distorted reflection of the findings of the Argentinean Courts. Both the Federal Court and the Supreme Court acknowledged the value of Roxin's theory for the situation under scrutiny, but revealed an incomplete understanding of the concept. The Federal Court explicitly used the qualification ' autor mediato', but in fact treated the accused as necessary participants. The Majority of the Supreme Court changed the mode of liability into 'necessary participation', but thus perpetuated the Federal Court's depiction of the accused as 'mere accessories'. Both courts did not fully grasp the scope of *Organisationsherrshaft* as a basis for responsibility as a perpetrator and its compatibility with Argentinean criminal law. See for a discussion of this confusion, Marcelo A. Sancinetti, *Los Derechos Humanos en la Argentina post-dictatorial* (Buenos Aires: Lerner, 1988), 26–30. I am indebted to my friend Prof. Dr. Alejandro Chehtman, and an anonymous reviewer for drawing my attention to this complex issue.
45. CSJ (Corte Suprema de Justicia), Sala Penal Especial, judgment of 7 April 2009, Exp. No. AV 19-2001. For an overview of the background of the case and a seminal legal analysis, see Ambos, 'The *Fujimori* Judgment'.
46. CSJ, note 45: § 731. For the original confirmation of the possibility of a chain of 'perpetrators behind the perpetrator' (*Tätern hinter dem Täter*), see Claus Roxin, *Täterschaft und Tatherrschaft*, Sechste Auflage (Berlin/New York: Walter de Gruyter, 1994), 248.
47. For a critical discussion, see Ambos, 'The *Fujimori* Judgment', 152.
48. CSJ, note 45: §§ 726–7.
49. I draw this background information from the article by Muñoz-Conde and Olásolo, 'The Application of the Notion of Indirect Perpetration', 128.
50. Judgment of the Peruvian National Penal Chamber, 13 October 2006, Case No. 560-03; confirmed by the Peruvian Supreme Court, Penal Chamber, 14 December 2007, Case No. 5385.
51. For a critical discussion of this approach, see Muñoz-Conde and Olasolo, 'The Application of the Notion of Indirect Perpetration', 130. Compare also Dino Carlos Caro Coria, 'Prosecuting International Crimes in Peru', *International Criminal Law Review* 10 (2010): 598–9, who correctly observes that the large membership of Shining Path did not necessarily imply that the direct perpetrators were expandable.
52. Sala de Reconocimiento de Verdad, Responsabilidad y de la Determinación de los Hechos y Conductas de la Jurisdición Especial de la Paz, 26 January 2021 (hereafter : SRVR). The institute is established in order to conduct pre-procedures, involving truth-finding, legal qualifications of crimes and identification of responsibility, with a view to excluding especially serious (international) crimes from the ambit of amnesties. For an extensive analysis of the nature of the SRVR, the procedure and its findings in the case under scrutiny, see Kai Ambos and Milena Schellenberger, *Primera Imputación en la JEP: toma de rehenas y otras privaciones graves de la Libertad, cometidas por las FARC-EP*, CAPAZ (Instituto Colombo-Alema por la Paz), Policy Brief, 10-2021.
53. The SRVR explicitly referred to the Rome Statute, particularly mentioning Art. 7(1), sub e (Imprisonment or other severe deprivation of physical liberty in violation of fundamental

rules of international law) and art. 8(2) c, sub 3 (Taking hostages as a serious violation of Common Article 3 to the Geneva Conventions); SRVR, note 52: §§ 718, 749.

54. SRVR, note 52, § 113.
55. Corte Suprema de Justicia, 22 May 2013, No. 40830: § 14.
56. SRVR, note 52: §§ 782–4.
57. SRVR, note 52: § 771. Concurring with the conclusion, Ambos and Schellenberger, *Primera Imputación en la JEP*, 11, although they censure the shallow discussion of the evidence that was advanced to sustain the point.
58. See, for instance, Corte Suprema de Justicia, Sala Penal. Sentencia de 12 de Febrero de 2014. Radicado 40.214 ; Corte Suprema de Justicia, Sala Penal. Sentencia de 02 de Septiembre de 2009. Radicado 29.221.
59. Ambos, 'The *Fujimori* Judgment', 152.
60. Katanga, Judgment, 1412.
61. Ibid, 1411; Ambos, 'The *Fujimori* Judgment', 152.
62. Katanga, Confirmation of Charges, 524–6.
63. See, for instance, Carolin Urban, *Mittelbare Täterschaft kraft Organisationsherrschaft; Eine Studie zur Konzeption und Anwendbarkeit, insbesondere im Hinblick auf Wirschaftsunternehmen* (Universität Osnabrück, 2019).
64. Katanga, Confirmation of Charges, 518. Emphasis added.
65. *Prosecutor v. Dominic Ongwen*, Trial Chamber Judgment, ICC-02/04-01/15, 4 February 2021: § 2914.
66. Ibid, 2915–8.

Acknowledgements

The author acknowledges the assistance of his academic friends, Kai Ambos, Alejandro Chehtman and Hector Olásolo.

Disclosure statement

No potential conflict of interest was reported by the author(s).

The role of Criminal Justice in dealing with past atrocities in the Spanish and Argentine transitions: Common grounds, but different pathways

Elena Maculan

ABSTRACT
The comparative study of relevant Argentine and Spanish legislation and jurisprudence offers a perfect picture of the debate surrounding the role and limits of Criminal Law in transitional contexts. An analysis of these two experiences, and of the different choices they have taken, allows to point out three controversial aspects: firstly, the clash between legislative choices (often implying amnesties or similar measures) and judicial decisions that may somehow attempt to 'correct' the former. Secondly, the concerns raised by this creative judicial activity, in terms of its compatibility with the principles of legality and non-retroactivity and the prohibition of arbitrariness. Thirdly, the extent of the duty to prosecute and punish gross human rights violations vis-à-vis the limits of Criminal Justice. The article suggests reminding that, in extraordinary (transitional) contexts, Criminal Justice can and should be combined with other complementary mechanisms aimed at granting truth, justice, reparation and the building of a shared memory.

1. Introduction

Spain and Argentina share the experience of having had a past dictatorship, during which massive human rights violations were committed, and the challenge posed by its legacy in the framework of the transition to democracy. Yet, their respective choices as to the way to deal with past atrocities have differed.

Argentina initially combined a limited criminal prosecution with a full disclosure of truth undertaken by a truth commission, but the 1986 Full Stop and 1987 Due Obedience Laws soon closed that path. The later declaration of the unconstitutionality of these Laws (in the 2005 *Simón* case) has led to the reopening of criminal trials, many of which are still taking place. Here, the common problems faced by domestic tribunals are the situation of the defendants in these late prosecutions and how to overcome the statutory limitations, due to the length of time that has passed since the facts occurred. Domestic courts have developed some creative interpretations to overcome this obstacle, the main one being to qualify the facts as crimes against humanity, either as the sole qualifying category or combined with domestic offences. Nevertheless, these interpretations amount to a challenge to the principles of legality and non-retroactivity.

Spain has opted, instead, for 'a model of total oblivion with partial rehabilitation',[1] in which the 1977 Amnesty Law was a core element, and Criminal Justice had no place. This strategy was confirmed in 2007 Historical Memory Law, where further measures have since been provided, but no criminal prosecution was envisaged. Despite some attempts to bring past crimes before domestic criminal tribunals (in particular, former judge Garzón's 2008 decision, later overruled by the Supreme Court in 2012), both the legislator and the judiciary have closed that path.

The 2022 Law on Democratic Memory contains no provisions about criminal prosecution either, and it focuses, instead, on other mechanisms through which to grant truth, justice, and reparation. Moreover, the Spanish Constitutional Court, in a 2021 decision, has rejected the classification of the facts as crimes against humanity as a ground upon which to apply the rules of non-statutory limitations and the non-applicability of amnesties, based on its incompatibility with the legality principle. The interpretation followed by this judicial body is therefore at odds with the main interpretative trend identified in the Argentine jurisprudence, although some recent judicial developments cast some doubts on this conclusion.

The comparative study of relevant Argentine and Spanish legislation and jurisprudence offers a perfect picture of the debate surrounding the role and limits of Criminal Law in transitional contexts and the wider debate about the scope of the international duty to prosecute and punish human rights abuses. In this analysis, I shall point out two main features: first, the clash between legislative choices (often implying amnesties or similar measures) and judicial decisions, which may somehow try to 'correct' these. Judges often use international crimes as an 'interpretive lockpick' to break down the wall created by the rules on statutory limitations (and, to a lesser extent, by amnesty provisions).

Second, I shall point out the concerns raised by this creative judicial activity, in terms of its compatibility with the principles of legality and non-retroactivity. The dilemma faced by judges, between respecting these principles while admitting impunity, or prosecuting the facts while infringing these principles, cannot find an easy solution. Besides considering the drawbacks of both solutions, I argue that, in extraordinary (transitional) contexts, Criminal Justice should be applied always granting the compatibility with Constitutional principles, and it could be combined with other complementary mechanisms aimed at granting truth, justice, and reparation.

2. The Argentine experience: Criminal Law as the key tool

2.1. A transitional process in three phases

In the transitional experience that followed the collapse of the military dictatorship of the *Juntas* in Argentina, three separate periods may be distinguished, in which the role of criminal prosecution has been framed in different fashions.[2] At the very beginning of the transition, in 1984, Alfonsín's Presidency adopted a combination of a (at least pretended) full discovery of truth entrusted to the Truth Commission CONADEP, and *selective* criminal prosecution of those who bore the main responsibility.[3] The unexpected opening of a higher number of criminal prosecutions, together with the serious threat of a new military *coup*, led to a shift in the strategy.

The 1984 Full Stop Law and the 1986 Due Obedience Law[4] opened therefore a second phase of impunity. Nevertheless, some alternative options were explored to overcome this situation: the opening of criminal prosecutions for offences that were expressly excluded from the scope of the two laws (such as the crime of the abduction of minors);[5] charges brought before tribunals of other States, by means of the principles of passive personality or of universal jurisdiction;[6] and the so-called truth-finding trials. The latter is a unique hybrid mechanism, in which tribunals with competence on criminal matters performed a truth-finding activity about past atrocities.[7] Although this allowed to satisfy the victims' right to truth in a moment in which the two impunity laws prevented any criminal prosecution, the mechanism has two main flaws: first, it mixed the goals, tools and limits of criminal proceedings with those more appropriate for a truth commission, in entrusting criminal tribunals with an activity where there was no defendant, nor charges, nor a judgment or a sentence, but where the limits, standards and safeguards of a criminal trial seemingly applied to a certain extent. Second, the truth-finding trials appeared as a judge-made mechanism, and the lack of a common regulation allowed each jurisdiction to decide which format giving to it, thereby causing significant differences and infringing the principle of equality before the law.[8]

In 2001, the first ruling declaring the unconstitutionality of the Full Stop and Due Obedience Laws was issued,[9] and later upheld by the Supreme Court in the seminal 2005 *Simón* judgment.[10] Both rulings grounded their findings mainly in the Inter-American jurisprudence and in its *Barrios Altos* precedent, which declared the incompatibility of the two Peruvian self-amnesty laws with the victims' rights to fair trial and to judicial protection and the duty to prosecute and punish serious violations of human rights protected under the American Convention on Human Rights, as well as under other human rights treaties.[11] This judgment opened the IACtHR rich jurisprudential line stating the States' duty to prosecute and punish international crimes or serious human rights violations and the parallel, absolute inapplicability of amnesties and similar weavers of punishment.[12] This interpretive line, which broadened the scope of the prohibition, from self-amnesties, to amnesties issued by a democratic Parliament (and even ratified in popular referendum),[13] to pardons issued after the sentence had been partially served,[14] has been paramount to the progressive consolidation of the duty to prosecute and punish serious human rights violations.

No international treaty expressly prohibits amnesty nor affirms a duty to punish;[15] yet, they both appear in some soft law instruments,[16] in some human rights bodies' decisions, such as the HRC,[17] in the ICTY seminal *Furundzija* Judgment,[18] in a SCSL decision[19] and in an ECCC decision, which found that treaty obligations prohibit amnesties and similar measures concerning genocide, torture, and grave breaches of the Geneva Conventions and that, in general terms, there is an emerging consensus on the prohibition of amnesties for serious international crimes.[20] Nevertheless, the IACtHR's strict understanding of this duty stands against an opposite, more flexible interpretation thereof, maintained, as we will explain further, by other judicial bodies and part of scholarly literature.

The *Barrios Altos* precedent has been widely applied by many Latin-American countries in assessing the admissibility of their amnesty provisions, by virtue of the doctrine of the control of conventionality, and has served as a ground to state the unconstitutionality of domestic impunity laws that were found incompatible with the rights and duties set out in the American Convention and in other human rights treaties.[21] This is exactly the core of the reasoning of the Argentine Supreme Court in the *Simón* case.

This new position, completed by the declaration of unconstitutionality of the pardons that had been granted, in the 2006 *Mazzeo* judgment,[22] paved the way for the reopening of criminal prosecutions under a new transitional phase.[23]

Since then, reopened criminal prosecutions dealing with the crimes of the past dictatorship have proliferated all over the country, under the coordination of a dedicated Unity created within the General Office of the Prosecution (*Procuración General de la Nación*, PGN) to assist the federal prosecutors all over the country in dealing with such complex cases.[24] These late criminal prosecutions face important challenges, such as the death or the old age of many alleged perpetrators (who may not be fit to stand trial), and the application of statutory limitations.

2.2. The reopening of criminal prosecutions: statutory limitations and judicial creativity

According to data collected by the PGN,[25] the reopening of criminal prosecutions dealing with the crimes of the dictatorship lead to investigations against 3631 people and to the conviction of 1088 people, including some high-profile perpetrators.[26] This is commonly seen as an achievement in terms of granting truth, acknowledgment and justice to victims,[27] and such judgments definitely perform a significant expressive function. In contrast, 1371 people died during the proceedings, before a judgment was issued, and this circumstance clearly frustrated the victims' expectations in terms of finding the truth about the crimes and having the corresponding criminal liability declared.

Moreover, there remains the problem that the length of time that has elapsed since the commission of the facts has time barred the offences, according to the rules on statutory limitations envisaged in Argentine legislation (art. 59 Penal Code). To overcome this obstacle, many tribunals have resorted to the classification of the facts as international crimes; more specifically, as crimes against humanity (CAH), deriving from this feature the inapplicability of statutory limitations.[28]

Qualifying the facts under this category mirrors also their higher seriousness, their massive and systematic nature, and their integration into a wider context of violence and criminality, which common offences cannot communicate properly.[29]

Nevertheless, CAH appeared in Argentine legislation with Law 24.584, promulgated on 23 November 1995, implementing the 1968 Convention on the Non-Applicability of Statutory Limitations to War Crimes and Crimes Against Humanity. This law does not even offer a true description of the category; rather, it refers to the text of the 1968 Convention, which in turn refers to the Statute of the International Military Tribunal. Applying an offence that was included in the Argentine legislation *after* the offences were perpetrated amounts, *prima facie,* to a violation of the principle of non-retroactivity of unfavourable legal provisions.

Many judgments[30] argue that CAH were part of international customary law and as such can be applied under Article 118 of the Argentine Constitution, which refers to crimes 'against the law of nations'. This interpretation is grounded on a concept of legality much wider and more flexible of that consolidated in the Argentine system and, in general terms, in systems belonging to Continental legal tradition.[31] Resorting to international treaties that define the offences at stake does not comply with the standards of certainty, clarity, and determination required by the principle of legality under this legal tradition. Treaties, by their very nature, contain only the prohibition of certain conducts that violate human rights. Moreover, the fact that they impose an obligation on States party thereto to take all necessary legislative measures to criminalise the conduct prohibited in the international text suggests that the Convention 'does not establish any criminal offence in accordance with the requirements of the principle of legality, but rather describes the elements that the criminal offence must contain'.[32]

Additionally, many of the international Conventions invoked by the courts in the judgments analysed (such as the 1994 Inter-American Convention on Forced Disappearance of Persons or the 2006 International Convention for the Protection of All Persons from Enforced Disappearance) were signed *after* the criminal acts judged in these proceedings occurred. The same can be said of the ICC Statute, the only international instrument to date that defines the category of CAH as a whole, as a set of different criminal conducts committed in the context of a widespread or systematic attack against the civilian population, and with the knowledge of that attack.[33]

The argument used by many domestic courts to repeal this objection considers that the treaty rules simply crystallise prohibitions already contained in international custom, and that, therefore, their application would be 'retrospective and not retroactive'.[34] However, nor is international custom fully compatible with the strict understanding of the principle of legality: not only because it is an unwritten source (and thus not complying with the *lex scripta* requirement), but also because its application should be subject to prior verification that a customary rule prohibiting the conduct in question actually existed at the time of the events,[35] a step that courts very often neglect. Thus, for example, the concept of CAH, in the 1970s-1980s, had not clearly emancipated itself from the need for a link to an armed conflict, nor was the requirement for a widespread or systematic attack expressly stated. In any case, the unwritten nature and progressive formation of international custom, as well as the plurality of the sources that contribute to it, impinge on its accessibility (as required for Criminal Law provisions) and make it very difficult for citizens to know in advance, with a satisfactory level of certainty, the exact content of the prohibited conduct and the consequences that its commission entails.[36] Although the *generically criminal nature* of such conducts was undoubtedly known at the time of their commission, there was no clear and precise definition of the specific constitutive elements that had to be met in order to classify them as international crimes.

A further problem is the lack, in both conventional and customary international norms, of the provision of the penalty corresponding to the crimes, which is also a requirement for the principle of legality (*nulla poena sine lege*).[37]

Some doubts as to the compatibility with the principle of legality arise, too, as regards the rule of the non-applicability of statutory limitations to international crimes. The provision has consolidated at a much later stage than the moment in which the atrocities of the dictatorship were committed. The only relevant normative provision in force at the time was the 1968 Convention on the Non-Applicability of Statutory Limitations, which is often considered as crystallising international custom, but which has been signed by a small number of States, making it unclear whether it actually reflects an *opinio juris.*

Facing this tension, domestic courts have developed some interesting interpretive proposals, none of which is, though, in my view fully convincing. A first option would be to admit a more relaxed or flexible concept of the principle of legality, in line with its understanding in International Law and, especially, with the provisions contained in Articles 14(2) ICCPR and 7(2) ECHR, according to which the principle of legality shall not prejudice the trial and punishment of conducts which, at the time of their commission, 'constituted an offence according to the general principles of law recognized by civilized nations' or 'by the community of nations', respectively.[38] This option, which has been explicitly or implicitly maintained by many domestic courts, in Argentina and elsewhere,[39] would create a sort of *double track* for international crimes.

In my view, such a flexible interpretation of the principle of legality should not be given priority over a stricter concept thereof, which is expressly stated in the Argentine Constitution (art. 18) and in many other Constitutions, and which grants a wider protection,[40] to the accused and to any citizen, against any possible misuse or abuse in the exercise of the *ius puniendi.*

Additionally, the provision for a stricter concept of the principle of legality in the Rome Statute (Articles 22 and 23) may be seen as a trend towards elevating the international understanding of the principle of legality to a stricter level,[41] virtually against what this view proposes.

Lastly, the creation of this double track would, in my opinion, require a clear determination of the core of offences to which it can apply by way of exception. The perimeter of these categories is not, though, in practice, as clearly fixed as might be thought, and it has been the object of several expansive interpretations. For example, both in the 2018 *Levin* judgment and in the 2022 *Almirón* judgment,[42] some episodes of torture, committed by police agents in 1976–1977 against some people who had been denounced by their bosses for alleged fraud, are labelled as CAH, even though the facts could hardly be linked to the context of attack against the civilian population furthered by the military dictatorship.

Similarly, two judgments issued by the Argentine *Cámara Federal de Casación Penal* came to qualify as CAH the conducts of forgery[43] and illegal occupation,[44] on the ground that they were part of the wider attack against the civilian population. The following step in both judgments was the declaration of the non-applicability of statutory limitations to the offences, although one might wonder whether these offences can properly fall under the 'other illegal acts of a similar nature' clause.

A second option proposed by some Argentine judicial decisions to grant the compatibility with the principle of legality is the 'dual classification of facts'.[45] This technique is based on the qualification of the facts under two criminal categories at once: as both an international crime and a domestic offence. The first category allows the declaration of the non-applicability of statutory limitations and, if needed, of amnesties and similar waivers of punishment; in contrast, the second category, insofar as it was already provided in domestic legislation at the time of the facts, would grant the compatibility with the principle of non-retroactivity, as well as the provision of the applicable sanction.

This technique, albeit interesting, has serious methodological flaws: firstly, it does not clarify the relationship existing between the two categories. Despite its usually being labelled as a case *of apparent concurrence of norms*, the solution does not follow the criterion that ordinarily applies to these cases (i.e. the *lex specialis* criterion), according to Continental legal systems.[46] This criterion would lead to the applying of just one of the concurring norms, namely, the most specific one, whereas the dual classification aims at applying both.

Secondly, as regards the international component, it still poses the same, unsolved challenges to the principle of legality that I have described above.

Lastly, since it applies both categories at once, it amounts to a judicial creation of a further criminal offence, which is not the same as either the domestic or the international one. Judicial creation of new criminal offences is clearly not allowed in Continental legal systems (to which Argentina belongs), and it no longer occurs in common law systems either.[47]

Actually, both the options that I have just described may amount, in my view, to judicial arbitrariness: 'The interpretive role of judges is not necessarily hostile to the rule of law. But there is a standing tension between that interpretive role, and the rule of law'.[48] Facing some legislative constraints that are perceived as *unfair,* judges develop some *ad hoc* interpretive solutions that fit neither within Constitutional principles nor in ordinary Criminal Law rules.

When facing the obstacle posed by the time-barring of the offences, tribunals have developed an interpretive trend that is clearly expansive, from a diachronic perspective, since it broadens the scope of CAH back in time.[49] Not only do these judges consciously create a sort of exceptional separate track along which to prosecute the offences committed under the dictatorship, they also use the categories of international crimes (especially of CAH) as an *interpretive lock pick* to break down the wall that prevents Criminal Law from displaying its full effects.

Judges act as substitutes for, as a 'double' of, a legislator whose political decisions are perceived as insufficient or unfair. Although this judicial activism is understandable, when facing the hard legacy of collective atrocities, it somehow deprives the legislative and the executive powers of their role, and of their corresponding *responsibility*, thereby questioning the rule of law. Furthermore, the special track thus created for a restricted number of atrocities is at constant risk of expanding beyond its original boundaries, and to broaden the scope of the exceptional measures there allowed to many other facts that fail to reach either the same level of seriousness, or its same widespread nature.

In this sense, I find much more correct another interpretive option that appears in some judicial decisions: namely, arguing that the time barring should be considered as suspended during the dictatorial regime in which the abuses were committed, due to the full suspension, under that rule, of all basic safeguards, and due to the impossibility of taking criminal action against those responsible for the offences.[50] This understanding would allow the overcoming of the obstacle posed by statutory limitations, without causing the tensions above described with the principle of legality and non-retroactivity. Moreover, it stresses the illegitimacy of the past regime that committed the atrocities, thereby giving grounds for the application of a special rule. Still, it would need further development, as to the determination of the moment when the limitation period ceases to be suspended, which should, ideally, be determined by means of a legislative provision.

Given this, outside all of these interpretive proposals, which share the ultimate goal of finding a way to allow *late criminal prosecutions*, there might be another way to give a response to past atrocities: that is, by admitting that, in transitional and post-transitional settings, taking into account the exceptionality of those circumstances and the intrinsic limits of Criminal Law, we could focus instead on other, extra-Criminal Law or even extra-judicial mechanisms, aimed at satisfying the claims for truth, justice (in a wider sense), and reparation.[51] Here is where the Spanish transition may offer some interesting ideas.

3. The Spanish experience: Amnesty, 'Historical Memory' and 'Democratic Memory' ... but no room for Criminal Law

The Spanish transitional experience has taken a direction very different from the Argentine choice. When the dictator Francisco Franco died, one of the first measures taken by the new democratic regime was the 1977 Law on Amnesty (Law 46/1977, of 15 October), which was passed with the votes of the 93.3% of the members of the Parliament, including those political parties that were the main target of the Francoist repression. The provision can therefore be classified as a democratic amnesty, and it provided for a general, bilateral amnesty (covering the offences committed by both the dictatorial regime and the opponents or dissident thereto), with a somewhat different scope depending on the date of the fact and with no conditions to grant the benefit.[52]

This law closed the way for criminal prosecution of the crimes committed during the Civil War and the Francoist dictatorship, while other normative provisions envisaged a wide range of measures of redress: monetary compensation, the rehabilitation of civil servants and military members who had been purged by Franco, and the return of exiled people.[53] Spain thus opted for a 'model of oblivion with partial rehabilitation'[54] and it is seen as the only country where a general impunity was explicitly declared and approved as such by all the democratic forces.[55] Albeit many scholars criticise this option as 'a third route towards impunity',[56] an 'amnesic transition'[57] or 'an imposed oblivion and granted impunity',[58] we should remind that it was taken in a historical moment in which the duty to prosecute and punish the alleged commission of international crimes, which we have recalled above, was far from being as firmly consolidated as it is nowadays.[59]

In Spain, the prevention of criminal prosecution thus imposed by the Amnesty Law was confirmed by the later Law on Historical Memory (Law 52/2007, of 26 December, LHM), which provided a set of very needed measures for reparation (such as the withdrawal of coats of arms, insignias, and other objects that glorified Francoism), for re-integration and for building memory, all outside the area of Criminal Law. One key measure was the imposition on Public Administration of a duty to assist relatives of disappeared people, which allowed the opening of mass graves, and the identification of the bodily remains.[60]

Part of the public opinion, victims' associations, and certain scholars have largely criticised the decision to exclude every option of criminal prosecution, as well as the investigation on the facts and the acknowledgment of responsibilities by, possibly, a non-judicial body, such as a truth commission.[61] In addition, the implementation of the LHM faced problems of coordination between central and local institutions, many of which did not cooperate in the activities of opening of mass graves, and problems with funding, after the cut abruptly imposed by the new political majority in 2011, thereby ultimately leaving the task of searching and identifying missing victims to private initiatives.[62]

3.1. Attempts to open criminal prosecutions

The criticism of the Amnesty Law and the dissatisfaction with the poor implementation of the LHM and the 'privatisation' of the search for mass graves led to the undertaking of some initiatives to open proper criminal prosecution for the crimes of the Civil War and the dictatorship.

In 2008, (then) Judge Baltasar Garzón issued a decision in which he classified some of those episodes as permanent offences of illegal detention perpetrated 'in the context of crimes against humanity'.[63] This qualification allowed him to declare that those offences could not be time-barred, nor benefit from the amnesty, besides grounding his competence over them. Although the category of CAH was included in the Spanish Penal Code only in 2003 (art. 607 bis Penal Code), the judge maintained (in a very similar vein to what we have seen in the Argentine jurisprudence) that CAH already existed, at the time of the facts, in international custom, crystallized in the 'Martens clause' in the 1907 Hague Convention, in the 1945 Nuremberg Principles and in the 1948 Genocide Convention. This factor would be sufficient, in his view, to comply with the standards of foreseeability required by the principle of legality. Furthermore, the decision also labelled the facts as common offences of illegal detention, envisaged in the Penal Code in force at that time, from which it obtained a detailed description of the illegal conduct and the applicable sanction, thus granting, in principle, the compliance with the principle of legality. This reasoning, based on the technique of the 'dual classification of facts' that we have previously recalled, led the judge to declare the inadmissibility of the Amnesty Law and of statutory limitations to the facts, and to order some investigative activities to ascertain responsibilities and to identify the remains in mass graves.

Nevertheless, the Supreme Court, in its judgment STS 101/2012, of 27 February, rejected this interpretation (while declaring Judge Garzón *not* guilty of the crime of breach of duty with which he was charged), deeming it incompatible with the principle of legality.[64] According to the judgment, the international norms to which the judge had resort neither comply with the requisite of determination, accessibility, and clarity of criminal law provisions, nor do they provide the applicable sanctions, thereby infringing the *nulla poena sine lege* mandate.

Moreover, the Supreme Court recalls that the rule of the non-applicability of statutory limitations to international crimes also emerged at a later stage than the moment in which the facts took place, it being envisaged in international treaties that Spain has ratified much later (such as the Rome Statute) or not ratified at all (such as the 1968 Convention), as well as in human rights bodies' decisions issued at a later moment. Since the rules about the time-barring of offences fall within substantive Criminal Law, according to the Court's consolidated jurisprudence, they are subject to the principle of the non-retroactivity of unfavourable provisions: as a result, the (unfavourable) provision on the non-applicability of statutory limitations cannot apply to previous facts.

Furthermore, the Supreme Court rejects the claim that the facts covered by the 1977 Amnesty Law were CAH and that, therefore, they cannot be the object of an amnesty. The Tribunal states that the rule of non-applicability of amnesties is still debated and it emerged in International Law after the facts occurred. Since it amounts to an unfavourable provision, it cannot be applied retroactively either. Besides this, the tribunal considers that the special needs and priorities of a transitional setting may allow the application of an amnesty, insofar as some minimum legitimacy conditions (such as being passed by a democratic Parliament and not being a blanket amnesty) are met, and it does not prevent the process from truth-seeking. The tribunal thus follows the position that, in general terms, allows, under certain circumstances, the passing of amnesties or other mechanisms that restrict or limit criminal prosecution, provided they fulfil some minimum legitimacy requirement,[65] as does the 1977 Amnesty Law.

The issue of the validity of the 1977 Amnesty Law has indeed been posed in a couple of cases before the European Court of Human Rights (ECtHR); however, the Court declared both cases inadmissible, without entering into a proper analysis of the subject matter,[66] possibly in line with its traditional self-restraint when deciding on the validity of amnesty provisions enacted by democratic institutions. In contrast to the IACtHR intrusive approach,[67] the ECtHR has maintained a more cautious position.[68] In its comparatively less abundant jurisprudence on the matter, the Strasbourg Court has generally applied a flexible approach to deference to states,[69] when examining not the validity of amnesty provisions *per se*, but their effects on individual rights.[70]

These opposing perspectives have been explained in light of a different understanding of criminal prosecution, which would be, according to the IACtHR, a form of reparation itself, to which victims are entitled, whereas the ECtHR considers it as an instrument with a preventive and deterrent purpose.[71] According to an even more convincing analysis, the Inter-American strict approach, and its resistance to granting margin of appreciation to states, is due to the historical situation of deficient local judiciaries and unreliable autocratic regimes in the region,[72] a circumstance which is not commonly found in the countries that fall under the jurisdiction of the ECtHR.

One can identify a progressive rapprochement between the Inter-American and the European position on amnesties, insofar as the former has not closed the door to amnesty provisions issued in contexts of ongoing conflicts, such as El Salvador and Colombia,[73] and the latter, in turn, has increasingly remarked the existence of a duty to prosecute serious human rights violations, especially when referring to torture cases.[74] Yet, the ECtHR has been cautious in admitting the existence of a 'a growing tendency for international, regional and national courts to overturn general amnesties enacted by Governments',[75] and has insisted, so far, on the need to leave the States a certain margin of appreciation as to the best means to tackle past human rights abuses.[76] A relevant concurring opinion by three of its judges states that 'international rules imposing a blanket ban on amnesties in cases of grave violations of human rights [are] liable, in some circumstances, to reduce the effectiveness of human rights protection' and, in certain cases, 'there may be practical arguments in favour of an amnesty that encompasses some grave human rights violations'.[77]

In a similar vein, the ICC, against the background of the silence of the Rome Statute on the issue, has not ruled out the possibility to pass an amnesty. In fact, the quite categorical stance by the PTC in the *Gaddafi* case, according to which 'there is a strong, growing, universal tendency that grave and systematic human rights violations – which may amount to crimes against humanity by their very nature – are not subject to amnesties or pardons under international law',[78] was somehow deflated by the Appeals Chamber which, albeit declaring that the amnesty law was not applicable to the specific case, cautiously affirmed that 'international law is still in in the developmental stage on the question of acceptability of amnesties'.[79]

This jurisprudence supports, in my view, the position in favour of a somehow flexible interpretation of the general duty imposed on States to prosecute and punish international crimes or serious human rights violations. This view, which I personally share, claims for the admissibility of a nuanced application of this duty in extraordinary contexts, in which amnesties, pardons or other leniency measures (provided they fulfil some legitimacy conditions) might be necessary for the transitional or peace-making process,[80] whereas a full criminal prosecution might turn even into an obstacle to it.[81]

Interestingly, we can found an example of this view in the recent decision issued by the Spanish Constitutional Court in 2021 about the legitimacy of the Amnesty Law.

3.2. The 2021 Constitutional Court decision on the validity of the Amnesty Law

On 15 September 2021 the Spanish Constitutional Court issued its first decision on the constitutionality of the Amnesty Law,[82] dealing with a writ of protection filed by Gerardo Iglesias Argüelles, a victim of torture while he was under police custody during the Francoist regime. The complaint he filed, claiming to have been the victim of crimes against humanity and injuries, was rejected by first and second instance tribunals, according to which those facts were both time-barred and covered by the Amnesty Law.

The Constitutional Court rejects the classification of facts as CAH, since the category was not provided in domestic legislation at the time of the facts, and international custom (which was the only normative source existing at that time where one can find a definition of the offence) does not comply with the mandates of *lex scripta, praevia et certa* stemming from the principle of legality. Once stated that the facts cannot be classified under that category, it follows that we cannot, either, apply the special regime attached to that category, especially the inapplicability of statutory limitations and of amnesties. As the tribunal literally says:

> In sum, the constitutional provisions about the principle of legality prevent us from applying, in our constitutional framework, offences that are defined, in frameworks that are partially alien to our legal systems, in an open, changing, non-homogeneous way, without it being consolidated in an exact provision and in which, moreover, no specific content can be found as to the applicable sanction. Since it is not possible to label the facts as crimes against humanity, the consequences that the applicant links to that classification to overcome some obstacles to their prosecution, namely, the non-applicability of statutory limitation and the amnesty, also disappear.[83]

This decision reminds us of the judgment issued by the Supreme Court back in 2012, which rejected the interpretation proposed by Judge Garzón, and goes against the position in favour of a complete ban of amnesties covering gross human rights violations. The Court refers to the ECtHR and ICC jurisprudence that we have recalled above,[84] as a support to a more flexible position regarding the international duty to prosecute and punish.

Interestingly, the tribunal points out, in a final remark, that the closure of criminal proceedings does not wholly prevent the looking for *truth and reparation* by means of *other mechanisms outside the criminal trial* (point 7): an option that would indeed be, in my view, not only needed, but also much more effective than insisting on the activity of criminal tribunals at all costs. Along the same line seemingly goes the new Law on Democratic Memory, which is the last step in the Spanish (post-)transitional experience.

3.3. The Law on Democratic Memory

The new Law on Democratic Memory (Law 20/2022, LDM) was passed on 19 October 2022 to take over from the LHM.[85] The aspects of concern that led to take this step were, basically, twofold: first, the diversity among the Spanish Autonomous Communities as to the activity and initiatives undertaken to deal with the pending issues of truth, reparation, and memory of the past abuses. Some Autonomous Communities have passed their own regional Laws on Historical Memory and have devoted great efforts to their implementation, while others have been rather inactive.[86] Second, some missions realised by international bodies and the following Reports have repeatedly insisted on the need for Spain to undertake a serious effort for the identification of victims of forced disappearances at the national level, as part of a comprehensive State policy.[87]

The new Law, which has been enacted after a heated debate, and amidst the tensions regarding the exhumation and removal of Franco's bodily remains from the monument *El Valle de los Caídos*,[88] does not invalidate the 1977 Amnesty Law. In contrast, it focuses mainly on mechanisms, either judicial or not, to enact policies of memory and to meet the claims for reparation, truth, and justice in a broader sense.

Thus, to comply with the goals of reparation, the Law provides, *inter alia,* for the disavowal of the *coup,* the declaration of nullity of all convictions and sentences handed down by the special tribunals created during the dictatorship, the investigation and acknowledgment of the seizures undertaken and the reparation to victims of forced labour.

As regards the goal of truth, the Law proposes to promote the exhumation and identification of disappeared people and the creation and maintenance of archives. As to the goal of memory, the Law insists on the revision and removal of Francoist symbols (which surprisingly still exist in many places); it proposes the study of measures at the educative level, the creation of archives and registers and the development of policies and places of democratic memory.

Furthermore, it envisages the creation of an independent Commission to which it entrusts 'the ascertaining of human rights violations (…), by means of collecting testimonies, information and documents' and the drafting of a Report 'to systematize the existing information' and to propose conclusions and recommendations (art. 57.5 LDM). The Commission should be an independent, temporary, non-judicial body of scholarly nature: i.e. it is conceived following the model of a (belated) Truth Commission.[89] The Law refers to a later Decree to determine the composition, timeframe, and mandate of such Commission, but this Decree has at the moment of writing not yet been passed.

Lastly, in view of the goal of justice, it envisages the creation of a 'Special Prosecutor for the Investigation of facts amounting to breaches of International Human Rights Law and International Humanitarian Law, including those that took place during the *coup*, the war and the dictatorship' (art. 28) and it affirms the 'right to investigate' those breaches (art. 29). These provisions call for an activity developed in the field of Criminal Law, but not necessarily for criminal trials as such. What is envisaged here is a specialised figure, within the Office of the Prosecutor, who undertakes and purports investigations about those facts, with no pretension of obtaining a conviction, nor of the imposition of a sanction. Actually, the reference to the duty of the new Special Prosecutor to protect 'legality and human rights' (art. 29.1) and the focus on the search and identification of disappeared victims seem to confirm this interpretation.

However, the LDM apparently contains a provision that may serve as a ground for maintaining the view that past crimes are not subject to amnesties nor are they time barred, much against the position held, until now, by the Spanish Supreme and Constitutional Court. Art. 2.3 of the Law states:

> All laws of the Spanish State, including the Law 46/1977, of 15th October, Law on Amnesty, shall be interpreted and applied in accordance with conventional and customary International Humanitarian Law, according to which crimes against humanity, war crimes, genocide and torture are considered as not subject to statutory limitations nor amnesties.[90]

This provision has been understood as a possible ground to argue the non-applicability of the 1977 Amnesty Law and of statutory limitations,[91] as it was, admittedly, the intention of the drafters of the provision. This view has been expressly maintained also by the Special Prosecutor on Human Rights and Democratic Memory, Ms. Dolores Delgado, in a recent Directive to a local Prosecutor dealing with a case of alleged torture committed during the Francoist regime.[92] The Special Prosecutor argues, against the criterion followed by the local Prosecutor, that the case cannot be closed at the initial stage, since a certain amount of investigation is needed to determine whether the facts can be labelled as CAH, and whether they are time barred and covered by the amnesty. She affirms that Art. 2.3 of the LDM 'expressly recognises the interpretive value of customary law and *jus cogens* about the most serious human rights violations, which imply the effects of non-applicability of statutory limitations nor of amnesties to crimes against humanity'.[93]

In my view, though, the impact of this provision is not so clear. To begin with, its drafting seems to me quite unfortunate, since it apparently suggests that the interpretation of legal provisions in Spain has been, until now, *not in accordance* with international norms. What we can find in the Spanish legal system is, instead, the same debate that still persists, in scholarship, international jurisprudence and other venues, between two competing positions about the admissibility of amnesty laws in transitional settings and about the exact content and scope of the duty to prosecute and punish serious human rights violations.[94] As Schabas notes, 'The amnesty pendulum [...] seems to be returning to equilibrium'.[95] In this unresolved conflict, the Spanish Supreme Court and the Constitutional Court by majority have opted for the more flexible position as to this duty, and for the adherence to a *maximalist* understanding of the principle of legality and legal certainty.

Furthermore, even admitting that the duty aforementioned and the parallel inapplicability of amnesties and of statutory limitations have consolidated in International Law, this does not automatically imply the possibility to apply them *retroactively*. The stricter understanding of the principle of legality, which both the Spanish Supreme and Constitutional Courts have clearly re-affirmed, prevents that retroactive application of the rules to facts occurred during the Civil War and the Francoist dictatorship, as the General Counsel of the Judiciary has stated in its Report on the LDM.[96]

More recently, in response to the aforementioned Directive issued by the Special Prosecutor on Human Rights and Democratic Memory, the competent Judge declared the inadmissibility of the claim, arguing that the LDM does not impose a duty of *criminal* investigation.[97]

Considering this, the provision apparently performs a mere symbolic function, with no practical impact to be expected. If that is correct, as Alicia Gil rightly points out, 'the worst part of this irresponsible game is that the legislator transfers again to tribunals the unpleasant task of frustrating the false expectations that have been created'.[98]

A further mechanism envisaged in the LDM that has strangely not attracted much attention, but that can be especially interesting, in my view, to satisfy the victims' rights to truth and justice, is the 'file of information for perpetual memory' (art. 29.2 LDM). It is a judicial procedure envisaged by Law 15/2015, about Voluntary Jurisdiction, which allows the obtaining of an *official declaration* about certain facts that occurred, insofar as there is no controversy and no need to open an adversarial process about them. The mechanism, regulated with more details in the Final Disposition 3rd of the LDM, is a judicial venue, but falls outside the scope of Criminal Law, belonging to the area of Civil Law. It might turn out to be a valid alternative pathway, in my view, towards meeting the victims' legitimate claims for truth, acknowledgment, and justice.

The mechanisms thus provided by the LDM are grounded on a wider concept of Justice, not limited to Criminal Law, and one which enhances the options for victims to satisfy their rights to have access to justice and to truth.[99] They can, in my opinion (and while waiting to see the real implementation of the recently passed Law), be a perfectly valid solution to complying with some key goals of transitional processes (truth, justice in a broad sense, and reparation), without forcing the limits and principles of Criminal Law nor the role of the judiciary, and without opening a way prone to arbitrary expansion and to being manipulated for political reasons.

4. Comparing the two experiences: common grounds, but different pathways

The transitional experiences in Argentina and in Spain share many common grounds: both stem from the overcoming of a dictatorial regime (plus a civil war, in the case of Spain), both face the challenge of dealing with the legacy of massive human rights violations, and both have opted, at least at some point, for a limitation on criminal prosecution with respect to those atrocities. However, while Argentina has eliminated the two impunity laws that paralysed criminal prosecution during a long period and has shifted to a classic Criminal Justice response, Spain still keeps its Amnesty Law in force. Even the recent events, including the passing of a new Law on Democratic Memory, or the issuing of a decision by the Constitutional Court about the legitimacy of the 1977 Amnesty Law, have not furthered the opening of criminal prosecutions.[100]

A first remark we can make is that the two experiences show a different dynamic between the respective judiciaries, the Constitutional Courts, and the legislative and executive powers. When it comes to validating political decisions about how to come to terms with the legacy of past atrocities, the judiciary may either support the strategy adopted by the legislator or may try to invalidate or even 'correct' it. The decisions issued by the Spanish Supreme Court and Constitutional Court confirm the validity of the 1977 Amnesty Law, acknowledging its importance for the successful transition to democracy, thus aligning themselves with the political decision not to pursue criminal prosecution but, rather, to focus on other mechanisms towards granting truth, reparation, and memory-building.

Argentine tribunals, instead, have clearly acted as *opponents* to the political decision not to prosecute (anymore) past atrocities: this is self-evident not only in the Supreme Court's *Simón* decision to declare the two impunity laws unconstitutional, but also in the following judgments that reinterpret the rules about statutory limitations, the definition of the crimes and the principles of legality very much against what domestic legislation says.

We may talk about *synergy* to define the dynamics between the judiciary and the legislative power in the transitional design in Spain, whereas the Argentine judiciary acts more as an opponent than an ally, under the idea of providing a *correction* of political strategies that are deemed to be wrong or unfair.

At a first glance, the overall Spanish strategy appears more prone to granting *impunity* to those responsible for the atrocities, and indeed has in this sense received much criticism. Still, I think that it is important to consider which would be the consequences of reopening the classic venues of criminal prosecution at this stage. Besides the fact that almost all those who took part in the offences have died or are very old (and might not be fit to stand trial), the long time passed since the facts imply that the crimes are time-barred, not to mention the doubts that might arise as to the significance of these late prosecutions in terms of deterrence or positive prevention. The legitimate victims' claims for truth, acknowledgment and justice (which can be met, to a certain extent, in the judgments following these late prosecutions) might find, instead, more satisfactory and less problematic responses in mechanisms and activities outside the classic Criminal Law venue.

The parallel experience in Argentina shows the significant challenges that a late prosecution of past atrocities poses to fundamental Criminal Law principles, especially the principle of legality and non-retroactivity and the rule of law. Here, judges face a very hard dilemma, between respecting key Criminal Law and Constitutional principles while admitting impunity, or prosecuting the facts even though this amounts to infringing those principles. Argentine jurisprudence has developed some interesting reasoning to ground the latter option; yet, at the end of the day, all of those proposals fall short of complying with the strict understanding of the principle of legality and non-retroactivity followed in Argentina and in Continental legal systems, and often amount to judicial arbitrariness.

Admitting a sort of double track, in which international crimes fall under a more relaxed principle of legality, has some dark sides. First, it amounts to accepting a less guarantee-based approach, which can be seen as going against the evolution of the principle of legality in International Criminal Law as a whole. Second, it opens a gap that, being intended only for the core international crimes, is likely to expand well beyond them, especially if we combine it with the expansive trend, in the Argentine jurisprudence itself, when interpreting the scope of this category. Third, the reasoning developed by the competent tribunals and their judgments might amount to arbitrariness, and therefore to a risk for the rule of law, as the foundation of any modern legal system.

Considering all of these problematic issues, the alternative proposal to argue for the suspension of time barring during the illegitimate dictatorial regime, which appears in some judicial decisions, looks more convincing. However, we might also wonder whether it would be wiser to focus on other mechanisms that equally help to achieve truth, reparation, and a wider concept of justice, and better serve victims' claims in this context. This approach requires acknowledging that the 'fight against impunity', so often evoked in the aftermath of atrocities, is not an end in itself, nor does it always serve the purpose of promoting peace and the consolidation of democracy. Further, there may be other venues for justice and punishment, *in a wider sense,* through which to pursue the purposes normally attributed to criminal sanction.[101]

Lastly, both Spain and Argentina still face debates and pending issues related to the legacy of past abuses, which Criminal Justice is not able to deal with by itself in any case. An overall, strong and long-lasting response to such experiences needs the implementation of a wide range of public policies fostering truth-finding, acknowledgment, education, and narrative- and memory-building.

Notes

1. Alicia Gil Gil, 'Spain as an Example of Total Oblivion with Partial Rehabilitation', in *The Role of Courts in Transitional Justice*, ed. Jessica Almqvist and Carlos Esposito (London: Routledge, 2011), 103.
2. Pablo Parenti, 'The Prosecution of International Crimes in Argentina', *International Criminal Law Review (ICLR)* 10 (2010): 491.
3. Before leaving the power, the military junta had passed a self-amnesty law (*Law for National Pacification,* of 22 September 1983, No. 222.924), but this was declared void by the Law 23.040 of 22 December 1983.
4. Law 23.492 of 12 December 1986, and Law 23.521 of 4 June 1987, respectively.
5. Art. 5, Law 23.492, and Art. 2, Law 23.521 expressly excluded from their scope the offences of kidnapping minors and falsifying birth records and/or adoption papers, which would continue 'according to their status'.
6. See, among others, the notorious *Scilingo* case in Spain (Tribunal Supremo, Sala de lo Penal, judgment 798/2007, 1 October 2007) and the *Astiz* case in Italy (Cassazione Penale, I Sezione, *Alfredo Ignacio Astiz,* judgment, 18 March 2009). Ezequiel Malarino, 'Argentina', in *Persecución penal nacional de crímenes internacionales en América Latina y España,* ed. Kai Ambos and Ezequiel Malarino (Montevideo: KAS, 2003), 35.
7. Sévane Garibian, 'Ghosts Also Die Resisting Disappearance Through the "Right to the Truth" and the Juicios por la Verdad in Argentina', *Journal of International Criminal Justice (JICJ)* 12 (2014): 515; Elena Maculan and Daniel Pastor, *El derecho a la verdad y su realización por medio del proceso penal* (Buenos Aires: Hammurabi, 2013).
8. Elena Maculan, 'Prosecuting International Crimes at National Level: Lessons from the Argentine "Truth-Finding Trials"', *Utrecht Law Review* 8, no. 1 (2012): 106.
9. Juzgado Nacional en lo Criminal y Correccional Federal 4 (Juez Cavallo), *Simón, Julio, Del Cerro, Juan Antonio* (8686/2000), 6 March 2001.
10. Corte Suprema de Justicia de la nación (hereafter, CSJN), *Simón, Julio Héctor y otros s/privación ilegítima de la libertad* (17.768), Judgment, 14 June 2005.

11. Christine Bakker, 'A Full Stop to Amnesty in Argentina: The Simón Case', *JICJ* 3 (2005): 1106, and, more critical, Ezequiel Malarino, 'La cara represiva de la reciente jurisprudencia argentina sobre graves violaciones de los derechos humanos', *IuraGentium* (2009).
12. Juan-Pablo León-Pérez-Acevedo, 'The Control of the Inter-American Court of Human Rights over Amnesty Laws and Other Exemption Measures: Legitimacy Assessment', *Leiden Journal of International Law* 33 (2020): 667; Louise Mallinder, 'The End of Amnesty or Regional Overreach? Interpreting the Erosion of South America's Amnesty Law', *International and Comparatively Law Quarterly* 65 (2016): 645; Christina Binder, 'The Prohibition of Amnesties by the Inter-American Court of Human Rights', *German Law Journal* 12 (2011): 1203.
13. IACtHR, *Gelman v. Uruguay*, Judgment, 24 February 2011.
14. IACtHR, *Barrios Altos and La Cantuta v. Peru*, Monitoring compliance proceedings, Resolution, 30 May 2018, calling for the revision of the pardon issued to the former president Fujimori.
15. Paolo Caroli, 'Transitional Amnesties: Can They Be Prohibited?', *Diritto penale contemporaneo* 4 (2018): 205.
16. Basic Principles and Guidelines on the Right to a Remedy and Reparation for Victims of Gross Violations of International Human Rights Law and Serious Violations of International Humanitarian Law (UN Doc. A/RES/60/147), 16 December 2005; Updated Set of Principles for the Protection and Promotion of Human Rights Through Action to Combat Impunity (UN Doc. E/CN.4/2005/102/Add.1), 8 February 2005.
17. HRC, *General Comment 20* (UN Doc. A/44/40), 10 March 1992, para. 15; *General Comment 31* (UN Doc. CCPR/C/21/Rev.1/Add.13), 29 March 2004, para. 18; *Rodríguez v. Uruguay*, Communication 322/1988, Views, 19 July 1994, para. 12.4.
18. ICTY, *Prosecutor v. Furundzija*, Judgment, IT-95-17/1-T, T.Ch., 10 December 1998, para. 155. The decision focuses on amnesties granted to cover acts of torture.
19. SCSL, *Prosecutor v. Kallon/Kamara*, Decision on Challenge to Jurisdiction, SCSL-2004-15-PT/SCSL-2004-16-PT, A.Ch., 13 March 2004, paras. 66–74. The Chamber declared the invalidity of the amnesty law provided in the Lomé Peace Agreement, due to the *ius cogens* nature of the international rules prohibiting and criminalising these crimes: Antonio Cassese, 'The Special Court and International Law: The Decision Concerning the Lomé Agreement Amnesty', *Journal of International Criminal Justice* 2, no. 4 (2004): 1130–40. The Court finds a 'crystallising international norm that a government cannot grant amnesties' for international crimes (para. 82).
20. ECCC, *Case 002*, Decision on Ieng Sary's Rule 89 Preliminary Objections, 002/19-09-2007/ECCC/TC, T.Ch., 3 November 2011, paras. 37–53. For an overall study of international instruments and rulings dealing with the prohibition of amnesties: Josepha Close, *Amnesty, Serious Crimes and International Law* (Oxon: Routledge, 2019); Gabriele Della Morte, *Le amnistie nel diritto internazionale* (Padova: Cedam, 2011).
21. Naomi Roth-Arriaza, 'After Amnesties are Gone: Latin American National Courts and the New Contours of the Fight Against Impunity', *Human Rights Quarterly* 37 (2015): 341.
22. CSJN, *Mazzeo, Julio Lilo y otros s/recurso de casación e inconstitucionalidad* (causa M.2333.XLII), Judgment, 13 July 2007.
23. Fabián Raimondo, 'Overcoming Domestic Legal Impediments to the Investigation and Prosecution of Human Rights Violations: The Case of Argentina', *Human Rights Brief* 18, no. 2 (2011): 15.
24. The Unity initially created was replaced, in 2013, by the *Procuraduría de Crímenes contra la Humanidad* (PGN Decision 163/04, 29 July 2013).
25. https://www.fiscales.gob.ar/lesa-humanidad/son-1088-las-personas-condenadas-por-crimenes-de-lesa-humanidad-en-286-sentencias-dictadas-desde-2006/. Data updated until the 9 September 2022.
26. The first conviction was issued against the former General Director of Investigations within the Police of the Province of Buenos Aires: *Tribunal Oral Federal en lo Criminal* (hereafter, TOFC) in La Plata, *Etchecolatz, Miguel Osvaldo* (2251/06), Judgment, 19 September 2006.

27. Roth-Arriaza, 'After Amnesties are Gone', 342–4.
28. This position was upheld by the Supreme Court: CSJN, *Arancibia Clavel, Lautaro s/ homicidio calificado y asociación ilícita y otros* (259), Judgment, 24 August 2004.
29. Some first-instance judgments also declare that the facts can be labelled as genocide, but this finding is usually reversed by the higher courts: Elena Maculan, 'La contribución iberoamericana a la ampliación de los grupos protegidos por el delito de genocidio', in *El legado Del Tribunal Penal Internacional para la ex Yugoslavia sobre la definición y aplicación del delito de genocidio*, ed. Hector Olásolo and Eirene de Prada (Valencia: Tirant, 2019), 209.
30. TOCF 1 of San Martín, *Riveros, Omar Santiago and others* (2046 and its accumulations 2208), Judgment, 5 May 2011, 282–3; TOCF of Neuquen, *Reinhold, Oscar Lorenzo* (666), Judgment, 1 Februuary 2009, 500 *ff.*, confirmed in second instance (*Cámara Federal de Casación Penal*, Chamber IV, *Reinhold, Oscar Lorenzo et al. on appeal* (10.609), Appeals Judgment, 13 February 2012); TOCF of Tucumán, *Romero Niklison María Alejandra* (401.118/04 and its accumulations 401.118/04), Judgment, 31 March 2011, 110; TOCF 1 of Córdoba, *Videla, Jorge Rafael and Others and Menéndez, Luciano Benjamín* (172/09 and M-13/09), Judgment, 22 December 2010, 295.
31. The understanding of this principle and its underlying implications differ significantly between domestic legal traditions, as well as in International and International Criminal Law: Kenneth Gallant, *The Principle of Legality in International and Comparative Criminal Law* (Cambridge: CUP, 2009); Mercedes Pérez Manzano and Juan Antonio Lascurain Sánchez (eds.), *La tutela multinivel del principio de legalidad* (Madrid: Marcial Pons, 2016); Marco Scoletta, 'El principio de legalidad penal europeo', in *Los derechos fundamentales en el derecho penal europeo*, ed. Luis Diez Picazo and Adán Nieto Martín (Madrid: Civitas, 2010), 277; Vico Valentini, *Diritto penale intertemporale: logiche continentali ed ermeneutica europea* (Milano: Giuffrè, 2012).
32. Dissenting vote of Judge Vasquez attached to the Argentine Supreme Court's ruling in the *Arancibia Clavel* case, para. 29 (*free translation*).
33. The *Draft Articles on Prevention and Punishment of Crimes Against Humanity*, adopted by the International Law Commission on 15 May 2019, apart from their being still at a draft stage, adopt the same definition of the category contained in Article 7 of the Rome Statute.
34. Luis Sánchez Rodríguez and Javier Chinchón Álvarez, 'Algunas consideraciones jurídico-internacionales acerca de la sentencia de la sala Especial de la Corte Suprema de la República del Perú contra Alberto Kenya Fujimori', *Revista de Estudios Jurídicos* 10 (2010).
35. In the same vein, Juan Pablo Montiel, 'La "mala costumbre" de vulnerar derechos humanos: análisis y pronóstico de la costumbre internacional como fuente de Derecho penal internacional', in *La crisis del principio de legalidad en el nuevo Derecho penal: ¿Decadencia o evolución?*, ed. Juan Pablo Montiel (Madrid: Marcial Pons, 2012), 399, 414.
36. Ward Ferdinandusse, *Direct Application of International Criminal Law in National Courts* (The Hague: TMC Asser Press, 2006), 236, despite suggesting that these problems are 'greatly mitigated by the fundamental character of many of the core crimes'.
37. Malarino, 'Argentina', 60.
38. Triestino Mariniello, 'The "Nuremberg Clause" and Beyond', *Nordic Journal of International Law* 82 (2013), 221.
39. In this line, the Colombian Supreme Court of Justice has gradually affirmed a *principle of flexible legality,* which should be applied exclusively to core international crimes: Colombian Supreme Court, Criminal Cassation Chamber, *Banquez Martínez, Úber Enrique* (33.039), Judgment, 16 December 2010.
40. Alicia Gil Gil, 'La excepción al principio de legalidad del n.° 2 del artículo 7 del Convenio Europeo de Derechos Humanos', *Anuario de Derecho penal y Ciencias penales* 63, no. 1 (2010): 143, 159.
41. Bruce Broomhall, 'Article 22', in *The Rome Statute of the International Criminal Court. A Commentary*, 4th ed., ed. Kai Ambos (München: C.H.Beck-Hart-Nomos, 2022), 1149; Héctor Olásolo, 'A Note on the Evolution of the Principle of Legality in International

Criminal Law', *Criminal Law Forum* 18 (2007): 301; Kai Ambos, *Treatise of International Criminal Law*, Vol. I (Oxford: OUP, 2013), 90.

42. CSJN, *Levin, Marcos Jacobo y otros s/ imposición de tortura* (CSJ1874/2015/RH1), Judgment, 18 September 2018 and *Almirón, Víctor Hugo y otros s/ imposición de tortura*, Judgment, 18 October 2022.
43. Cámara Federal de Casación Penal (CFCP), Sala III, *Labarta Sánchez, Juan Roberto et al. s/ recurso de casación* (14.282), 8 February 2013.
44. CFCP, Sala III, *Albornoz, Roberto et al. s/ rec. De casación* (13.085/13049), 8 November 2012.
45. Elena Maculan, 'International Crimes or Ordinary Crimes? The "Dual Classification of the Facts" as an Interpretive Method', *International Criminal Law Review* 21, no. 3 (2021): 403.
46. Kai Ambos, *Treatise on International Criminal Law*, Volume II (Oxford: OUP, 2014), 248–89.
47. Leena Grover, *Interpreting Crimes in the Rome Statute of the International Criminal Court* (Cambridge: CUP, 2014), 188.
48. Timothy Endicott, 'The Coxford Lecture. Arbitrariness', *Canadian Journal of Law and Jurisprudence* XXVII, no. 1 (2014): 49. Similarly, Anthony K. Thompson, 'The Rule of Law, Arbitrariness and Institutional Virtue', *Alternative Law Journal* 44, no. 2 (2019): 159–63, warns about arbitrariness as the real 'enemy' of the rule of law, since it prevents citizens from predicting 'the public outcomes in their lives without fear'.
49. Elena Maculan, *Los crímenes internacionales en la jurisprudencia latinoamericana* (Madrid: Marcial Pons, 2019), 96.
50. Juzgado de Primera Instancia en lo Penal, 7° turno, *Bordaberry Arocena, Juan María*, Judgment, 9 February 2010, and (Peruvian) Tribunal Constitucional, *Contreras Roberto* (00218-2009-PHC/TC, *Accomarca* case), 11 November 2010.
51. Elena Maculan and Alicia Gil Gil, 'The Rationale and Purposes of Criminal Law and Punishment in Transitional Contexts', *Oxford Journal of Legal Studies* 40, no. 1 (2020): 132.
52. Alicia Gil Gil, *La justicia de transición en España. De la amnistía a la memoria histórica* (Barcelona: Atelier, 2008), 49.
53. Ibid., 62; Paloma Aguilar Fernández, *Memoria y olvido de la guerra civil española* (Madrid: Alianza, 1996); Santos Juliá, *Transición* (Barcelona: Galaxia Gutenberg, 2017).
54. Gil Gil, 'Spain as an example'.
55. Paolo Caroli, *Transitional Justice in Italy and the Crimes of Fascism and Nazism* (London: Routledge, 2022), 182.
56. Luc Huyse, 'Justice after Transition: On the Choices Successor Elites Make in Dealing with the Past', *Law and Social Inquiry* 51 (1995): 76.
57. Manuel Reyes Mate, *Justicia de las víctimas* (Barcelona: Anthropos, 2009); Caroli, *Transitional Justice*, 215.
58. Ramón Sáez Varcácel, 'Justicia transicional y España. ¿Se puede juzgar la Historia?', in *Memoria histórica: ¿Se puede juzgar la historia?* (Madrid: Fundación Antonio Carretero, 2009), 86.
59. John Vervaele, 'Delitos Internacionales: Del Ius (Non) Puniendi del Estado-Nación a un Deber Puniendi Imperativo de Ius Cogens', *Inter-American and European Human Rights Journal* 6 (2013): 104.
60. Josep Tamarit Sumalla, 'Transition, Historical Memory and Criminal Justice in Spain', *JICJ* 9 (2011): 729.
61. Javier Chinchón Álvarez, *El tratamiento judicial de los crímenes de la Guerra Civil y el franquismo en España* (Donostia: Universidad de Deusto, 2012). From a sociological perspective: Paloma Aguilar Fernández, Luis Balcells and Héctor Cebolla-Boado, 'Las actitudes de los españoles ante las medidas de justicia transicional relativas a la Guerra Civil y al franquismo', *Revista Internacional de Sociología* 69, no. 1 (2011): 59.
62. Josep Tamarit Sumalla, 'Justicia transicional y Derecho penal en España', in *Memoria histórica: ¿Se puede juzgar la historia?*, (Madrid: Fundación Antonio Carretero, 2009), 129, 139.
63. Juzgado Central de Instrucción 5, Audiencia Nacional de Madrid, *Diligencias Previas Proc. Abreviado 399/2006 V*, Decision, 16 October 2008.

64. Elena Maculan, 'Límites a la expansión de la persecución por crímenes internacionales y del papel del juez-historiador: La aportación de la STS 101/2012', *Revista de Derecho penal y Criminología* 8 (2012): 497.
65. Kai Ambos, 'The Legal Framework of Transitional Justice: A Systematic Study with a Special Focus on the Role of the ICC', in *Building a Future on Peace and Justice*, ed. Kai Ambos et al. (Berlin: Springer-Verlag, 2009).
66. ECtHR, *Gutiérrez Dorado y Dorado Ortiz v. Spain*, Decision on inadmissibility, 27 March 2012; *Canales Bermejo v. Spain*, Decision on inadmissibility, 8 November 2012.
67. Pérez-León-Acevedo, 'The Control of the Inter-American Court', 680–1.
68. Kai Ambos and Laura Böhm, 'Tribunal Europeo de Derechos Humanos y Corte Interamericana de Derechos Humanos: Tribunal tímido y tribunal audaz?' in *Sistema interamericano de protección de los derechos humanos y Derecho penal internacional*, vol. II, ed. Kai Ambos et al. (Montevideo: KAS, 2011), 55.
69. For instance, in *Makuchyan and Minasyan v. Azerbaijan and Hungary* (App.17247/13, Judgment, 26 May 2020), the ECtHR remarked that 'pardons and amnesties are primarily matters of member States' domestic law' (para. 160).
70. Miles Jackson, 'Amnesties in Strasbourg', *Oxford Journal of Legal Studies* 38, no. 1 (2018); Juan-Pablo Pérez-León-Acevedo, 'The European Court of Human Rights (ECtHR) vis-à-vis Amnesties and Pardons: Factors Concerning or Affecting the Degree of ECtHR's Deference to States', *International Journal of Human Rights* 26, no. 6 (2022): 1107. Although, as the Author points out, the degree of this deference to states varies depending on four main factors: '(i) the national process of adoption, application, and/or validation of amnesties/pardons; (ii) ECtHR's consideration of the margin of appreciation or discretion given to states; (iii) state compliance with international obligations on human rights; and (iv) potential impact on transitions to peace, reconciliation, democracy, and/or the rule of law' (1108).
71. Anja Seibert-Fohr, *Prosecuting Serious Human Rights Violations* (Oxford: OUP, 2009), 118.
72. Pérez-León-Acevedo, 'The European Court of Human Rights', 1110.
73. IACtHR, *El-Mozote v. El Salvador*, Concurring Opinion Judge García-Sayán, 25 October 2012; *La-Rochela-Massacre v. Colombia*, Judgment, 11 May 2007. This trend has been pointed out by Louise Mallinder, 'The End of Amnesty or Regional Overreach? Interpreting the Erosion of South America's Amnesty Law', *International and Comparatively Law Quarterly* 65, no. 3 (2016): 657.
74. ECtHR, *Association 21 December 1989 v. Romania* (App.33810/07), Judgment, 24 May 2011, para. 144: 'an amnesty is generally incompatible with the duty incumbent on the States to investigate acts of torture [...] and to combat impunity for international crimes. This is also true in respect of pardon'.
75. ECtHR, *Margus v. Croatia* (App.4455/10), Judgment, 13 November 2012, para. 74.
76. ECtHR, *Tarbuk v. Croatia* (App.31360/10), Judgment, 11 December 2012, para. 45. Pérez-León-Acevedo, 'The European Court of Human Rights', 1118-23.
77. ECtHR, *Margus v. Croatia* (App.4455/10), GC, Judgment, 27 May 2014, Joint concurring opinion of Judges Šikuta, Wojtyczek, and Vehabović, para. 9.
78. ICC, *Prosecutor v. Saif Al-Islam Gaddafi*, PTC, 'Decision on the Admissibility Challenge' (ICC-01/11-01/11-662), 5 April 2019, para. 61.
79. ICC, *Gaddafi*, AC, 'Judgment on the Appeal' (ICC-01/11-01/11-695), 9 March 2020, para. 96.
80. Close, *Amnesty*; Caroli, *Transitional Amnesties,* 210; Christine Bell, 'The "New Law" of Transitional Justice', in *Building a Future on Peace and Justice,* ed. Kai Ambos et al. (Berlin: Springer, 2009), 105, 123 (defending the need for an element of 'legal mess' on the point in transitions); Louise Mallinder, 'Can Amnesties and International Justice be Reconciled?', *International Journal of Transitional Justice* 1 (2007): 208. Jackson, 'Amnesties in Strasbourg', warns that the latest trend in ECtHR jurisprudence on amnesties implies 'the exclusion of conflicting interests from the Court's analysis; the closing down of the margin of appreciation; the limiting of judicial deference to political decision makers' (17). Christian Tomuschat, 'The Duty to Prosecute International Crimes Committed by Individuals', in

Tradition und Weltoffenheit des Rechts, Festschrift für Steinberg, ed. Hans-Joachim Cremer (Berlin: Springer, 2002), 315, also suggests: 'It would seem to be wrong, however, to provide categorical answers to this issue. [...] We agree with those authors who are of the view that such amnesties, if they have been responsibly enacted by a people wishing to make a fresh start after having lived through a period of national cataclysm, should also be respected by other States and by the institutions of the international community' (344 and 347). Similarly, Daniel Pastor, 'El sistema penal internacional del Estatuto de Roma. Aproximaciones jurídicas críticas', *Estudios sobre justicia penal*, ed. David Baigún (Buenos Aires: Editores del Puerto, 2005), 699, 711.

81. Maculan and Gil, 'The Rationale and Purposes', 157. Ezequiel Malarino, 'Transición, derecho penal y amnistía', *Revista de Derecho Penal y Criminología* 9 (2013): 205, suggests the following motto: 'as much [criminal] justice as peace allows' (211).
82. (Spanish) Tribunal Constitucional, 'Auto sobre recurso de amparo 5781-2018, *Gerardo Iglesias Argüelles*', 15 September 2021.
83. Para. 4 (free translation). Two judges sign a dissenting opinion, in which they claim for an interpretation closer to the idea of the applicability of international custom as a sufficient incriminating source, and the following inadmissibility of statutory limitations and amnesties.
84. See section 3.1 above.
85. The terminological shift from the concept of 'historical memory' to that of 'democratic memory' is significant in itself: Artemi Rallo Lombarte, 'Memoria democrática y Constitución', *Teoría y Realidad Constitucional* 51 (2023): 109, 116.
86. JuanManuel López Ulla, 'Del derecho a la verdad al deber de memoria: a propósito de la nueva Ley de Memoria Democrática', *Revista de Derecho Político* 117 (2023): 99, 101. The Author also argues that the LDM focuses on building a *collective* memory based on the knowledge of truth, much more than the former LHM (113). *See* the official map of mass graves https://www.mpr.gob.es/memoriademocratica/mapa-de-fosas/Paginas/index.aspx.
87. Report of the Working Group on Enforced or Involuntary Disappearances; Follow-up report to the recommendations made by the Working Group, Human Rights Council. Missions to Chile and Spain (A/HRC/36/39/Add.3), 7 September 2017; Report of the UN Special Rapporteur on the Promotion of Truth, Justice, Reparation and Non-repetition Guarantees, Pablo de Greiff, after his Mission to Spain, 22 July 2014.
88. BBC News Mundo, 24 October 2019, https://www.bbc.com/mundo/noticias-internacional-50144938.
89. López Ulla, 'Del derecho a la verdad', 123 agrees on this point, but he cautions against the underlying idea that such Commission should somehow impose an 'official' narrative about the past.
90. Free translation.
91. López Ulla, 'Del derecho a la verdad', 124–5; Marc Carillo, 'La Memoria y la calidad democrática del Estado', *Revista de las Cortes Generales* 114 (2022): 183, although the latter Author admits that, to get that result while complying with the principle of legality, Spain should previously ratify the 1968 Convention (205–6).
92. Fiscal de Sala en materia de Derechos Humanos y Memoria Democrática, 'Diligencias Indeterminadas n. 438/2022 Juzgado de Instrucción no. 18 de Barcelona' (M.D.20/2023), 13 September 2023.
93. Ibidem, free translation.
94. See sections 2.2 and 3.1 above.
95. William Schabas, 'Of Amnesty, Pendulums, and Peremptory Norms', *FIU Law Review* 15 (2021): 83, noting that the recent developments regarding amnesties have refuted the SCSL's forecast according to which the norm prohibiting amnesties was crystallising.
96. Consejo General del Poder Judicial (Pleno), *Informe sobre el Anteproyecto de Ley de Memoria democrática*, 7 June 2021.
97. Juzgado de Instrucción 18 de Barcelona, DP 1500/2023, Decision, 5 October 2023.
98. Alicia Gil Gil, 'Humo', *Fonte limpa* 54 (2022): 8–10 (free translation).

99. Similarly, Ana I. Pérez Machío and Norberto J. de la Mata Barranco, 'Vulnerabilidad de las víctimas de motivación política herramientas de lucha contra la impunidad', in *Personas vulnerables y tutela penal*, ed. Ana I. Pérez Machío and Norberto J. de la Mata Barranco (Valencia: Tirant, 2023), 267.
100. It is noteworthy that both countries opened investigations about the past atrocities committed in the other country; yet, whereas the criminal investigation opened in Spain about crimes committed in the Argentine dictatorship ended with the conviction of Adolfo Scilingo, the opening of a criminal investigation in 2010, before an Argentine tribunal, about crimes committed in the Francoist regime ('*Querella argentina*'), is still ongoing, and has not really met the cooperation of Spanish authorities: Manuel Sánchez-Moreno, 'Memorias y justicia a través del océano. Argentina y España frente a sus últimas dictaduras', *Memoria y narración* 1 (2018): 52.
101. Mark Drumbl, 'Impunities', *The Oxford Handbook on International Criminal Law* (Oxford: OUP, 2020), 230.

Disclosure statement

No potential conflict of interest was reported by the author(s).

The ping-pong strategy: Confronting atrocities from the exile

Valeria Vegh Weis

ABSTRACT
This article will focus on the still marginal topic of atrocity crimes, and it will do so by building upon Southern studies, which expose how global power inequalities have helped present knowledge from a small number of Northern societies as universal, timeless and placeless while disregarding valuable knowledges and experiences from the South. Moreover, this article will also dispute the 'static' perspective in the literature of atrocities that has largely focused on either domestic or global issues of concern, but without enough attention to the dialogues, connections normative transfers, and even shared practices between the South and the North. Furthermore, it will do so by focusing on a particular unattended actor: those in exile and their role in the confrontation of the atrocities back home. Altogether, this article will go beyond the European-centred and static approaches and instead look at points of dialogue and encounters between Europe and Latin America and the role of the diaspora/exile as a legal and dynamic protagonist in the struggle against atrocities. Particularly, the research will look at the role of Argentinean activists in the European exile and their struggle against the dictatorship that ruled the country between 1976 and 1983, as well as their activism against impunity laws once democracy was re-established.

1. Introduction

Atrocities have been responsible for massive suffering historically and worldwide. Encompassing all types of international crimes, including genocide, war crimes, crimes against humanity and the crime of aggression, these crimes can be attributed to state agents acting either deliberately (e.g. via the persecution of groups labelled as rebels or enemies of the people) or by omission (e.g. not intervening in a civil conflict between two factions or even in case of lack of effective oversight of agents on the ground by the higher-ups).[1] Despite the foremost severity of these crimes, the literature on criminology and human rights in the context of mass atrocities has been marginal and scarce to the point that it was only after Chambliss' 1988 discourse at the American Society of Criminology that these crimes became a topic of criminological studies.[2] In Hagan and Rymond-Richmond's words, it has taken criminology a long time to 'confront its more deadly neglected topics, namely genocide, war crimes, and crimes against humanity'.[3] Indeed, such is the scope of the academic silence about these crimes that Morrison refers to this phenomenon as a 'criminological apartheid'.[4]

Remarkable exceptions include efforts to foster dialogue between war and military studies, criminology,[5] sociology, criminology and humanitarian law,[6] victimology, criminology and atrocities,[7] criminology and human rights studies,[8] criminology and transitional justice studies,[9] criminology and memory studies,[10] criminology and international criminal,[11] micro-meso-macro studies on why ordinary people engage in mass atrocities at all[12] and attention to genocide and the Holocaust in particular.[13] However, a core shortcoming in the literature points to the fact that it has largely focused on the 'European Powers' as drivers of the human rights framework aimed at stopping atrocities,[14] downplaying Southern contributions. Even when Southern cases are being discussed (e.g. South Africa, Colombia, Rwanda), those theorising the experiences are usually located in Northern institutions. Moreover, the accountability processes themselves (e.g. the special tribunal for Rwanda) are located in the Global Nort (e.g. The Hague). Notably, this occurred even though crucial struggles against atrocities, human rights legal developments, and the most remarkable transitional justice processes happened in the South.[15] Going further, even when part of this literature analyses cases in the South, it has been written by Northern scholars and practitioners, silencing Southern voices.[16]

Breaking with this tradition, this article will focus on the still marginal topic of atrocity crimes, and it will do so by building upon Southern studies, which expose how global power inequalities have helped present knowledge from a small number of Northern societies as universal, timeless and placeless while disregarding valuable knowledges and experiences from the South.[17] Moreover, this article will also dispute the 'static' perspective in the literature of atrocities that has largely focused on either domestic or global issues of concern, but without enough attention to the dialogues, connections normative transfers, and even shared practices between the South and the North. Furthermore, it will do so by focusing on a particular unattended actor: those in exile and their role in the confrontation of the atrocities back home.[18] Indeed, even when ground-breaking works, such as Keck and Sikkink on 'transnational advocacy network', have tried to go beyond the static analyses,[19] they failed to pay attention to the role of those in exile forming their own networks.

Altogether, this article will go beyond the European-centred and static approaches and instead look at points of dialogue and encounters between Europe and Latin America and the role of the diaspora/exile – an actor in-between spaces- as a legal and dynamic protagonist in the struggle against atrocities, i.e. war crimes, crimes against humanity and genocide, as regulated in the Rome Statute.[20] Particularly, the research will look at the role of Argentinean activists in the European exile and their struggle against the dictatorship that ruled the country between 1976 and 1983, as well as their activism against impunity laws once democracy was re-established. Throughout, activists in Europe worked in engagement with those based in Argentina through a 'ping-pong strategy'. Adolfo Perez Esquivel, leader of SERPAJ and later Nobel Prize Laureate, explains:

> We formed networks to support each other. … to articulate groups in continuous movement … We tried to articulate the work through the "politics of pin pong": the social

organizations in Latin America bounced the information to Europe, where the exiles spread the news from wherever they were.[21]

Besides working with secondary sources, particularly from Argentinean historians specialised in exile,[22] the study will build upon 12 interviews with victims engaged in activism against the perpetrated atrocities from the European exile along with archive research conducted in Argentina from 2019 to 2022, which will be deployed for illustrative purposes. Part 2 deals with the atrocities perpetrated in Argentina as well as with the victims' organisations created in the European exile. Part 3 will introduce the work done by these organisations during state terror, highlighting the ping-pong strategy consisting of sharing and disseminating information across continents. Part 4 moves the argument forward to discuss the role of these organisations once democracy was re-established, but impunity made accountability legally impossible. This section also zooms in and looks at how the ping-pong strategy continued as the trials in Europe fuelled justice back home, and the other way around.

2. State terror in Argentina and the creation of diaspora networks centred on human rights

The most recent Argentinean dictatorship occurred between 1976 and 1983, in the context of Operation Condor, a network of repressive South American regimes coordinated backed up by the United States amid the geopolitics of the Cold War. Set up in 1975, it included Argentina, Bolivia, Chile, Paraguay and Uruguay, while Brazil, Peru and Ecuador joined later. The goal was to facilitate the kidnapping and assassination of those deemed as political opponents throughout the region.[23] Following this global setting, the coup was notably different from previous ones (1930, 1943, 1955, 1962 and 1966). The military junta brought about a drastic and destructive economic transformation, including a seven-fold increase in the nation's external debt and extreme liberalisation of the economy.[24] Official publicity campaigns celebrated the possibility of buying foreign goods over local ones, disparaging them for their allegedly poorer quality. Additionally, even though the coup was carried out by the military, the media and other corporations supported and took advantage of the repression either by suppressing unions or by acquiring assets from victims of the regime.[25]

Furthermore, this last dictatorship was unusual in terms of the extent and the features of the human rights violations perpetrated, including unlawful imprisonment in hundreds of clandestine detention centres spread throughout the country, where unprecedented forms of torture were carried out. In particular, the military enforced a plan of 'forced disappearances'.[26] Human rights organisations state that 30,000 were kidnapped, tortured, and murdered, while their final whereabouts have never been disclosed.[27] Another criminal innovation of the military was the operation to abduct at least 500 children from pregnant women and young mothers who had been detained and forcibly disappeared, unlawfully giving them up for adoption under false identities.[28] As soon as 1978 and building upon grassroots fact-finding driven by the victim organisations, the Inter-American Commission of Human Rights made its first-ever visit to a country undergoing atrocity crimes and issued a devastating report exposing the dramatic situation.[29]

State terror forced many people to flee. Exile was emotionally and financially challenging but it allowed to take advantage of the civil and political rights denied back home, such as the rights to association and freedom of expression, to denounce the crimes of the dictatorship. Networks were formed throughout Europe, in the USA and Latin America. The ones in Europe, the focus of this article, included CADHU (Argentinean Commission of Human Rights/Comisión Argentina de Derechos Humanos) which consisted of lawyers as well as renowned people from very different disciplines and backgrounds, and CO.SO.FAM (Commissión de Solidarité des Parents des Prisonniers, Disparus et Tués en Argentine), which was exclusively formed by direct victims of the dictatorship and their relatives, among many others.[30] While other organisations thought that it was necessary to discuss politics openly, these two argued for a discussion in terms of solidarity and human rights. Rodolfo Mattarollo, the co-founder of CADHU, states: 'I was among those who thought that discussing and working on solidarity and human rights was the highest form of politics that was possible during those years because it was a way of isolating [the Argentinean government] in the international arena, and that was certainly important'.[31]

Indeed, the global political context was marked by Jimmy Carter as the new President of the United States (1977–1981) and the expansion of a human rights agenda in the West, to show a contrast with the arguably totalitarian regimes of the East. In this context, many of those in exile discovered the brand-new relevance of international human rights and international human rights law, and the benefits of developing a legal left-wing human rights activism to 'denounce repression and torture' back home.[32] In this vein, human rights were deployed in the form of actual legal initiatives as well as a framing for contentious activities. To exemplify the latter, one of the first campaigns led by CO.SO.FAM in Madrid in December 1977 claimed a 'Christmas with Justice', understanding 'justice' as the appearance of the disappeared, and the release of those in detention who should be judged according to the National Constitution and laws.[33]

This multidimensional human rights-centred strategy proved to be the most successful way to dispute power with the military government in the international arena. Mattarollo recalls that, indeed, in one of the first press conferences of the military government that was published in the main Argentinean newspapers, the Military Junta pointed at CADHU – naming each of the members and their country of activism – as the most responsible actor of the anti-Argentinean campaign, aimed at delegitimizing the country. Moreover, the creative deployment of human rights and the rule of law helped to open access to a wider range of spaces than what would have resulted from a narrower left-wing political approach. As explained by Vicente Zito Lema, writer and co-founder of CADHU:

> [Accessing government officials and renowned people was possible because] we presented ourselves as human rights organizations, and, when discussing human rights, they always receive you with a good face and recognise your work. CADHU and particularly Duhalde and Gustavo Roca were particularly smart in exploiting the bourgeois contractions and their double moral standards.[34]

Furthermore, this human rights-based strategy was probably relevant also to overcome political differences among those in exile. In this vein, the human rights-centred discourse allowed to displacement and replace prior political identities, that were in crisis as a result of the defeat of the left-wing organisations at the hands of the military.[35]

Francisco Pompeyo Ramos Marrau, who was in exile in Germany, recalls how people were coming from different political groups, which, in the beginning, complicated the chances of working together. However, at one point, 'we [those in exile in Germany] came to the conclusion … that we needed to prioritize a plural perspective … the importance thing was to have two or three ideas and work together on them, and the rest was dialogue, dialogue, dialogue and dialogue … '.[36] These efforts culminated with the formation of the CAD (Argentine Committee for Democracy), which was aimed at 'strengthening the institutions and human rights organizations back in Argentina'.[37] This goal was shared across the different organisations in exile, which worked with the conviction that their role was to 'soften the massacre and guarantee the lives of those imprisoned' at home.[38] In the words of Juan Mendez, who was a political prisoner and fled to the United States, where he became the head of Human Rights Watch: 'Many people, regardless of their political origins, realised that the most important thing was what was done from within Argentina and to help from outside'.[39] Under this logic, a ping-pong of human rights-based mechanisms to confront atrocities took place across the Atlantic.[40]

3. The role of the diaspora during state terror: fact-finding, denunciation, international solidarity and accountability

The Military Junta imposed strict censorship that constrained Argentinean national media from reporting the actual human rights violations taking place. Moreover, at the core of the military programme, was the explicit decision of providing no information about the situation of the political prisoners or the fate of the disappeared and the abducted children. To respond to this denial, the brand-new organisations in exile devoted their efforts to fact-finding, denunciation, international solidarity and accountability.

In terms of fact-finding, and because of the reigning censorship, information was mostly coming from survivors. In other words, taking into account that 'the military has never organically released any information', those who arrived in exile became the 'fundamental source of information'.[41] Clandestine sources were also crucial. A particularly relevant one came from the renowned journalist, writer, activist and later disappeared Rodolfo Walsh, who created the Agency of Clandestine News (*Spanish* Agencia de Noticias Clandestina/ANCLA) based in Buenos Aires. Walsh gathered a network of key informants, including lawyers who could let him know the numbers and fate of the habeas corpus, members from corporations who could reveal information about negotiations among powerholders and hidden socio-economic data, and occasional witnesses of kidnappings and extrajudicial killings. The leaks were then sent condensed in microfilms to the domestic and international press and to the survivors' organisations working in the exile, who backed up the work done in Argentina.[42] The organisations in exile put together this clandestine information, the testimonies of survivors and relatives of the victims, reports from lawyers working back home and letters from political prisoners. As a result, as early as August 1976 (less than five months after the coup), the first document with the names and information of those detained-disappeared and executed between March and June was made available.[43] Different publications followed, including Latin-American Summary, which, published by CADHU, became the most widespread newsletter in exile and still exists in the Netherlands, Venezuela, Cuba, and Argentina.[44] Other relevant publications included the report edited by the filmmaker and producer Elias Querejeta entitled 'Argentina: A Process toward Genocide', the book 'From Prison' with essays, drawings and poems written by political prisoners.[45]

Denunciation took form in the publication of independent newsletters along with articles in the European press. In the words of Ana Jaramillo, a journalist exiled in Europe, 'we had to work to make a living and when we finished our job, we devoted our time to write and disseminate through any possible means the disappearance of our peers … We knew well that our only possibility was to disseminate what we knew abroad'.[46] Mattarollo confirms: 'we had a dynamic activity in terms of solidarity and fight for human rights based fundamentally on information and denounce'.[47] Concerning European media, the connections with Le Monde Diplomatique were crucial and, very early on, the newspaper published an article entitled The Killing Machine which had a huge impact on the European public.[48]

Public demonstrations and activities were also held as another strategy to create awareness among the local civil society and pressure foreign governments to confront the Argentinean dictatorship. For example, a big demonstration with people carrying images with the figures of the disappeared went from the Netherlands to France.[49] Meanwhile, in the Rambla de Barcelona, CO.SO.FAM organised a permanent exhibition with pictures of the disappeared.[50] Another striking example is the group formed in France in solidarity with the Madres of Plaza de Mayo, i.e. the network of mothers of those who had been forced disappeared. Replicating the weekly protest that Madres of Plaza de Mayo have been performing in Argentina since their first meeting on April 30, 1977, the group started weekly gatherings before the Argentinean Embassy in Paris, which went on for seven years. Artists contributed to the aesthetics of the struggle; for example, Jorge Errandonea designed a flag with the symbol of Madres de Plaza de Mayo that was carried every Thursday, while figures such as Julio Cortazar took part in the protest.[51] A particularly active period in terms of activities and engagement with the European civil society took place before the Football World Cup in Argentina in 1978. Even in the exile, some thought that opposing the World Cup would position the activist movement as 'anti-Argentineans' – as the Military Junta was claiming-; however, most groups agreed that denouncing the sports competition was an opportunity to call international attention to the ongoing crimes.[52] Eduardo Luis Duhalde commanded COBA, the Committee of Boycotting the Football World Cup in Argentina, which included Argentineans in exile, the student movement and solidarity networks in Europe. This Anti-World Cup campaign meant that they were not just a handful of activists claiming against atrocities, but a translational movement demanding to change the location of the tournament, the liberation of the political prisoners and the reestablishment of the rule of law.[53] Even famous artists joined the campaign. For example, Zito Lema 'hosted an event with the actress Catherine Deneuve in 1978 to create awareness about the situation back home'.[54]

In addition to these events, international solidarity was also fostered through meetings with a wide range of actors, from members of international organisations and state agents to artists and athletes. The first actions included contacting the Red Cross and Amnesty International,[55] followed by meetings with Human Rights Watch and the United Nations. Also, a member of CADHU, 'Eduardo Luis Duhalde was received by the government in the Netherlands and the Solidarity Committee requested the Dutch Ministry of Foreign Affairs to stop trading with Argentina. We told them that Dutch planes were used to kill activists in an atrocious manner [though the death flights]'.[56] Slepoy also recalls how they achieved a declaration of the Spanish parliament repudiating the Military Junta. In turn, Zito Lema remembers that together with his wife Regine Bergmeijer, 'we visited schools, the Crown, universities, local communitarian festivities and gathering, the soccer and hockey national team to inform them what was happening in Argentina'. Also, Matilde Herrera, mother of three disappeared children and wife of a renowned artist in the French exile, contacted Jean-Paul Sartre and Simone de Beauvoir. This renowned international solidary not seldomly worked as a lifejacket. In the words of Pérez Esquivel: 'I was in exile in Switzerland, Belgium, France, Ecuador, but in 1977 we were expelled, so I returned to Argentina and here I was detained. ... .[my detention] had a lot of international resonance. I am a survivor thanks to the networks we have been working with for so long'.[57]

During this period, the exile also worked to help members of the human rights movement in Argentina travel abroad to denounce the ongoing crimes and gather support by themselves. The aid went from fundraising and providing them with housing to arranging meetings with European leaders. Hebe de Bonafini, leader of Asociación Madres de Plaza de Mayo, clarifies that the organisation was committed to travel following three guidelines: without doing any touristic activity, without asking for money, and always talking in representation of the 30,000 forced disappearance (rather than of their cases). She also recalls how, in one of their trips to Italy, those in exile arranged a meeting with the then president of the country, Sandro Pertini, who issued a public declaration against the Military Junta. In that opportunity, Madres also met with Italian parliamentary members who promised to create a commission to pressure the Argentinean government.[58] The Argentinean networks in Europe also promoted awards for human rights organisations as a means to disseminate the situation in the international arena.[59] In 1980, Madres and Abuelas were nominated for the Nobel Prize and shortly after they received the Norwegian Prize of the People for having qualified for the Nobel Prize.[60] Finally, in 1980, Pérez Esquivel, was the one receiving the Nobel Prize, although explicitly sharing it with the other human rights organisations.[61] The legitimation brought by the award to this, yet, not well-known figure, was a great impulse for the campaign against the ongoing atrocities. As Pérez Esquivel later said: 'The award opened many doors and windows in many places where we did not have access before, and it allowed us to continue our struggle. It was a breath of fresh air amid the dictatorship asphyxia'.[62] Even the secret files of the United States recognised that the award was a 'bomb' against the dictatorship, 'a brilliant political strike', and 'a new turn in the international pressure against the dictatorship'.[63]

Finally, those in the European exile also worked toward the development of legal mechanisms to make perpetrators accountable. At the end of the 1970s and the beginning of the 1980s, they started to think about the potential of an 'Argentinean Nuremberg'.[64] The idea was to use international legal tools to create a new criminal offence on enforced disappearance applicable to the crimes perpetrated in Argentina that, as a result, would be suitable for international prosecution as international crimes. Among the most crucial events in this regard was the First Colloquium on Forced Disappearances organised in the French Senate in 1981.[65] The original motivation for the activity was to demand the renewal of the mandate of the Working Group on Enforced Disappearance of the United Nations, but the event surpassed that initial goal and became 'a crucial landmark in the exile'.[66] A total of 500 lawyers from all over the world joined efforts to define the crime of forced disappearance and submit the conclusions to the United Nations.[67] Two former presidents, Arturo Humberto Viñas and Aguilar de Bolivia, chaired the event, while Pérez Esquivel, Cortazar and Louis-Edmond Pettiti, who was the Dean of the Lawyers Forum in Paris, coordinated it. The discourse of Cortazar would be later published as a memorable essay under the title 'The Rejection of Oblivion'.[68] Human rights organisations, including Elida de Galleti from Madres de Plaza de Mayo, also took part in one of them, intervening and arguing that forced disappearances must be considered a crime against humanity.[69] Emilio Mignone and Augusto Conte, lawyers whose children disappeared, presented their ground-breaking manuscript 'The Global Parallel': using solid evidence based on testimonies, they exposed how the military was operating on a double basis, composed of a legal display to cover an unlawful network of criminality. In Mignone's words: the strategy of the dictatorship consisted of 'acting harshly but within a legally sanctioned system, based on the operation of ordinary military courts with extended jurisdiction and the application in certain cases of extreme measures' to avoid or reduce 'external influences and pressures'.[70]

4. The role of the diaspora in democracy: fostering trials abroad via universal jurisdiction to overturn impunity

In 1982, amid the increasing international and local denunciation of the committed atrocities – including massive protests, the loss of the Malvinas war against the UK, and an economic crisis, the Military Junta called for elections.[71] Particularly crucial was the 'Demonstration for Democracy' of December 16, 1982, with 100,000 people, including representatives of all political parties, demanding the end of the military regime. Raúl Alfonsin, a member of the Radical Party and part of the human rights movement, won the polls promising an agenda committed to truth and justice.

With the re-establishment of democracy, the role of those in exile changed completely. In the words of Bertolucci: 'The day of [President Raúl] Alfonsin' triumph, we experienced it second by second talking permanently on the phone and listening to the shouting in Buenos Aires, the happiness and all. It was a huge happiness. It was the possibility of coming back'.[72] Also, Mattarollo explains that 'when democracy was re-established and Alfonsin decided to foster a human rights agenda, we decided to come back to Argentina, even though our material situation in France was very good'.[73]

Despite the initial excitement, the return was far from easy. As Bertolucci states: 'Coming back means that you will remain split'.[74] The identity-shaping process was particularly relevant for the ones unaware of the reactions that those who stayed had about them. Sosa explains: 'When I came back, the first thing I did was to go to Plaza de Mayo. It was very important to meet the relatives and partners of those with whom I engaged in activism and who died. Hugging the Madres, and partners was very important. I felt peace after many years of exile. I needed their forgiveness'.[75] On a different level, for those who decided to stay, the transition to democracy was also a turning point in their identity. As explained by Carlos Pipino Martínez: 'In 1983, we stop being 'exilees'. The ones who decided to stay became 'immigrants''.[76]

Meanwhile, the Argentinean government was ambivalent in terms of dealing with past atrocities. Alfonsin promoted the first truth commission worldwide, the CONADEP (National Commission on the Disappearance of Persons),[77] and the prosecution of the most prominent figures of the dictatorship in a civilian court in what become known as the Junta Trials.[78] However, after further tensions with the members of the dictatorship and military uprisings threatening democracy, the government enacted impunity laws. Deploying techniques of neutralisation,[79] Alfonsin expressed that the decision was not damaging accountability efforts but, instead, was a positive path to strengthen democracy and 'leave the house [the country] in order'.[80] In December of 1986, Congress passed Act 23,492, known as Full Stop Act, which imposed a deadline to present new cases for crimes committed during the dictatorship. As the Criminal Code allows civil parties to initiate cases, victims' organisations took advantage of the time left to bring as many cases as possible before the courts. This further irritated lower-ranking officers and, as a result, Act 23,521, known as Due Obedience Act, was approved, getting everybody below the rank of Colonel off the hook.[81]

After a political and economic crisis, Alfonsin called for elections before the expected date and Carlos Menem, a representative of the Peronist Party, came into power. The president-elected enjoyed a stronger stand about the military threats but, nevertheless, promoted policies of impunity through Decrees 1.002, 1.003, 1.004 and 1.005,[82] which established the pardon of civilians and military personnel convicted in the former trials, including the leaders sentenced in the 1985 Juntas Trial. Announcing the pardons on the balcony of the government palace, Menem resorted again to self-justifying techniques of neutralisation and said it was good news because they would allow the nation to be rebuilt in peace. At the same time, the president made certain concessions in terms of truth and reparations, which were seen by some human rights organisations as 'blood money'.[83] It was necessary to wait until the 2003 Presidency of Nestor Kirchner for the impunity laws to be finally overturned.

However, this did not mean that no accountability was achieved during the years between the impunity laws and Kirchner's presidency. Both from Argentina and abroad the human rights movement played an important role in creating awareness about existing impunity as a 'serious political and social problem that undermines our fragile democracy'[84] and looking for accountability opportunities. On the one hand, the strategy focused on disseminating information about the disappearance of European citizens, including Swedish Dagmar Hagelin, Finn Hanna Hietala and two French nuns, Alice Domon and Leonie Duquet – four cases that involved Navy member Captain Alfredo Astiz. On the other hand, the legal strategy centred on the deployment of universal jurisdiction to seek accountability abroad, particularly in Sweden, France, Italy, Germany and Spain. This legal instrument proved to be a suitable tool for the organisations of former exiles to move justice forward by providing evidence gathered through fact-finding and even presenting themselves as civil parties at a scale that was unlikely to take place in international tribunals. Moreover, the organisations placed in Argentina were opposed to any international intervention and, at first, were even reluctant to accept that justice should be soaked outside the country through universal jurisdiction.[85] However, they rapidly ended up engaging with this legal instrument, conceiving it as an in-between tool, a ping-pong strategy, to fuel justice abroad while pressuring Argentinean authorities to ensure accountability in the country.

Spain was the most suitable European country to open trials. There, universal jurisdiction was broad as in Germany – in contrast to France and Italy, where only cases with national victims were accepted – while there was a big Argentinean network. In 1989, those still in Spain created the Asociación Argentina pro Derechos Humanos de Madrid (AAPDH-M) to develop specific legal strategies based on universal jurisdiction to enforce human rights treaties and make them a reality. Ramos Marrau argues 'the UN Declarations and Conventions after the war were wet paper, nobody enforced them'.[86] Likewise, Slepoy adds:

> We started to work with the legislation that existed in Spain and many other countries but that has not yet been put into practice … as many other norms that look beautiful on the paper but that are not enforced … The law established that the Spanish tribunals had jurisdiction over certain crimes perpetrated outside the country when they met a series of elements that made them international crimes.[87]

One of the first initiatives of the AAPDH-M in this regard was the organisation of the First Latin-American Seminar against Impunity in the offices of the European Parliament in Madrid together with Asociación Pro Derechos Humanos in España, Amnesty International and UNESCO.[88] Meanwhile, it was necessary to create awareness among the Spanish population. Slepoy recalls how he published articles in El País and other newspapers with signatures from renowned artists, athletes, politicians and intellectuals to gather support for eventual trials. The cases finally moved forward when, in March 1995, Captain Adolfo Scilingo confessed he had thrown people who were alive from Navy planes (the so-called death flights) and that this methodology was authorised by the Church as a 'Christian way of death'.[89] As AEDD (Association of Former Detainees-Disappeared), an association composed of survivors from clandestine detention centres, states, a perpetrator needed to confirm the extent of the systematic killings for the public to react. In their words: 'Just then what those of us who have been imprisoned and liberated had been detailing almost step by step acquired the status of 'truth''.[90] The hierarchy of truth located the words of the perpetrator at a higher stage than the ones of those who suffered the crimes themselves.

Following the scandal of this declarations, Spanish Prosecutor Carlos Castresana Fernández, on behalf of the Union of Progressive Spanish Prosecutors (Unión de Fiscales Progresistas de España) presented a case before the Spanish Audiencia Nacional in 1996. He invoked article 23.4 of the Organic Law of the Spanish Judicial Power (Ley Orgánica del Poder Judicial español, 6/1985) to foster a broad understanding of universal jurisdiction, arguing that even though the case involved crimes perpetrated by Argentines against Argentines, they harmed the entire humanity and could be judged wherever it was possible. Still, the Audiencia Nacional needed to accept the case. AAPDH-M kept on looking for support for the trials, arranging meetings in different cities, making agreements with NGOs, and collecting signatures. They gathered more than 300,000 signatures in support of the criminal proceeding as well as a vigil against impunity before the Audiencia Nacional, which culminated with the unanimous acceptance of the jurisdiction that was celebrated with 'hugs and crying' in the streets.[91]

Yet more documentation, testimonies, case material and legal arguments were needed to move the case forward and the organised victims' networks in Argentina and Europe were the ones providing them. Following the acceptance of the trials, AAPDH-M continued publishing articles in Spanish newspapers and organising seminars. One of the most important ones was the Conference for Universal Jurisdiction organised in the School of Medicine in Madrid, with the participation of judges, prosecutors, lawyers, victims and activists from Germany, the UK, France, Argentina and Spain. Many of the human rights organisations leaders from Argentina attended, including Horacio Verbitsky, Estela de Carlotto and Adolfo Perez Esquivel.[92] In turn, survivors from Argentina travelled to Spain to give testimony in the trials; this included AEDD members Susana Calloni, Graciela Daleo, Adriana Calvo, Ana María Careaga and Eduardo Lardies.[93] The AAPDH-M organised housing and support.

Inside and outside the courts, the role of the diaspora was crucial. As Ramos Marrau claims, 'who presented the denounces? Who was there as a civil party? Who engaged in activism so that the Spanish society supported the cases and the Audiencia Nacional accepted jurisdiction to judge non-Spanish people?'. And he answers:

> It was mainly the Argentine exile who fostered these trials under the accusation of genocide … I am neither a lawyer nor anything like that but one starts to understand a little bit these legal figures, what is universal jurisdiction that makes an Argentinean who perpetrated a crime against humanity can be detained in Mexico, as it happened with Ricardo Gabriel Cavallo, and that he can be extradited to Spain.[94]

He explains that the prosecutor needed to present evidence and that evidence was mainly based on testimonies and how that worked relied basically on the shoulders of the diaspora: it meant, identifying the witnesses, contacting them, preparing their trip, hosting them, preparing their testimonies, arranging meetings, and also giving comfort to the survivors and relatives of the disappeared for whom the whole experience was emotionally intense. 'They stayed at my home, we spent all night talking and even the strongest ones, the ones who would you think that they would never hug you, at some point, collapsed, and started to cry like children when going over all the details that have to be part of the testimony'.[95] Even though the process was advancing, it was not possible to convict Scilingo if he was not there. Then, Graciela Lois, a member of Familiares, presented herself as a civil party and played a key role in getting Scilingo to travel to Spain, arguably as a protected witness, so that the case could move forward.[96] Finally, on November 4, 1998, the Sala Penal de la Audiencia Nacional convicted Scilingo and, fostering the genocide argument, stated that, through the forced disappearances and other crimes, the Military tried to destroy a 'national group', a part of the Argentine society that was questioning the status quo.[97] Later on, in 2000, Miguel Angel Cavallo was arrested in Mexico and extradited to Spain.

When in 1998 President Menem travelled to Europe seeking investments, he found that the European press and the authorities were concerned about the reigning impunity. Following with the ping-pong dynamic, even if the efforts of networks in Europe were not enough to make room for the extraditions – which were denied –, they did fuel justice back home. To respond to foreign pressure, President Menem pushed the local judiciary to move forward and got Judge Marquevich to order the detention of one of the leaders of the Military government, Jorge Rafael Videla, in a case dealing with the abduction of children, which was excluded from the impunity laws.[98] Videla's detention in 1998 allowed, on the one hand, to start breaking reigning impunity in Argentina while, on the other hand, benefited Menem's stand in Europe, portraying him as a defender of the rule of law. Indeed, President Menem declared before European reporters: 'this is one more sign that we have one of the best justice systems in the world'.[99] One year later, in November 1999, Spanish judge Baltasar Garzón ordered the prosecution of almost 100 members of the Argentine military for dictatorship-era crimes, requesting the extradition of 48 of them.[100] Notably, this happened in an international context in which Argentina played a relevant role in the negotiations of the Rome Statute between 1994 and 1998, which further raised the country's prominence in international criminal justice.

Cases under this dynamic also moved forward in other European countries. In France, the relatives of the French nuns, Alice Domon and Léonie Duquet, tortured and murdered in Buenos Aires in 1977 presented a case against Astiz in June 1982. Argentinean authorities did not respond to the court's extradition request, but Astiz was convicted in absentia in 1990 to life in prison.[101] Even years later, French President Jacques Chirac, both publicly and in private conversation with Argentinean President Menem, expressed that he was committed to obtaining the extradition. Likewise, from the mid-1990s, HIJOS Sweden – the Swedish branch of the Argentinean network of children of the victims of the dictatorship – pushed for accountability against Astiz for the case of Dagmar Hagelin.[102] In Germany, a group of relatives of 85 German citizens and Argentineans of German descent killed or disappeared by the Argentinean military, together with Pérez Esquivel, formed the Koalition gegen Straflosigkeit (Coalition against Impunity) in 1998. The coalition also includes INGOs, protestant groups and human rights organisations.[103] This same year they initiated a case on behalf of ten of the victims before a federal judge in Nuremberg against 89 military officers.[104] In 2001, a German court issued an international arrest warrant for Suárez Mason for the suspected murder of German citizen Elisabeth Kasemann in 1977, while another ten cases of German-Argentine victims against Junta leaders are under investigation. At the same time, diaspora efforts toward accountability also took place in Italy, which was a privileged place to initiate criminal cases because the legislation makes it possible to host trials '*in absentia*' and to bring to justice criminal cases against Italian victims even if perpetrated abroad. Lita Boitano from Familiares and Juana Bettanin from the Asociación Familiares de Desaparecidos Italianos had already gathered in 1983 a list of Italian-Argentinean victims of the dictatorship. A few years later, in 1988, relatives of disappeared with Italian citizenship gathered in Montevideo, Uruguay, in the office of SERPAJ to discuss the possibility of litigating in Italy. These efforts materialised through a case presented before the Rome Tribunal in 1999 to investigate the disappearance of 44 Italian citizens and 277 people with double citizen (Argentinean-Italian), all between 17 and 29 years old.

Again, the ping-pong strategy, meant that, to repeal this foreign pressure, but still present himself as law-abiding, Menem had to make local concessions in terms of accountability. He then connected with other abiding judges to order the pretrial detention of the Military Junta leader, Admiral Emilio Massera, for the systematic abduction of the babies born in the clandestine detention centres, the loophole in the impunity laws.[105] The context and timing of both Videla's and Massera's arrests suggest that President Menen and the Argentinean judges may have been influenced by foreign trials.[106] The international legal precept brought up in these trials was that a state must either extradite or try the accused domestically. Confronted with this dilemma and 'to fend off political pressures to extradite many officers, the Argentine government apparently decided to place under preventative detention a few high-profile figures, but now politically marginalized officers'.[107]

Meanwhile, trials continued abroad. In December 2000, the Italian court convicted seven perpetrators, including General Carlos Guillermo Suarez Mason, based on the intense contributions of those providing testimonies and evidence.[108] In that year, Italian authorities also arrested Jorge Olivera, responding to an international arrest warrant issued by a French judge for the enforced disappearance of the French citizen Anne-Marie Erize Tisseau in 1976. After forging the death certificate of the victim, he was released and escaped to Argentina. In turn, a Swedish prosecutor started an investigation based on universal jurisdiction and issued an international arrest warrant against Astiz in 2001.[109] Back home, building upon Videla and Massera's detentions, the human rights movement back home took advantage of the opportunity opened by the trials for illegal appropriation of children to show a fundamental contradiction|| in the judicial system. That is, the system allowed the investigation and punishment of the crimes perpetrated against the babies, while it prevented the investigation and punishment of the disappearance of their parents. In March 2001, Judge Gabriel Cavallo accepted the claim and declared the impunity laws unconstitutional. In November, the Federal Court confirmed the decision and in June 2005, the Supreme Court of Justice followed the same reasoning, settling the path to reopen the trials.

Overall, the role of those networks in Europe in a ping-pong display with the organisations based in Argentina was relevant in terms of breaking the reigning impunity back home and fostering accountability abroad. In the words of Smulovitz: 'Beyond the relevance that Judge Cavallo´s decision had in the reopening of past human rights cases, it should also be highlighted the role that the search and use of legal loopholes by human rights organisations and victims had in the reactivation of the legal strategy'.[110] In 2003, as a result of these transatlantic efforts and domestic political changes, impunity laws were repealed. By September 2021, Argentina had convicted 1044 people in 264 sentencings for crimes against humanity, while 281 other cases with 581 defendants were in pre-trial, 67 cases were awaiting trial and 19 trials were on the make.[111]

5. Brief conclusions

The article seeks to go beyond the mainstream Northern-centered perspective on atrocity confrontation and, instead, looks at the Global South as vital agents and not just recipients of help. In other words, while many crucial atrocities happened in the South (e.g. South Africa, Cambodia, Timor East, etc.), it is the case that the accountability processes that followed massive violence were intensively shaped by Northern powers either through special tribunals located and design in the North or through the involvement of international experts. Instead, the case of Argentina illustrates a process that was predominantly shaped by local actors – either at home or in exile-, based on legal innovations that, in turn, shaped international law. In this vein, looking into the case of Argentina and the struggle against the crimes against humanity perpetrated during the dictatorship that reigned from 1976 to 1983, the study shed light on the role of the grassroots organisations as innovators in deploying a human rights-based approach to dealing with the most severe crimes, against odds. Moreover, challenging the South-North dichotomy, the article also exposed how the atrocities perpetrated in Argentina have been challenged through a ping-pong strategy that involved denunciation, fact-finding, network-building and accountability initiatives built upon a permanent dialogue between actors on both sides of the Atlantic. In other words, the article drove attention to the fact that the struggle against atrocities cannot be reduced to one geographic space but, instead, it has been the result of a ping-pong strategy between Argentina and the (European) exile.

In this vein, networks in Europe in cooperation with the human rights movement in Argentina took a leading role in fostering justice mechanisms. The study highlights the entangled work across continents in mobilising international human rights law and the human rights framing to disseminate information about ongoing crimes and develop innovative legal initiatives to hold the military accountable. Once democracy was re-established in 1983 but the government passed impunity laws, those who remained abroad kept on working with the movement in Argentina by deploying universal jurisdiction and soaking to foster a boomerang effect aimed at fuelling justice back home. Moreover, through this analysis, the research also contributes to overcoming the marginal attention to the exiles – an actor in-between spaces-, who have been largely ignored or viewed with suspicion. Indeed, in Argentina, it was only with the revalorisation of the 1970s activism since 2003 – when trials reopened after thirty years of impunity laws – that those who had gone into exile started to be seen in a political and activist dimension and, as a result, that the children born or raised in exile become also recognised as political actors.

Notes

1. William A. Schabas, 'Crimes Against Humanity as a Paradigm for International Atrocity Crimes', *Middle East Critique* 20, no. 3 (September 2011): 253–69, https://doi.org/10.1080/19436149.2011.619762; Alette Smeulers and Roelof Haveman, *Supranational Criminology: Towards a Criminology of International Crimes* (Antwerp: Intersentia, 2008).
2. William Chambliss, '*State-Organized Crime—The American Society of Criminology, 1988 Presidential Address*', *Criminology* 27, no. 2 (1989): 183–208. Ray Michalowski, *Order, Law and Crime* (New York: Random House, 1985); David Kauzlarich, Rick A. Matthews, and William J. Miller, 'Toward A Victimology of State Crime', *Critical Criminology* 10 (2001): 173–94; Ronald C. Kramer and Raymond J. Michalowski, 'War, Aggression and State Crime', *The British Journal of Criminology* 45, no. 4 (2005): 446–69.
3. John Hagan and Wenona Rymond-Richmond, 'Darfur and the Crime of Genocide', in *Darfur and the Crime of Genocide*, 2008, 503.
4. Wayne Morrison, *Criminology, Civilisation and the New World Order* (Routledge/Cavendish, 2006).
5. Ruth Jamieson, 'Towards a Criminology of War in Europe', in *The New European Criminology*, ed. Vincenzo Ruggiero, Nigel South, and Ian Taylor (1998), 480–506; Ross McGarry and Sandra Walklate, *A Criminology of War?, The British Journal of Criminology* (Bristol University Press, 2019).
6. John Hagan, Heather Schoenfeld, and Alberto Palloni, 'The Science of Human Rights, War Crimes, and Humanitarian Emergencies', *Annual Review of Sociology* 32 (2006): 329–49.
7. Nicole Rafter and Sandra Walklate, 'Genocide and the Dynamics of Victimization: Some Observations on Armenia', *European Journal of Criminology* 9, no. 5 (2012): 514–26.
8. Stanley Cohen, *States of Denial: Knowing about Atrocities and Suffering* (Oxford: Blackwell, 2001).

9. Stephan Parmentier, 'The Missing Link: Criminological Perspectives on Transitional Justice and International Crimes', in *What is Criminology?* ed. M. Bosworth and C. Hoyle (Oxford, UK: Oxford University Press, 2011).
10. Suzanne Karstedt, 'The Life Course of Collective Memories: Persistency and Change in West Germany between 1950 and 1970', *Polish Sociological Review* 165, no. 1 (2009): 27–38.
11. Frank Neubacher, *Kriminologische Grundlagen Einer Internationalen Strafgerichtsbarkeit: Politische Ideen- Und Dogmengeschichte, Kriminalwissenschaftliche Legitimation, Strafrechtliche Perspektiven* (Mohr Siebeck, 2005).
12. John Hagan, Wenona Rymond-Richmond, and Patricia Parker, 'The Criminology of Genocide: The Death and Rape of Darfur', vol. 43, 2005; Hagan and Rymond-Richmond, 'Darfur and the Crime of Genocide', 2; Olaoluwa Olusanya, 'A Macro-Micro Integrated Theoretical Model of Mass Participation in Genocide', *The British Journal of Criminology* 53, no. 5 (2013): 843–63.
13. Barbara Harff, 'Genocide as State Terrorism', in *Government Violence and Repression: An Agenda for Research*, ed. Michael Stohl and George A. Lopez (New York: Greenwood, 1986), 165–88; David O Friedrichs, 'The Crime of the Century? The Case for the Holocaust', *Crime, Law and Social Change* 34, no. 1 (2000): 21–41; Alexander Alvarez, 'Adjusting to Genocide: The Techniques of Neutralization and the Holocaust', *Social Science History* 21, no. 2 (1997): 139–78; Annika Van Baar and Wim Huisman, 'The Oven Builders of the Holocaust: A Case Study of Corporate Complicity in International Crimes', *The British Journal of Criminology* 52, no. 6 (1 November 2012): 1033–50.
14. Karl Härter and Valeria Vegh Weis, 'Transnationales Strafrecht in Transatlantischer Perspektive (1870–1945). Ein Dialog Zwischen Dem Globalen Norden Und Dem Globalen Süden', *Max Planck Institute for Europan Legal History*, 2018.
15. Diego Zysman Quirós, 'Punishment, Democracy and Transitional Justice in Argentina (1983–2015)', *International Journal for Crime, Justice and Social Democracy* 6, no. 1 (1 March 2017).
16. John Braithwaite, 'Criminology, Criminology, Peacebuilding and Transitional Justice: Lessons from the Global South', in *The Palgrave Handbook of Criminology and the Global South*, ed. Kerry Carrington Hogg Russell Scott John and Sozzo Máximo (London: Palgrave, 2018), 971–90. See Kathryn Sikkink, *The Justice Cascade.*
17. Kerry Carrington, Russell Hogg, and Máximo Sozzo, 'Southern Criminology', *The British Journal of Criminology*, 2016, 1–20.
18. Larissa Van Den Herik, 'Diasporas and International Law', *ESIL Reflections* 7, no. 6 (24 September 2018).
19. Margarete E. Keck and Kathryn Sikkink, *Activists Beyond Borders* (London: Cornell University Press, 1998).
20. William A. Schabas, 'Crimes Against Humanity as a Paradigm for International Atrocity Crimes', *Middle East Critique* 20, no. 3 (September 2011): 253–69.
21. Adolfo Perez Esquivel, Interview, July 10, 2019, Buenos Aires, Argentina.
22. Marina Franco, 'Algunas Reflexiones En Torno al Acto de Exilio En El Pasado Reciente Argentino', in *Problemas de Historia Reciente Del Cono Sur*, ed. Bohoslavsky Ernesto, Franco Marina, and D. Lvovich (Buenos Aires: UNGS-Prometeo, n.d.); S Jensen, 'Los Exiliados Argentinos Y Las Luchas Por La Justicia (1976–1981)', *Estudios* 38 (2017): 13–30.
23. Francesca Lessa, *The Condor Trials Transnational Repression and Human Rights in South America* (NH: Yale University Press, 2022).
24. Augusto Conte McDonnell and Emilio F. Mignone, *Estrategia Represiva de La Dictadura Militar. La Doctrina Del Paralelismo Global* (Buenos Aires: Colihue, 2006); Horacio Verbitsky and Juan Pablo Bohoslavsky, *The Economic Accomplices to the Argentine Dictatorship. Outstanding Debts* (Cambrigde: Cambrigde University Press, 2015).
25. Leigh A. Payne, Gabriel Pereira Pereira, and Laura Bernal-Bermúdez, 'International Pressure for Corporate Accountability', in *Transitional Justice and Corporate Accountability from Below*, ed. Leigh A. Payne, Gabriel Pereira, and Laura Bernal-Bermúdez (Cambridge University Press, 2020), 61–112.

26. International Convention for the Protection of All Persons from Enforced Disappearance, 2006.
27. The lack of certainty about the final number of disappeared people responds to the very nature of the crime, in terms of the refusal of the perpetrators to give the official documents that account for the disappearances. The CONADEP registered less than 10,000 cases, but it received no response to hundreds of requests for information from the military and police about those enforced disappeared. CONADEP, *Nunca Más* (Buenos Aires: Eudeba, 1984). Moreover, one bishop alone tracked 2,800 cases for a single diocese in Greater Buenos Aires, nearly a quarter of the CONADEP's total for the entire country, which shows that the cases published by the are not representative of the total number of cases. Alison Brysk, *The Politics of Human Rights in Argentina: Protest, Change, and Democratization* (Stanford: Standford University Press, 1994).
28. Félix Luna, *Los Golpes Militares (1930–1983). El Peronismo En Sus Fuentes* (Buenos Aires: La Nación, 2003).
29. Comisión Interamericana de Derechos Humanos, Informe de Pais – Argentina 1980, OEA/Ser.L/V/II.49 (11 April 1980); T. Piñeiro, 'Visita de La Comisión Interamericana de Derechos Humanos a La Argentina', APDH, Materiales de la Secretaría, 2020, https://www.apdh-argentina.org.ar/lesa-humanidad/materiales-de-la-secretaria/85.
30. Marina Franco, 'Testimoniar e Informar: Exiliados Argentinos En París (1976–1983)', *Amerique Latine Histoire & Memoire*, no. 8 (2004).
31. Rodolfo Mattarollo, Interview, Memoria Abierta.
32. Rodolfo Mattarollo, Interview, Memoria Abierta; Jensen, 'Los Exiliados Argentinos Y Las Luchas Por La Justicia (1976–1981)', 22.
33. COSOFAM -Madrid, La paz se construye con la justicia, diciembre 1977. En. AMORÓS,ob cit, 2011, p. 126.
34. Vicente Zito Lema, Interview, August 22, 2019, Buenos Aires, Argentina.
35. Marina Franco, *Argentinos En Francia Durante La Dictadura* (Buenos Aires: Siglo XXI, 2008).
36. Francisco Pompeyo Ramos Marrau, Interview, Memoria Abierta.
37. Francisco Pompeyo Ramos Marrau, Interview, Memoria Abierta.
38. Carlos Slepoy, Interview, Memoria Abierta.
39. Juan Mendez, Interview January 29, 2019, Washington DC, USA.
40. Dora Salas, Interview June 19, 2018, Berlin, Germany.
41. Rodolfo Mattarollo, Interview, Memoria Abierta.
42. Pablo Yankelevich, *Ráfagas de Un Exilio. Argentinos En México, 1974–1983* (Buenos Aires: FCE, 2010).
43. Guillermo Mira Delli-Zotti and Frrnando Esteban, 'La Construcción de Un Espacio Político Transnacional Iberoamericano de Defensa de Los DDHH: El Caso de La Asociación Argentina pro Derechos Humanos de Madrid', *HAOL* 14 (2007): 57–66.
44. Vicente Zito Lema, Interview, August 22, 2019, Buenos Aires, Argentina.
45. Camillo Robertini, 'Las Relaciones Bilaterales Entre Italia y Argentina Durante La Última Dictadura Militar 1976–1983. The Internacional Relationship between Italy and Argentina during the Last Military Dictatorship 1976–1983', *Historia Unicap* 3, no. 5 (2016): 42; Yankelevich, *Ráfagas de Un Exilio. Argentinos En México, 1974–1983.*
46. 'El Mundo Es Un Pañuelo - Tomo I', https://www.editorial.unlp.edu.ar/derechos_humanos/el_mundo_es_un_panuelo_i-18135 (accessed September 17, 2023).
47. Rodolfo Mattarollo, Interview, Memoria Abierta.
48. Rodolfo Mattarollo, Interview, Memoria Abierta; Carlos Slepoy, Interview, Memoria Abierta.
49. Rodolfo Mattarollo, Interview, Memoria Abierta.
50. Mira Delli-Zotti and Esteban, 'La Construcción de Un Espacio Político Transnacional Iberoamericano de Defensa de Los DDHH: El Caso de La Asociación Argentina pro Derechos Humanos de Madrid'.
51. Marta Ungaro, Interview, Memoria Abierta.

52. Rodolfo Mattarollo, Interview, Memoria Abierta.
53. Raanan Rein, 'Solidaridad Internacional y Protestas Transnacionales Contra La Copa Mundial de Fútbol 1978', *Cuadernos de Aletheia* 3 (2019): 29–42.
54. Vicente Zito Lema, Interview, August 22, 2019, Buenos Aires, Argentina.
55. Carlos Slepoy, Interview, Memoria Abierta.
56. Vicente Zito Lema, Interview, August 22, 2019, Buenos Aires, Argentina.
57. Adolfo Perez Esquivel, Interview, July 10, 2019, Buenos Aires, Argentina.
58. 'El Mundo Es Un Pañuelo - Tomo I', 25–6.
59. Iain Guest, *Behind the Disappearances: Argentina's Dirty War against Human Rights and the United Nations* (Philadelphia: University of Pennsylvania Press, 1990).
60. Familiares Archive.
61. See https://www.nobelprize.org/prizes/peace/1980/esquivel/26126-adolfo-perez-esquivel-nobel-lecture-1980/
62. See https://www.memo.com.ar/poder/por-que-accion-le-otorgaron-a-adolfo-perez-esquivel-el-premio-nobel-de-la-paz-en-1980/
63. See https://www.comisionporlamemoria.org/project/40-anos-del-premio-nobel-de-la-paz-a-adolfo-perez-esquivel/
64. Jensen Silvina, *Los Exiliados : La Lucha Por Los Derechos Humanos Durante La Dictadura Militar* (Buenos Aires: Sudamericana, 2010).
65. See the original document at https://www.cels.org.ar/common/documentos/Coloquio_Paris_paralelismoglobal.pdf
66. Rodolfo Mattarollo, Interview, Memoria Abierta.
67. Adolfo Perez Esquivel, Interview, July 10, 2019, Buenos Aires, Argentina
68. See https://cortazar.nakalona.fr/items/show/1154
69. 'El Mundo Es Un Pañuelo – Tomo I'.
70. Mario Amoros, *Argentina En El Archivo de IEPALA (1976–1983)* (Madrid: IEPALA, 2011).
71. See https://www.youtube.com/watch?v=vaQfoXeq_Ys
72. Laura Bertolucci, Interview, Memoria Abierta.
73. Rodolfo Mattarollo, Interview, Memoria Abierta.
74. Laura Bertolucci, Interview, Memoria Abierta.
75. Juan Sosa, Interview, Memoria Abierta.
76. Carlos Pipino Martínez, Interview, Memoria Abierta.
77. CONADEP, *Nunca Más* (Buenos Aires: Eudeba, 1984).
78. Rebecca Lichtenfeld, 'Accountability in Argentina 20 Years Later, Cases Studies' (ICTJ, 2005), Carlos Nino, 'The Human Rights Policy of the Argentine Constitutional Government: A Reply', *Yale Journal of International Law* 11, no. 1 (1985), https://openyls.law.yale.edu/handle/20.500.13051/6144.
79. See 'Si te he visto no me acuerdo – Alfonsín: "La casa está en orden"', https://www.youtube.com/watch?v=tbGNIvsrtA0
80. Emilio Crenzel, *La Historia Politica Del Nunca Mas. La Memoria de Las Desapariciones En La Argentina* (Buenos Aires: Siglo XXI, 2008).
81. Carlos S. Nino, *Juicio al Mal Absoluto* (Buenos Aires: Emecé, 1997).
82. Decreto Nacional 1.002/1989, 1.003/1989, 1.004/89 y 1.005/89, Buenos Aires, 6 de octubre de 1989.
83. Valeria Vegh Weis, 'The Relevance of Victims' Organizations in the Transitional Justice Process: The Case of the Grandmothers of Plaza de Mayo in Argentina', *Intercultural Human Rights Law Review* 60 (2017): 1–70.
84. Martín Abregú, 'Human Rights After The Dictatorship Lessons From Argentina', *NACLA Report on the Americas* 34, no. 1 (July 2000): 12–18, 13.
85. Carlos Pipino Martínez, Interview, Memoria Abierta.
86. Francisco Pompeyo Ramos Marrau, Interview, Memoria Abierta.
87. Carlos Slepoy, Interview, Memoria Abierta.
88. Mira Delli-Zotti and Esteban, 'La Construcción de Un Espacio Político Transnacional Iberoamericano de Defensa de Los DDHH: El Caso de La Asociación Argentina pro Derechos Humanos de Madrid'.

89. CELS, *Derechos Humanos En Argentina. Informe 2013* (Buenos Aires: Siglo XXI, 2013).
90. AEDD Tantas voces tantas vidas a. 3, nro. 7, mayo 2003 pp. 27/31.
91. Francisco Pompeyo Ramos Marrau, Interview, Memoria Abierta.
92. Francisco Pompeyo Ramos Marrau, Interview, Memoria Abierta.
93. Horacio Verbitsky, *Civiles y Militares. Memoria Secreta de La Transición* (Buenos Aires: De Bolsillo, 1987); Lauriane Bouvet, 'The Italian Operation Condor Trial: Limits of the Criminal Approach to the Transnational Repressive Coordination in the Trial Attempts Justice from Abroad', *Revista Científica de Estudios Sociales Iberoamericanos* IX (2017): 40–75.
94. Francisco Pompeyo Ramos Marrau, Interview, Memoria Abierta.
95. Francisco Pompeyo Ramos Marrau, Interview, Memoria Abierta.
96. Graciela Lois, Interview Dec. 7, 2018, Buenos Aires, Argentina.
97. Emilio Crenzel, 'Entre La Historia y La Memoria. A 40 Años Del Golpe de Estado En La Argentina', *História: Questões & Debates* 64, no. 2 (14 December 2016): 39–69.
98. Since illegal appropriation of children had not been part of the crimes judged during the Junta Trials and the subsequent criminal processes, it was not included in the presidential pardons and impunity laws. This loophole allowed Abuelas to initiate in 1996, and despite the Due Obedience Law, lawsuits against those who directly appropriated the children and also those who gave the orders, including several ex-high-ranking officials.
99. 'Cuatro Historias Escandalosas En El Legajo Del Juez Marquevich', https://www.clarin.com/politica/historias-escandalosas-legajo-juez-marquevich_0_HkNXemgAFe.html (accessed September 20, 2023).
100. Argentina Author and Rita Arditti, 'The Grandmothers of the Plaza De Mayo and the Struggle against Impunity in Argentina', *Source: Meridians*, vol. 3, 2002.
101. Astiz, Arrêt, N° 1893/89, Cour d'assises de Paris, 16 mars 1990.
102. Alexandra Barahona De Brito, Carmen Gonzalez Enriquez, and Paloma Aguilar, *The Politics of Memory: Transitional Justice in Democratizing Societies* (Oxford: OUP, 2001).
103. Amnesty International, Franciscans, Pax Christi, Miserior, Diakonisches Werk, Republican Lawyers' Association, Freiburg Human Rights Association and the Nuremberg Human Rights Centre, among others. See http://www.menschenrechte.org/straflosigkeit.htm#koa
104. Cases of "disappeared" facing judicial closure in Germany, April 2000, https://kipdf.com/argentina-cases-of-disappeared-facing-judicial-closure-in-germany-introduction_5b222333097c47d1648b4689.html
105. Lauriane Bouvet, 'The Italian Operation Condor Trial: Limits of the Criminal Approach to the Transnational Repressive Coordination in the Trial Attempts Justice from Abroad'.
106. Martín Abregú, 'Human Rights After The Dictatorship Lessons From Argentina'.
107. Kathryn Sikkink and Carrie Booth Walling, 'La Cascada de Justicia y El Impacto de Los Juicios de Derechos Humanos En América Latina', *Cuadernos Del Claeh* 31, no. 96–7 (2008), https://ojs.claeh.edu.uy/publicaciones/index.php/cclaeh/article/view/16.
108. Francesca Lessa, 'Operation Condor on Trial: Justice for Transnational Human Rights Crimes in South America', *Journal of Latin American Studies* 51, no. 2 (2019): 409–39.
109. On 5 December 2001, then President Fernando de la Rúa issued Decree 1581/2001, which blocked extraditions in such cases, arguing double jeopardy and sovereignty (it was only when President Kirchner was elected that the Decree was overturned).
110. Catalina Smulovitz, 'I Can't Get No Satisfaction||: Accountability and Justice for Past Human Rights Violations in Argentina' (Paper prepared for the Project: —Comparing the Effectiveness of the Accountability Mechanisms in Eastern Europe and Latin America|| jointly organized by El Colegio de México and the United Nations University in association with Oxford University, 2008), 12.
111. See http://www.museositioesma.gob.ar/inauguracion/memoria-verdad-y-justicia/

Disclosure statement

No potential conflict of interest was reported by the author(s).

Impunity in cases of serious human rights violations: Three relevant aspects of contention in the jurisprudence of the Inter-American Court of Human Rights

Harold Bertot Triana and Elena C. Díaz Galán

ABSTRACT
The Inter-American Court of Human Rights (IACtHR) is a pioneer in international human rights law in developing jurisprudence against impunity. Since the 1970s, the American continent has been prone to political and policymaking processes to ensure impunity for those responsible for serious human rights violations. This impunity has aimed at, among others, enforcing amnesty and self-amnesty laws or implementing procedural institutions (such as the *ne bis in idem* principle) that intend to prevent the investigation and punishment of those responsible for serious human rights violations. The paper examines the jurisprudence of the IACtHR to determine some fundamental lines of argument that seek to combat impunity in cases of serious human rights violations. To this end, it emphasizes the particularities of the duty to investigate established by the IACtHR, the development of *jus cogens* in relation to these serious situations, and the scope of reparations. From a comparative perspective, it also highlights the need for other international Courts, such as the European Court of Human Rights, to assume these jurisprudential approaches to combat impunity in cases of serious violations.

Introduction

The Inter-American Court of Human Rights (IACtHR), the judicial institution responsible for interpreting and applying the American Convention on Human Rights provisions, has played an important role in combating impunity for serious human rights violations in the Americas. Its work began in the face of a daunting prospect of human rights in the American continent in the 1970s and 1980s.[1] It was a complex scenario, plagued by military dictatorships, forced disappearances, covert operations to eliminate political adversaries, weak democratic institutions, huge problems in the administration of justice, among others. All this was prone to impunity for serious human rights violations. Between 1978 and 1989, in view of serious and systematic human rights violations, the so-called 'impunity laws' came into force, resulting in the implementation of institutions that avoided investigating or punishing the perpetrators, and which took the form of amnesties, pardons, criminal statutes of limitation, etc.[2]

Democratisation in several States of the continent did not improve the situation. In the 1990s, together with a growing impunity in situations involving massacres or other human rights violations, there were some attempts to abandon the Inter-American system and, fundamentally, to avoid the IACtHR jurisdiction.[3] This scenario of serious and systematic human rights violations in the context of dictatorships had a significant impact on the jurisdiction of the Court. Furthermore, the so-called 'Operation Condor', which had awful effects on the American continent, has been highlighted, as well as those cases that later became part of the IACtHR's jurisdiction, namely the 'Cycles of Massacres'.[4]

In this context, the IACtHR launched jurisprudential lines of significant importance to prevent impunity in the Americas. One of the rulings that would have the greatest impact on international human rights law was the judgment on the merits of 14 March 2001, *Case Barrios Altos v. Peru*, which became the *leading case* on self-amnesty laws and serious human rights violations. Since then, other judgments (*Almonacid Arellano et al. v. Chile, La Cantuta v. Peru*, among others) have developed a *uniform jurisprudence* to prevent national practices and regulations that lead to impunity.

The implementation of these institutions was not weakened when the Court analysed facts within the framework of transitional justice processes in cases such as El Salvador or recently in Colombia. These processes allowed some authors to consider a certain flexibility in the amnesty standards even in cases of serious violations of human rights. This paper will address these examples to reaffirm how the Inter-American Court does not consider it compatible with human rights obligations to apply amnesty or any other measure that seeks impunity in cases of serious human rights violations.

However, the application of these institutions against impunity in the Inter-American system has been at the centre of discussions about 'judicial activism' in the Inter-American Court, which is not compatible with the ACHR. This discussion is addressed in this paper from a conciliatory perspective among victims, civil society, and the State. It also considers a reflection that does not lose sight of the particular regime within international law where the ACHR is inserted and the interpretative work of the Inter-American Court.

Nowadays, these approaches of the IACtHR have been strengthened in the context of the 'Inter-Americanization' of protection standards, and of mechanisms such as 'conventionality control' that have greatly reinforced the guidelines or standards of international protection of human rights.[5] It is a control that public authorities in all State parties must carry out on the compatibility of the norms to be applied with respect to the American Convention on Human Rights (ACHR) and the jurisprudence of the IACtHR.[6]

This paper examines the development of three fundamental topics in the jurisprudence of the IACtHR, linked to deter impunity in the Americas: the concretisation of the duty to investigate in the case of serious violations, the implementation of *jus cogens* norms, and reparations. In this way, the work presents three jurisprudence of the IACtHR with particular emphasis in combating impunity in the Americas in case of serious human rights violations: (1) the implementation and particular impact of the State's obligation to prevent, investigate and punish serious human rights violations; (2) the extension of *jus cogens* norms to other areas that accentuate the obligation to prevent, investigate and punish in order to deter regulations or practices that lead to impunity; and (3) the gradual expansion of the concept of reparation as an indispensable scope against impunity.

The article highlights these three elements along with a brief comparison with the jurisprudence of the European Court of Human Rights. Thus, it is possible to emphasis the development of the IACtHR's jurisprudence within the framework of international human rights law and which serves to combat impunity in cases of serious human rights violations. In this way, it raises the existence of certain areas that should be strengthened or considered by the European Court, and which will result in more effective judicial responses and greater depth in eradicating any vestige of impunity for serious human rights violations.

The scope of the duty to prevent, investigate and punish serious violations of human rights in the jurisprudence of the Inter-American Court

The Inter-American Court has developed the scope of the obligations to respect and guarantee rights contained in Article 1(1) of the American Convention. The obligation to 'respect' implies compliance with the established norm in a direct manner, either with an abstention or with an act. The obligation to 'guarantee' implies actions by the State to allow the free and full exercise of rights, and this has consequences for how the State is organised and structured to achieve these objectives. This means that the State must establish an organisation of public power to enable the free and full exercise of the Convention rights. In a landmark judgment on the *Case of Velásquez Rodríguez v. Honduras*, the Court derived from the obligation to 'ensure' granted by Article 1.1 of the ACHR, on States obligation to 'prevent, investigate and punish any violation of the rights recognized by the Convention'.[7]

The Court has developed a broad conception of impunity. In the *Case of 'White Van' (Paniagua Morales et al.) v. Guatemala*, impunity is defined as 'the total lack of investigation, prosecution, capture, trial and conviction of those responsible for violations of the rights protected by the American Convention'.[8] The 'chronic recidivism' of human rights violations and the 'helplessness of victims' is related to the obligation of the State to use all legal means at its disposal to avoid these situations.[9]

Impunity in the jurisprudence of the Inter-American Court is related to several situations for which a State can be responsible under the protection of the ACHR. These may cover the violation of Articles 8 and 25 in cases of 'deficient direction of the judicial proceedings', 'delays' and 'obstructions effected to prevent punishment all those responsible'.[10] Emphasis has been placed on essential or necessary aspects to give full effect to the State's obligation to investigate and punish all those responsible for human rights violations. Among them the elimination of *de facto* and *de jure* obstacles, efficient investigations and proceedings, and adequate security guarantees for all involved parties (victims' families, investigators, witnesses, judicial officials, etc.).[11]

In relation to situations involving serious human rights violations, the obligation to prevent, investigate and punish has a particular scope and impact.[12] This includes prohibitions of certain conducts that rise to the status of *jus cogens* of general international law. The IACtHR often refers to such conduct as 'serious human rights violations', 'grave human rights violations' or 'crimes under international law', which may include, as appropriate 'forced disappearances', 'extrajudicial executions', 'torture', 'crimes against humanity', 'slavery', among others. To classify these conducts, it must be observed 'the systematic pattern of grave and massive human rights violations.[13] In some cases, the Court prohibits the State in view of the existence of some of these conducts which 'violate non-derogable rights recognized by international human rights law',[14] and in others, it appeals directly to its prohibition with the status of *ius cogens* in international law.[15]

In the *Velásquez Rodríguez v. Honduras* case, it was also stated that the obligation to guarantee rights extended to those acts not directly attributable to the State. These were acts of private individuals for which the State may be responsible for not acting with 'due diligence to prevent the violation or to respond to it as required by the Convention'.[16] This is of particular importance in the discussion of State responsibility for serious human rights violations by organised crime. In *Pueblo Bello Massacre v. Colombia*, the Court specified that the responsibility of the State is not unlimited in the face of any act of private individuals. The particularities of the case must be taken into account in order to adjust the scope of the obligations for this type of situation. In this sense, the Court has indicated a set of conditions: (1) *knowledge of a situation of real and immediate risk to individuals or a group of persons*; and (2) *preventing or avoiding the risk within reasonable possibilities.*[17]

The debate in these cases of organised crime on the breach of the obligation to guarantee, in cases of forced disappearance, for example, may be due to the lack of prevention before the events occurred, or due to the lack of action when there was knowledge of a real and immediate risk for the victims[18]; or in those cases in which the State is the creator of the risk that it does not control afterwards.[19] In the case of *Gonzalez et al. ('Campo Algodonero') v. Mexico*, despite considering that the women in Ciudad Juarez were in a situation of vulnerability, and that this did not imply an 'unlimited responsibility for any unlawful act against such women', it nevertheless considered that the State was responsible for 'a failure of the State to comply in general with its obligation of prevention' because of 'the absence of a general policy which could have been initiated at least in 1998 – when the CNDH warned of the pattern of violence against women in Ciudad Juarez'.[20]

In contexts of enforced disappearances, such as the Mexican case, it has been argued that the correct approach of the Court to determine the responsibility of the State should be to take into account the role of the State in the creation of risk and structural situations of violence.[21] This approach of a State creating risk is present in the jurisprudence of the Court in these situations, and certain facts have been directly attributed to the State for failure to comply with the obligation to respect, as in the case of *Vereda La Esperanza v. Colombia*, due to 'the support and acquiescence provided by members of the security forces for the actions of the paramilitary forces'.[22]

In any case, some aspects of greater specificity of the State's obligation to prevent, investigate and punish serious human rights violations refer to the fact that it is impossible for certain factual and legal situations to be obstacles or impediments to the full effectiveness of compliance. It is worth highlighting issues of the jurisprudence of the Inter-American Court in cases of serious human rights violations, and in particular, the unconventionality of some institutions: amnesties, statutes of limitations on criminal actions for international crimes, 'fraudulent *res judicata*', and extradition and its improper application.

Against amnesty and other institutions of impunity in the jurisprudence of the Inter-American Court

On 3 November 1991, a massacre of 'alleged' members of *Sendero Luminoso* (Shining Path Group) took place in the neighbourhood known as Barrios Altos in Lima (Peru). It was carried out by the Colina Group, a well-known 'death squadron' that belonged to Peruvian military intelligence and Army.[23] However, subsequent laws gave amnesty coverage to people related to this type of human rights violation.[24] In dealing with this case, the IACtHR, in its judgment on the merits, was kind enough to state with respect to these laws:

> This Court considers that all amnesty provisions, provisions on prescription and the establishment of measures designed to eliminate responsibility are inadmissible, because they are intended to prevent the investigation and punishment of those responsible for serious human rights violations such as torture, extrajudicial, summary or arbitrary execution and forced disappearance, all of them prohibited because they violate non-derogable rights recognized by international human rights law.[25]

The court considered the said laws incompatible with the American Convention, and 'lack legal effect'.[26] It upheld the same approach in later cases, as in *Almonacid Arellano v. Chile,* judgment of September 2006 and *La Cantuta v. Peru,* judgment of 29 November 2006.[27] In *Barrios Altos v. Peru*, the prohibition of amnesty for the specific case derived from the legal obligations granted by Articles 1(1) and 2 of the ACHR with respect to Articles 8(1) and 25.[28] In *Almonacid Arellano v. Chile*, the Inter-American Court considers the existence of the duty to prevent, investigate and punish derived from Article 1(1) as a legal obligation under international law.[29] The Court upholds this reasoning in subsequent cases which is supported by reference to organs or bodies in international law. In the *Case of Gelman v. Uruguay*, for example, before reviewing the current state of international law, the Inter-American Court refers to how certain international bodies have ruled on the incompatibility of amnesty laws related to serious violations of human rights with international law and the international obligations of States.[30]

This jurisprudential position has been vital for the development of international law in this area. The European Court of Human Rights has adopted the jurisprudence of the IACHR as a pioneer in this matter. For instance, in the *Case of Lexa V. Slovakia* (2008), as part of international law and its practice, reference is made to the well-known paragraph 41 of the Court's judgment in the *Barrios Altos*,[31] as well as to *Bulacio v. Argentina* (2003) where specific reference is made to avoiding obstacles that hamper the investigation and punishment of those responsible for human rights violations.[32]

In *Margus versus Croacia* (2014) -where the following cases are cited *in extenso Barrios Altos, Almonacid, La Cantuta, Anzualdo Castro, Gelman v. Uruguay*, among others[33]- this interpretation is explicitly stated in accordance with international human rights law. The case dealt with the amnesty of a person involved in serious violations of fundamental human rights (international murder of civilians and severe injury to a child).

According to the ECtHR, Article 4 of Protocol No. 7 to the Convention was not applicable, and the existence of a fresh formal accusation to try that person for war crimes against the civilian population was in conformity with the requirements of Articles 2 and 3 of the European Convention on Human Rights (ECHR).[34]

After *Barrios Altos*, the jurisprudence of the Inter-American Court consolidated the prohibition of other legal institutions. This would be the case of the *ne bis in idem* principle and 'fraudulent *res judicata*'. The *ne bis in idem* principle is acknowledged by the IACtHR as a 'human right' enshrined in Article 8.4, although without an 'absolute character'.[35] Moreover, it is logically linked to the *res judicata principle*, so it is possible that the relative nature of this right destroys this principle if the process is flawed or leads to impunity. The 'fraudulent *res judicata*' is related to *respect for* 'the rules of due process' or 'when judges have not acted with independence and impartiality',[36] and in *Almonacid Arellano et al. v. Chile*, this notion is developed in the context of serious human rights violations and events aimed at achieving impunity. The Inter-American Court considered some circumstances in which the *ne bis in idem* principle was not applicable, such as exempting an accused from criminal responsibility for violations of human rights and international law with the acquittal or dismissal of the case, as well as lack of impartiality and independence in judicial processes or seeking to ensure that those responsible avoid justice when this is the real intention of the state authorities.[37]

On another issue related to the prohibition of legal institutions that seek impunity, in *Barrios Altos,* paragraph 41 of the judgment also extends to the impossibility of provisions to avoid the non-applicability of statutes of limitations to serious human rights violations.[38] This applies to crimes against humanity, torture, slavery, summary, extralegal or arbitrary executions, and forced disappearances, among others.[39] Due to the seriousness of conduct, the IACtHR stresses the need 'to maintain the State's punitive power in effect for actions which, because of their seriousness, must be stopped and also to avoid their repetition'.[40]

Although in *Bulacio v. Argentina,* pursuant to the American Convention, the imprescriptibility of crimes was not limited to the commission of serious violations,[41] it is a consolidated jurisprudence.[42] In this sense, Inter-American case-law has also recognised the imprescriptibility of the right to redress for victims of serious human rights violations. Accordingly, criminal actions to investigate and punish those responsible for these violations will not only be imprescriptible, but also civil lawsuits for damages to redress the victims.[43]

Finally, it is convenient to include in this topic an issue recently developed by the jurisprudence of the Inter-American Court, such as the improper application of extradition or other figures. As will be expressly demonstrated later, treating serious human rights violations as violations of *ius cogens* norms, and access to justice as *jus cogens* norm in inter-American jurisprudence, has had a substantial impact on strengthening inter-State cooperation to avoid impunity. This jurisprudence relates eliminating impunity to the obligation of the international community to guarantee interstate cooperation.[44] Hence, the Inter-American Court has established that 'a State cannot grant direct or indirect protection to those accused of crimes against human rights by the undue application of legal mechanisms that jeopardize the pertinent international obligations'.[45]

In this eventual 'undue application of legal mechanisms', the *extradition* takes place within the context of cooperation between States. In several cases, the IACtH has positively assessed the application of this figure which lies within the State's duty to investigate when the extradition of alleged perpetrators in cases of serious human rights violations is requested.[46] For the Court, this is an 'important tool to eradicate impunity' in such cases.[47] However, on many occasions the implementation of this figure promotes impunity when investigations are obstructed, or prosecution of the events is impeded. As a result, the Court has established that 'the concept of extradition cannot consist, either, in a means to favor, foster or guarantee impunity' and 'in the decisions regarding the application of certain procedural concepts to one person, the accusation of serious human rights violations must prevail'.[48]

During the oversight of compliance with judgment issued in the *Case of Mapiripán Massacre v. Colombia*, the Inter-American Court analysed the decision of the Colombian President on 14 May 2008 to extradite to the United States the former top commander of the United Self-Defense Forces of Colombia, requested for drug trafficking along with 13 other paramilitaries, at a time when the criminal investigations against him for the facts of the case in question were being jeopardized. To prevent extradition from becoming a factor for impunity, the Court considered that it was incumbent upon Colombia 'to clarify the mechanisms, instruments and legal concepts that shall be applied to guarantee that the extradited person will collaborate with the investigations into the facts of the instant case, as well as, if applicable, to guarantee the due process'.[49]

The Court held the same view for those cases of political asylum where the prohibition of extradition applies. In the advisory opinion *The Institution of Asylum, and its Recognition as a Human Right under the Inter-American System of Protection* and, following the Latin American tradition, it had expressed the view regarding an institution of asylum (territorial and diplomatic asylum) aimed at protecting people persecuted for political or related common crimes, or those persecuted for political reasons. However, at this point, it stated that its application should not be *denaturalized* in the sense that 'this figure cannot be used as a way to favor, procure, or ensure impunity in cases of serious violations of human rights'.[50] In this regard, and in line with the *Annual Report of the Inter-American Commission on Human Rights 2000,* in which was a *Recommendation on Asylum and International Crimes*,[51] the IACtHR stated that 'the protection provided through asylum and the prohibition of extradition in cases of political or related crimes cannot be conceived to protect people who seek to evade their responsibility as masterminds or perpetrators of international crimes'.[52]

Flexibilisation of amnesty in transitional justice processes for cases of serious human rights violations?

In the jurisprudence of the Inter-American Court of Human Rights, the prohibition of amnesty was relaxed to support certain negotiation processes in Latin America following non-international armed conflicts. In this context, a *harmonious interpretation*[53] was chosen between elements of international humanitarian law and the obligations established in the American Convention. In the *Mozote case*, following the cessation of non-international armed conflicts, the possibility of amnesty laws was recognised according to international humanitarian law in pursuit of peace (Article 6.5 of Additional Protocol II to the Geneva Conventions of 1949). However, this position continued to encounter limits in cases of international crimes (war crimes and crimes against humanity).[54]

A disturbing line of reasoning has been suggested with the concurring opinion of several judges in the aforementioned *El Mozote case*. They referred to 'the anomalous and exceptional situation of a non-international armed conflict' which also required 'exceptional mechanisms of response', including judicial and non-judicial mechanisms, designs of appropriate procedures according to 'the specificity of a process of negotiated solution to a non-international armed conflict', as well as a priority and specific procedure for war crimes or crimes against humanity, under the understanding that 'this is not necessarily the same for other crimes or human rights violations'.[55]

Hence, it has been argued that with this case, the Inter-American Court of Human Rights opened the possibility that 'not all serious human rights violations must be necessarily investigated, judged, and punished', and therefore the Court's reasoning limited the scope of this obligation solely to 'international crimes'.[56] This is a highly risky interpretation. As expressed in this paper, the Inter-American Court has used various terms to refer to situations of serious human rights violations, and it often equates these with the existence of international crimes. Thus, it can be misleading to take the Court's expressions in this matter literally to draw an absolute distinction between 'serious human rights violations' and 'international crimes'. This is further corroborated by the expressions used by the Court itself in its compliance monitoring resolutions in this case, where it generally refers to the obligation to investigate, judge, and punish for the 'serious violations' perpetrated in this case.[57]

But beyond this first problem, the really debatable question is determining what situations of 'serious human rights violations' may be in which the amnesty would be compatible with the norms of the American Convention. It does not seem that the interpretation made by the Inter-American Court in the aforementioned case opens the door for amnesty in any case of serious violations of human rights. The search to reconcile the interests at stake in a transitional justice process may entail adjustments in the designs of justice mechanisms, giving priority to the most serious human rights violations, etc., but in no way can it be assumed as a process of impunity through amnesty in cases of any 'serious violation of human rights'. This is not the meaning of the Inter-American Court in its jurisprudence or in this *El Mozote* case itself. This means that the purposes of reconciliation, negotiated paths to peace, cannot in any case extend the amnesty for serious acts that constitute international crimes. Here the Inter-American Court, it can be argued, has assumed a kind of absolutization of the amnesty, which in no way can be weakened in the weighing of the interests at stake (reconciliation, on the one hand, and truth, justice and reparation on the other).

Similarly, in the framework of transitional justice in Colombia following the Peace Agreement between the government and the FARC-EP guerrillas, the idea of recognition by the Inter-American Court of a 'margin of appreciation by the State' in cases involving the State's duty to investigate and punish has been defended.[58] The purpose of this is for the Inter-American Court to be deferential to the position taken by the national authorities in the transitional justice process in accordance with the *design of the agreement* and *its implementation*.[59] If this margin of appreciation[60] refers to issues such as the modality of the sentence,[61] or within the strategy of prioritisation or selection of cases, it does not seem to be a problem for the Court to recognise this discretion to the State. This discretion has been recognised in the cases *Vereda la Esperanza v. Colombia* and *Integrantes y Militantes de la Unión Patriótica v. Colombia*.[62] But it does in those cases in which the design and implementation may lead to impunity in accordance with the standards established by the Court in serious situations of human rights violations.

An exorbitant 'judicial activism' in *Barrios Altos* and other cases against the ACHR?

It has been criticised by some authors as 'judicial activism' of the Court positions regarding the prohibition of amnesty, and that it can be extended to the possibility of application of other figures such as *ne bis in idem* principle, 'fraudulent *res judicata*', *non-applicability of statutes of limitations, misapplication of extradition* or other figures. The Convention does not expressly contain provisions on issues such as amnesty, for example, and this has been interpreted as 'a clear example of a judicially created norm'.[63] The court uses expressions on the prohibition of amnesty as 'manifestly incompatible with the aims and spirit of the Convention' (although in the Spanish version of the judgment it is referred to as incompatible with the 'letra' (*wording*) of the treaty text instead of the 'aims').

This type of criticism sometimes seems to limit international judges in their task of interpretation to nineteenth century French 'exegetical legalism': 'Texts first', 'The whole law, but nothing but the law'.[64] But can it really be considered excessive to conclude on the prohibition of amnesty in cases of serious human rights violations on the basis of the duty of States to investigate and punish those responsible for these violations? If it is assumed without any reticence that this duty to investigate and punish derives from Article 1(1) and is linked to Article 2 in order to avoid regulations that hinder the State's compliance with this obligation, is it unreasonable to assume as an excessive judicial creation and contrary to the obligations assumed by the States this position that prohibits amnesties or other institutions that seek impunity? Is there or is there not a direct connection between amnesty laws and factors that hinder the State from complying with its duty to investigate and punish? Where such direct connections of this kind exist, the path to exorbitant judicial creation is narrower.

An important element cannot be lost sight of. The Inter-American Court is an international court, which, in a complementary manner, must be assisted by general international law in the interpretation of the provisions of the Convention, but which contains specific rules of interpretation (Article 29 of the ACHR). Article 62 of the ACHR establishes that 'the jurisdiction of the Court shall comprise all cases concerning the interpretation and application of the provisions of this Convention', and this interpretation must be placed in the context of the international law regime in which it is located.

International human rights law has achieved the status of a specific regime in the process of fragmentation of international law, precisely because it has developed 'specialized and (relatively) autonomous rules or rule-complexes, legal institutions and spheres of legal practice'.[65] Human rights treaties are treaties conceived where 'the States can be deemed to submit themselves to a legal order within which they, for the common good, assume various obligations, not in relation to other States, but towards all individuals within their jurisdiction'.[66] This reality in turn impacts on the interpretation of their provisions.

It is true that sometimes this 'judicial activism' in the Inter-American Court has gone beyond interpreting the American Convention to establish international obligations to the States when they expressly have not wanted, such is the case of the direct and autonomous justiciability of social, economic, cultural and environmental rights.[67] The main challenge in the work of the IACHR Court is to seek a balance between 'judicial activism', which places the victims at the centre of its reflections, and conventional mutations by way of its interpretation. This is not an easy task. The line dividing the two situations is very thin. But human rights courts must have a vocation for 'judicial activism', especially if they want to make their provisions effective. It is a task in which they must seek to balance the legitimacy of an inseparable triad: *victims*, *civil society* and *States*.

Another no less important issue must be taken into account when assessing the activism of tribunals such as the Inter-American Court. The specific situation where the work of these tribunals is located. Latin America is a region in which a passive or withdrawn attitude of the IACHR Court is a back to the victims of extremely complex situations. This has prompted several authors to reject the application of institutions such as the 'national margin of appreciation'[68] and this same position applies to understand judicial activism that seeks to make the American Convention a normative text for victims. All this, it is good to insist, within moderation and restraint to avoid over-expanding the possible responsibility of States. This is vital to gain the legitimacy of the States, a fundamental component for the vitality, consolidation and survival of the inter-American system.

An extension of *ius cogens* to areas or zones that hinder impunity

The right to access to justice is widely recognised in international human rights law.[69] In the jurisprudence of the IACtHR, international human rights law is a key instrument to avoid impunity in cases of serious human rights violations. The recognition of the right to access to justice results from the interpretation of the judicial guarantees and legal protection enshrined in Articles 8 and 25 of the ACHR and conceptualised in some cases as a non-absolute right.[70] Thus, for example, due process, which finds expression in the judicial guarantees under Article 8 of the ACHR, *inter alia*, has been broadly reflected since it is related to the notion of 'justice' to go beyond any formalistic or restricted interpretation of the right to access to justice.[71]

In the jurisprudence of the IACtHR, the right to access to justice has been consolidated as an 'expansion of the material content of *jus cogens*'.[72] In cases involving gross human rights violations or 'systematic violation of human rights' the right to *access to justice* is recognised as a *jus cogens* norm. This interpretation has a special connection with the considerations of the IACtHR on the dire consequences for the material and psychological human rights of the victims, when justice has been denied in situations of serious human rights violations.[73]

This has allowed the Court to accentuate or broaden the scope of States' obligations under the ACHR in cases of serious human rights violations. However, its recognition has not had the same fate in general international law,[74] as in some international jurisprudence.[75] It has a significant impact on two fundamental dimensions: at the domestic level, it obliges States to strengthen mechanisms and instruments to combat impunity;

and at the international level, it establishes a framework of legal obligations that reinforces cooperation among States with the same purpose of preventing impunity.[76]

Accordingly, the jurisprudence of the IACtHR deepens the duty of cooperation between States when it comes to the violation of 'peremptory norms of international law (*jus cogens*)'.[77] Widely recognised in general international law,[78] the IACtHR has reinforced it in the framework of the 'mechanisms of collective guarantee' established in the American Convention and, 'together with the regional and universal international obligations on this issue, bind the States of the region to collaborate in good faith in this respect'.[79]

Furthermore, this express recognition of *jus cogens* norms results in establishing a basis of legal obligations to avoid obstacles that could lead to impunity and that obligate the State regardless of whether it is subject to a particular treaty. *Almonacid Arellano et al. v. Chile* is an example of the implementation of general international law with the recognition of *ius cogens* norms, regardless of a State's treaty obligations. As for the imprescriptibility of international crimes, such as crimes against humanity, the IACtHR found that Chile had not ratified the *Convention on the Non-Applicability of Statutory Limitations to War Crimes and Crimes against Humanity*. However, the Court stated that 'the non-applicability of statutes of limitations to crimes against humanity is a norm of General International Law (*ius cogens*), which is not created by said Convention, but it is acknowledged by it', hence 'Chilean State must comply with this imperative rule'.[80]

This principle is directly related to the consideration that in such cases States have an obligation to initiate *ex officio* investigations. It becomes a vital component in situations where rights such as life, personal integrity or personal freedom are seriously or systematically violated. Thus, the IACtHR requires the State to initiate investigations *ex officio* when they involve prohibition of human rights violations recognised as *jus cogens norm*. In *Goiburú et al. v. Paraguay*, a case of extrajudicial executions, forced disappearances and other serious human rights violations, the court recalled that the *ex officio* investigation should be 'prompt, serious, impartial and effective'.[81]

This broad recognition of *jus cogens* norms, which has impacted the IACtHR jurisprudence against impunity in cases of serious human rights violations, is enhanced when comparing the development of these two areas with the jurisprudence of the ECtHR. Even though the influence of the IACtHR jurisprudence on the ECtHR is expressed in certain specific conducts involving serious human rights violations, such as forced disappearances, it is not always possible to find the same type of conduct in the ECtHR.[82] The European Court's recognition of *jus cogens* has been less far-reaching than that of the American court.[83] Hence, even if it were to be held that, in certain situations, the prohibition of amnesty in cases of serious violation of rights arises from the scope of several provisions of the ECtHR, it is not as convincing as the American court is.[84]

The extent of reparations ordered by the Inter-American Court of Human Rights in cases of serious violations of human rights

Impunity is a process that lasts beyond full reparations for the victims. Impunity cannot be eliminated if victims cannot be redressed for the violation of their rights. In *Barrios Altos*, the IACtHR recognised that self-amnesty laws have direct implications on access to justice, the right to truth and reparations for victims and their families.[85] In the context of serious violations, reparations have a particular role. The scope of reparations, the modalities in which they are recognised, and the possibilities that they can be made in domestic law mark the debate on the continuity or eradication of impunity in such cases.

In this regard, the jurisprudence of the IACtHR is packed with comprehensive measures to provide redress to victims in cases of serious human rights violations. The Court has assumed a criterion of 'comprehensive reparation' that is not restricted to pecuniary compensation.[86] These reparations have resulted in several modalities involving various actions to be carried out by the State. The IACtHR has insisted on 'the need to grant different measures of reparation in order to redress the damage caused integrally' and to this end, it is essential 'pecuniary compensation, measures of restitution and satisfaction and guarantees of non-repetition'.[87] Although its jurisprudence is seen as 'aggressive',[88] and with excessive 'intrusion' o 'interference' in States internal affairs,[89] it becomes a better instrument or vehicle to conceive a comprehensive model of reparation for victims of gross human rights violations.[90]

There are many factors underlying differences with other regional systems, such as the European system, which deal with obstacles or impediments to avoid impunity when it comes to reparations: in terms of interpretation, the existence of much more permissive and enabling legal provisions in the ACHR than in the ECtHR[91]; excessive 'intrusion' o 'interference' of the jurisprudence of the Inter-American Court in States internal affairs,[92] in contrast to the European sphere, which is marked by a much stricter interpretation of the principle of subsidiarity in the functioning of the international bodies, which results, *inter alia*, in the recognition of 'margins of national appreciation'; and a greater 'judicial activism' in the Inter-American Court in jurisprudential constructions.

It has already been stated that for the IACtHR, the denial of justice in cases of serious human rights violations and in case of massacre, results in damages to be considered, both individually and collectively, and of a material and psychological nature.[93] Regarding indigenous peoples, there may be an impact on the 'community life project' not only because of the absence of justice, but also because of the lack of 'acknowledgement of the damage suffered' or the 'remembrance of the victims'.[94] In these cases, the 'non-pecuniary damage' suffered by relatives stands out, either because of the absence of justice or because of the incapacity to provide a burial in accordance with their customs.[95] In this regard, due to the seriousness of these situations and the collective dimension of the damages, the IACtHR emphasizes the 'special relevance' of comprehensive redress along with various measures: pecuniary compensation, satisfaction, restitution, rehabilitation, and guarantees of non-repetition.[96]

By way of example, it is worth recalling that the Court ordered the State to adopt measures such as: healthcare expenses, the granting of scholarships and educational materials, construction of monuments,[97] the erection of plaques in public places,[98] the implementation of a housing program,[99] the implementation of programmes for the study and dissemination of indigenous cultures,[100] the implementation of a sewage and potable water supply system,[101] the publication in the mass media of the attempt to identify victims,[102] the creation of a genetic information system to determine the identification or affiliation of victims,[103] training of the armed forces through programmes on human rights and international humanitarian law,[104] among others.

Within this framework of reparations, measures ordered by the IACtHR as guarantees of non-repetition consolidate the transformative impact on the realities of the States. To this end, in many cases, States may acknowledge the context of structural discrimination to determine the scope of reparations.[105] These measures, whose compliance by the State is controlled by the IACtHR itself through its oversight of compliance with judgment,[106] has led to relevant measurable changes in the States of the region, such as *legislative reforms, public policies* and the implementation of State practices in line with Inter-American standards.[107]

Standards of the IACtHR have also been important in terms of the identification of victims. According to article 2.33 of the Rules of Procedure of the IACtHR which came into force in December 2009, a 'victim' is defined as a 'person whose rights have been violated, according to a judgment emitted by the Court'.[108] In this regard, it is up to the Inter-American Commission on Human Rights to identify the victims,[109] which 'must be indicated in the brief submitting the case and in the Commission's report'.[110] However, to prevent this rule from leading to impunity due to the inability to redress victims of serious and massive human rights violations, there is an exception in Article 35.2 of the Regulation itself. It states that:

> When it has not been possible to identify one or more of the alleged victims who figure in the facts of the case because it concerns massive or collective violations, the Tribunal shall decide whether to consider those individuals as victims.[111]

Accordingly, the Inter-American Court has found that this article applies when it is 'difficult to identify and individualise each presumed victim' as they have been for 'massacres perpetrated in seven different places', due to 'the nature of the events and the circumstances surrounding them' or because 'the time that has passed'.[112] In this context, it has considered 'difficulties to identify or contact all the presumed victims' in the event of 'presence of armed conflict, displacement or when the bodies of the presumed victims have been destroyed by fire, or in cases in which entire families have been disappeared, so that nobody could speak on their behalf'.[113]

Conclusions

In this paper, the implementation of the Inter-American Court of Human Rights' jurisprudence on impunity is analysed from three relevant jurisprudential lines. Together, these three lines serve to contain the impunity of serious human rights violations. They are not the only lines created for this purpose but are a reflection of the success achieved by the Inter-American Court of Human Rights in combating impunity in the Americas. On this basis, the paper delves into the recognition of *ius cogens* norms as an element that enhances the duty of States to investigate and sanction those responsible for serious human rights violations. It also argues that there can be no complete eradication of impunity without mechanisms or means to achieve comprehensive reparation for the victims.

In the IACtHR jurisprudence, the obligation to prevent, investigate and punish has great impact in situations of serious human rights violations. This comes when institutions or mechanisms that seek to prevent the investigation, prosecution, or implementation of mechanisms of non-repetition, or the punishment of those responsible for these serious violations, are understood as unconventional. In an environment marked by impunity, where national legal systems cannot provide justice and reparations to the victims, it is owing to this jurisprudence that the IACtHR has become an institution of considerable significance for the life of the States in Latin America, and especially for civil society, social movements, and human rights defenders.

This same obligation of States to prevent, investigate and punish is strengthened with the 'expansion of the material content' of *ius cogens* in the IACtHR jurisprudence. In particular, the consideration of the right to access to justice as an *ius cogens* norm, extends *erga omnes* to other States the obligation to investigate and punish serious human rights violations, which they must comply with through Inter-State cooperation mechanisms. Likewise, it reinforces the recognition of certain conducts as international crimes prohibited by *ius cogens* norms. This makes it possible to acknowledge that, in order not to breach American Convention, States are bound by *ius cogens* norms regardless of whether they have consented to be bound by a particular treaty.

By understanding impunity as a process, this paper focuses on reparations. However, it is not enough just to investigate and punish those responsible for serious human rights violations. Impunity is eradicated when victims are given the opportunity to obtain full reparation, which must be 'comprehensive', considering the pecuniary and non-pecuniary damage caused. In this line, the jurisprudence of the Inter-American Court is avant-garde, advanced, revolutionary, and specifically when compared to other international Courts, such as the European Court of Human Rights.

Furthermore, Inter-American jurisprudence has an impact on the work of other international Courts, especially the European Court of Human Rights, and constitutes a reference in the development of these issues, not only at the regional level, but also at the international level. This paper is a nod to areas in which dialogue between international human rights Courts should be strengthened to avoid impunity for serious human rights violations. Therefore, with this recognition of *ius cogens* norms, as well as reparations, the IACtHR jurisprudence takes a pioneering position, with the best guarantees of providing mechanisms and tools to avoid impunity. Other international human rights Courts should work in that direction, although this requires regulatory reforms, jurisprudential changes, and a fresh approach to the principle of subsidiarity of human rights protection mechanisms.

Notes

1. Thomas Buergenthal, 'Recordando los inicios de la Corte Interamericana de Derechos Humanos', *Revista IIDH* 39 (2004): 13.
2. See the work of Robert E. Norris on this topic, and the examples given from Chile (1978), Brazil (1979), Honduras (1981–1991), Guatemala (1982–1987), Argentina (1983–1990), Uruguay (1986–1990), El Salvador (1987), Nicaragua (1987–1990), Suriname (1989). Robert Norris, 'Leyes de Impunidad y los Derechos Humanos en las Américas: Una Respuesta Legal', *Revista del Instituto Interamericano de Derechos Humanos* 15 (1992): 47–121. See also: Manuel E. Ventura Robles, *Estudios sobre el sistema interamericano de protección de los derechos humanos* (San José, Costa Rica, 2007), 345–70.
3. This was the case in Peru, for example, when Peru on July 9, 1999 tried to withdraw the declaration of recognition of the optional clause of submission to contentious jurisdiction. This was accompanied by decisions of the courts to declare 'unenforceable' judgments of the Inter-American Court of Human Rights, in the cases of *Loayza Tamayo Vs. Peru* and

Castillo Petruzzi et al. Vs. Peru in 1999. See: *Loayza Tamayo v. Peru*. Monitoring Compliance with Judgment. Order of the Inter-American Court of Human Rights of November 17, 1999, considering paragraphs 1 and 2; *Castillo Petruzzi et al. v. Peru*. Monitoring Compliance with Judgment. Order of the Court of November 17, 1999, para. 2; Douglass Cassel, 'El Perú se retira de la Corte: ¿Afrontará el reto el sistema interamericano de derechos humanos?', *Revista IIDH* 29 (1999): 71.

4. These were made up of the *Case of Barrios Altos Vs. Peru* (2001), the *Case of Caracazo Vs. Venezuela* (1999 and 2002), the *Case of the Plan de Sánchez Massacre Vs. Guatemala* (2004), the *Case of the 'Mapiripán Massacre' Vs. Colombia* (2005), the *Case of the Pueblo Bello Massacre Vs. Colombia* (2006), the *Case of the Ituango Massacres Vs. Colombia* (2006), and the *Case La Cantuta Vs. Peru* (2006), among others. See, for example: Antônio Augusto Cançado Trindade, 'La misión de los Tribunales internacionales contemporáneos en la humanización del Derecho Internacional', in *Inauguración del Año Judicial Interamericano* (Costa Rica, San José, 2018), 44.
5. See, in this sense, for example: Mariela Morales Antoniazzi, 'Interamericanización como mecanismo del Ius Constitutionale Commune en derechos humanos en América Latina', in *Ius Constitucionale Commune en América Latina. Textos básicos para su compresión*, coord. Armin von Bogdandy, Mariela Morales Antoniazzi, Eduardo Ferrer Mac-Gregor (México: Instituto de Estudios Constitucionales del Estado de Querétaro, Max Planck Institute for Comparative Public and International Law, 2017), 418.
6. See, in this sense: Harold Bertot Triana, *Estudios sobre jurisprudencia de la Corte Interamericana de Derechos Humanos. Cavilaciones al hilo de temas actuales del Sistema Interamericano de Derechos Humanos* (Santiago de Chile: Editorial Olejnik, 2023), 123.
7. On this obligation to prevent, investigate and punish, see for example: Ludovic Hennebel and Hélène Tigroudja, *The American Convention on Human Rights: A Commentary* (Oxford University Press, 2022), 29–40; Eduardo Ferrer Mac-Gregor Poisot and Carlos María Pelayo Möller, 'Artículo 1. Obligación de respetar los derechos', in *Convención Americana de Derechos Humanos, Comentario* (Konrad Adenauer Stiftung, 2019), 31–105; Oscar Parra Vera, 'La jurisprudencia de la Corte Interamericana respecto a la lucha contra la impunidad: algunos avances y debates', *Revista Jurídica de la Universidad de Palermo* 1 (2013): 5–51.
8. *'White Van' (Paniagua Morales et al.) v. Guatemala*, IACtHR, Judgment of March 8, 1998 (Merits), para. 173; *Blake v. Guatemala*, IACtHR, Judgment of January 22, 1999 (Reparations and Costs), para. 64; *Trujillo Oroza v. Bolivia*, IACtHR, Judgment of February 27, 2002 (Reparations and Costs), para. 101.
9. Ibid.
10. *Myrna Mack Chang v. Guatemala*, IACtHR, Judgment of November 25, 2003 (Merits, Reparations and Costs), para. 271.
11. *Pueblo Bello Massacre v. Colombia*, IACtHR, Judgment of January 31, 2006 (Merits, Reparations and Costs), para. 268; *Cantoral Huamaní and García Santa Cruz v. Peru*, IACtHR, Judgment of July 10, 2007 (Preliminary Objection, Merits, Reparations and Costs), para. 190; *Valle Jaramillo et al. v. Colombia*, IACtHR, Judgment of November 27, 2008 (Merits, Reparations and Costs), para. 232; *Río Negro Massacres v. Guatemala*, IACtHR, Judgment of September 4, 2012 (Preliminary Objection, Merits, Reparations, and Costs), para. 257.
12. *Gelman v. Uruguay*, IACtHR, Judgment of February 24, 2011 (Merits and Reparations), para. 183.
13. *Río Negro Massacres v. Guatemala*, IACtHR, Judgment of September 4, 2012 (Preliminary Objection, Merits, Reparations, and Costs), para. 257. Regarding the relationship between the name 'serious violations of human rights' used by the Inter-American Court and crimes against humanity, see: Juan Pablo Pérez-León Acevedo, 'The Close Relationship Between Serious Human Rights Violations and Crimes Against Humanity: International Criminalization of Serious Abuses', *Anuario Mexicano de Derecho Internacional* 17 (2017): 145–86.
14. *Barrios Altos v. Peru*, IACtHR, Judgment March 14, 2001 (Merits), para. 41.

15. *Hacienda Brasil Verde Workers v. Brazil*, IACtHR, Judgment of October 20, 2016 (Preliminary Objections, Merits, Reparations and Costs), para. 454; *Members of the Village of Chichupac and neighboring communities of the Municipality of Rabinal v. Guatemala*, IACtHR, Judgment of November 30, 2016 (Preliminary Objections, Merits, Reparations and Costs), para. 216; *Almonacid Arellano et al. v. Chile*, IACtHR, Judgment of September 26, 2006 (Preliminary Objections, Merits, Reparations and Costs), para. 153.
16. *Velásquez Rodríguez v. Honduras*, IACtHR, Judgment of July 29, 1988 (Merits), para. 172; *González et al. ('Campo Algodonero') v. Mexico*, IACHR, Judgment of November 16, 2009 (Preliminary objection, Merits, Reparations and Costs), para. 236; *Kawas Fernández v. Honduras*, IACHR, Judgment of April 3, 2009 (Merits, Reparations and Costs), para. 137; *Anzualdo Castro v. Peru*, IACHR, Judgment of September 22, 2009 (Preliminary Objection, Merits, Reparations and Costs), para. 6.
17. *Pueblo Bello Massacre v. Colombia*, IACHR, Judgment of January 31, 2006, para. 123; *López Soto et al. v. Venezuela*, IACHR, Judgment of September 26, 2018 (Merits, Reparations and Costs), paras. 139–41.
18. *González et al. ('Campo Algodonero') v. Mexico*, IACHR, Judgment of November 16, 2009 (Preliminary objection, Merits, Reparations and Costs), para. 282.
19. *Pueblo Bello Massacre v. Colombia*, IACHR, Judgment of January 31, 2006, para. 151.
20. *González et al. ('Campo Algodonero') v. Mexico*, IACHR, Judgment of November 16, 2009 (Preliminary objection, Merits, Reparations and Costs), para. 282.
21. Lene Guercke, 'State Responsibility for a Failure to Prevent Violations of the Right to Life by Organised Criminal Groups: Disappearances in Mexico', *Human Rights Law Review* 21 (2021): 329–57.
22. *Vereda La Esperanza v. Colombia*, IACHR, Judgment of August 31, 2017 (Preliminary Objections, Merits, Reparations and Costs), para. 168.
23. *Barrios Altos v. Peru*, IACtHR, Judgment March 14, 2001 (Merits), para. 2.
24. Ibid.
25. Ibid., para. 41.
26. Ibid., decision 4.
27. *La Cantuta v. Peru*, IACtHR, Judgment of November 29, 2006 (Merits, Reparations and Costs).
28. *Barrios Altos v. Peru*, IACtHR, Judgment March 14, 2001 (Merits), para. 42–43.
29. *Almonacid Arellano et al. v. Chile*, IACtHR, Judgment of September 26, 2006 (Preliminary Objections, Merits, Reparations and Costs), para. 110.
30. *Gelman v. Uruguay*, IACtHR, Judgment of February 24, 2011 (Merits and Reparations), para. 195.
31. *Lexa V. Slovakia*, ECtHR Fourth Section, Judgment, 23 September 2008, para. 97.
32. Ibid., para. 98.
33. *Case of Marguš v. Croatia*, Grand Chamber, (Application No. 4455/10), Judgment, Strasbourg, 27 May 2014, párrs. 60, 62, 111, 138.
34. *Marguš v. Croatia*, ECtHR Grand Chamber, Judgment, 27 May 2014, para. 139. This position was subsequently upheld in *Mocanu and Others v. Romania*, ECtHR Grand Chamber, Judgment, 17 September 2014, para. 191. 'The Court has also held that in cases concerning torture or illtreatment inflicted by State agents, criminal proceedings ought not to be discontinued on account of a limitation period, and also that amnesties and pardons should not be tolerated in such cases'. Ibid., para. 326.
35. *Almonacid Arellano et al. v. Chile*, IACtHR, Judgment of September 26, 2006 (Preliminary Objections, Merits, Reparations and Costs), para. 154.
36. *Carpio Nicolle et al. v. Guatemala*, IACtHR, Judgment of November 22, 2004 (Merits, Reparations and Costs), para. 131; *Nadege Dorzema et al. v. Dominican Republic*, IACtHR, Judgment of October 24, 2012 (Merits, Reparations and Costs), para. 196.
37. *Almonacid Arellano et al. v. Chile*, IACtHR, Judgment of September 26, 2006 (Preliminary Objections, Merits, Reparations and Costs), para. 154.
38. See: *Barrios Altos v. Peru*, IACtHR, Judgment March 14, 2001 (Merits), para. 41.

39. In *Almonacid* it was pointed out that 'a crime against humanity (...) is neither susceptible of amnesty nor extinguishable.' *Almonacid Arellano et al. v. Chile*, IACtHR, Judgment of September 26, 2006 (Preliminary Objections, Merits, Reparations and Costs), para. 152; *Ibsen Cárdenas and Ibsen Peña v. Bolivia*, IACtHR, Judgment of September 1, 2010 (Merits, Reparation and Costs), para. 207; *Hacienda Brasil Verde Workers v. Brazil*, IACtHR, Judgment of October 20, 2016 (Preliminary Objections, Merits, Reparations and Costs), para. 454.
40. *Ibsen Cárdenas and Ibsen Peña v. Bolivia*, IACtHR, Judgment of September 1, 2010 (Merits, Reparation and Costs), para. 207.
41. *Bulacio v. Argentina*, IACtHR, Judgment of September 18, 2003 (Merits, Reparations and Costs), para. 117.
42. See, for example: *Albán Cornejo et al. v. Ecuador*, IACtHR, Judgment of November 22, 2007 (Merits, Reparations and Costs), para. 111; *Ibsen Cárdenas and Ibsen Peña v. Bolivia*, IACtHR, Judgment of September 1, 2010 (Merits, Reparation and Costs), para. 207.
43. See: *Órdenes Guerra et al. v. Chile*, IACtHR, Judgment of November 29, 2018 (Merits, Reparations and Costs), para. 92. On this point, the I/A Court HR considered 'rationale' the argument of the Inter-American Commission on Human Rights in the case of Órdenes Guerra et al. v. Chile, on the application of the same standard to the prescription of criminal action in serious cases. human rights violations as well as the statute of limitations regarding reparation for these cases. Ibíd., para. 88.
44. *Goiburú et al. v. Paraguay*, IACtHR, Judgment of September 22, 2006 (Merits, Reparations and Costs), para. 131.
45. Ibid., para. 132.
46. See: *La Cantuta v. Peru*, IACtHR, Judgment of November 29, 2006 (Merits, Reparations and Costs), para. 159 and 227; *Goiburú et al. v. Paraguay*, IACtHR, Judgment of September 22, 2006 (Merits, Reparations and Costs), para. 127, 130 and 132; *Las Dos Erres Massacre v. Guatemala v. Guatemala.* Monitoring Compliance with Judgment. Order of the Inter-American Court of Human Rights of July 6, 2011, para. 12; *12 Guatemalan's Cases v. Guatemala.* Monitoring Compliance with Judgment. Order of the Inter-American Court of Human Rights of November 24, 2015, para. 153; *Pueblo Bello Massacre, Case of the Ituango Massacres and Case of Valle Jaramillo et al. v. Colombia.* Request for Provisional Measures and Monitoring Compliance with Judgment. Order of the Inter-American Court of Human Rights of September 3, 2020, para. 25.
47. *Miguel Castro Castro Prison v. Peru.* Monitoring of Compliance with Judgment. Order of the Inter-American Court of Human Rights of March 31, 2014, para. 24. In this case, the Inter-American Court referred to the request for the extradition of former President Alberto Fujimori for his alleged responsibility in the facts of the case that 'Peru must move forward and take the necessary steps with extreme diligence so as to put in place the extension of the extradition of the former president and ensure that the fact that it remains pending does not constitute an impediment to the continuation of the investigation and determination of other matters involving criminal responsibility'. Ibid., para. 24.
48. *Mapiripán Massacre v. Colombia.* Monitoring Compliance with Judgment. Order of the Inter-American Court of Human Rights of July 8, 2009, para. 40–41; *Ituango Massacres v. Colombia.* Monitoring Compliance with Judgment. Order of the Inter-American Court of Human Rights of July 7, 2009, para. 19.
49. *Mapiripán Massacre v. Colombia.* Monitoring Compliance with Judgment. Order of the Inter-American Court of Human Rights of July 8, 2009, para. 41.
50. *The institution of asylum, and its recognition as a human right under the Inter-American System of Protection (interpretation and scope of Articles 5, 22(7) and 22(8) in relation to Article 1(1) of the American Convention on Human Rights)*, IACtHR, Advisory Opinion OC-25/18 of May 30, 2018, para. 91.
51. See note 92 of this advisory opinion.
52. *The institution of asylum, and its recognition as a human right under the Inter-American System of Protection (interpretation and scope of Articles 5, 22(7) and 22(8) in relation to*

Article 1(1) of the American Convention on Human Rights), IACtHR, Advisory Opinion OC-25/18 of May 30, 2018, para. párr. 91.

53. Concurring opinion of judge Diego Garcia-Sayán, Judgment of the Inter-American Court of Human Rights, *Massacres of El Mozote and surrounding areas v. El Salvador*, IACHR, Judgment of October 25, 2012 (Merits, Reparations and Costs), para. 16.
54. *Massacres of El Mozote and surrounding areas v. El Salvador*, IACHR, Judgment of October 25, 2012 (Merits, Reparations and Costs), para. 286.
55. Concurring opinion of judge Diego Garcia-Sayán, Judgment of the Inter-American Court of Human Rights, *Massacres of El Mozote and surrounding areas v. El Salvador*, IACHR, Judgment of October 25, 2012 (Merits, Reparations and Costs), para. 22–24.
56. Juana Inés Acosta-López, 'The Inter-American Human Rights System and the Colombian peace: Redefining the fight against impunity', *AJIL Unbound* 178 (2016): 180.
57. *Vid.*, for example: *Massacres of El Mozote and surrounding areas v. El Salvador*, IACHR, Supervision of Compliance with Judgment. Resolution of the Inter-American Court of Human Rights of April 30, 2024, para. 1.
58. Ibid., para. 182.
59. Ibid.
60. On the disadvantage of assuming the national margin of appreciation in the Inter-American system, see: Harold Bertot Triana, 'Margen de apreciación nacional en el sistema interamericano, activismo judicial y deferencia estatal: ¿afianzar o deconstruir el camino ya andado?', *Anuario iberoamericano de justicia constitucional* 27, no. 2 (2023): 415–44.
61. See also: Natalie Sedacca, 'The "turn" to Criminal Justice in Human Rights Law: An Analysis in the Context of the 2016 Colombian Peace Agreement', *Human Rights Law Review* 19 (2019): 330.
62. 'The Court notes, in the first place, that the need to use the "prioritization" mechanism to rationalize criminal prosecution is not a matter of dispute between the parties and the Commission. Moreover, it is consistent with the views of different international bodies, such as the U.N. Special Rapporteur on the Promotion of Truth, Justice, Reparation and Guarantees of Non-recurrence; the MAPP-OAS, and the Inter-American Commission itself.' *Vereda La Esperanza v. Colombia*, IACHR, Judgment of August 31, 2017 (Preliminary Objections, Merits, Reparations and Costs), para. 228; *Members and Militants of the Unión Patriótica v. Colombia, IACHR*, Judgment of July 27, 2022, (Preliminary Objections, Merits, Reparations and Costs), para. 485.
63. Ezequiel Malarino, 'Judicial Activism, Punitivism and Supranationalisation: Illiberal and Antidemocratic Tendencies of the Inter-American Court of Human Rights', *International Criminal Law Review* 12, no. 4 (2012): 670.
64. *Vid.*, Abelardo Torré, *Introducción al Derecho* (Editorial Reus, S.A., 2003), 2003, 425.
65. International Law Commission. Fragmentation of International Law: Difficulties Arising from the Diversification and Expansion of International Law, Document A/61/10. Yearbook of the International Law Commission, 2006, para. 6.
66. *The effect of reservations on the entry into force of the American Convention on Human Rights*, IACHR (Advisory Opinion OC-2/82 of September 24, 1982), para. 29.
67. Elena Díaz Galán and Harold Bertot Triana, 'Caso cuscul pivaral y otros vs. Guatemala, sentencia de 23 de agosto de 2018 de la corte interamericana de derecho humanos: Un paso más de una línea jurisprudencial polémica en la protección de los derechos sociales, económicos y culturales', *Revista Electrónica Iberoamericana* 13, no. 2 (2019): 63–88.
68. Antônio Cançado Cançado Trindade, *El derecho internacional de los derechos humanos en el siglo XXI* (Jurídica de las Américas, México, 2009), pp. 389 y ss.
69. See in this sense: Antônio Augusto Cançado Trindade, *The Access of Individuals to International Justice* (Oxford University Press, 2011), 71 y ss.; Janneke H. Gerards and Lize R. Glas, 'Access to Justice in the European Convention on Human Rights System', *Netherlands Quarterly of Human Rights* 35, no. 1 (2017): 11–30; Celestine Nchekwube Ezennia, 'Access to Justice Mechanisms for Individuals and Groups under the African Regional Human Rights System: An Appraisal', *African Journal of Legal Studies* 8, no. 1-2 (2015): 115–44.

70. 'This Court considers that while the right of access to a court is not an absolute and therefore may be subject to certain discretional limitations set by the State, the fact remains that the means used must be proportional to the aim sought.' *Cantos v. Argentina*, IACtHR, Judgment of November 28, 2002. Series C No. 97 (Merits, Reparations and Costs), para. 54.
71. *Rights and guarantees of children in the context of migration and/or in need of international protection*, IACtHR, Advisory Opinion OC-21/14 of August 19, 2014, para. 109.
72. Antônio Augusto Cançado Trindade, *International Law for Humankind Towards a New Jus Gentium* (Brill Nijhoff, 2020), 299 y ss.
73. In the *Case of the Dos Erres Massacre v. Guatemala*, the Inter-American Court recalls the enormous material and psychological impact on the victims in this type of case. *Vid.*, *Las Dos Erres Massacre v. Guatemala*, IACtHR, Judgment of November 24, 2009 (Preliminary Objection, Merits, Reparations and Costs), para. 226. See also: *Pueblo Bello Massacre v. Colombia*, IACtHR, Judgment of January 31, 2006 (Merits, Reparations and Costs), para. 256; *Mapiripán Massacre v. Colombia*, IACtHR, Judgment of September 15, 2005 (Merits, Reparations and Costs), para. 288; *Ituango Massacres v. Colombia*, IACtHR, Judgment of July 1, 2006 (Preliminary Objection, Merits, Reparations and Costs), para. 390 y ss.
74. For example, this right of access to justice was not recognized in the 'non-exhaustive' list of the recent Draft conclusions on identification and legal consequences of peremptory norms of general international law of the International Law Commission (ILC). Conclusion 23. International Law Commission, 'Draft conclusions on identification and legal consequences of peremptory norms of general international law (*jus cogens*) 2022', in *Yearbook of the International Law Commission*, 2022, vol. II, Part Two.
75. It has been taken as a reference in courts such as the Special Court for Lebanon in the *Order Assigning Matter To Pre-Trial Judge in El Sayed*, in which its president, Judge Antonio Cassese, expressly recognized this jurisprudence of the Inter-American Court. *Vid.*, *El Sayed, Case No. CH/PRES/2010/01, Order of 15 April 2010 assigning Matter to Pre-Trial Judge*, para. 29.
76. *Goiburú et al. v. Paraguay*, IACtHR, Judgment of September 22, 2006 (Merits, Reparations and Costs), para. 131.
77. *La Cantuta v. Peru*, IACtHR, Judgment of November 29, 2006 (Merits, Reparations and Costs), para. 160; *Gelman v. Uruguay*, IACtHR, Judgment of February 24, 2011 (Merits and Reparations), para. 233–34.
78. See, for example: Article 4.2 of Resolution 2625 of October 24, 1970 of the United Nations General Assembly, concerning the 'Declaration of Principles of international law relating to friendly relations and cooperation between States in accordance with the Charter of United Nations'. In jurisprudence, see the International Court of Justice (ICJ) in advisory opinions such as *Legal Consequences of the Construction of a Wall in the Occupied Palestinian Territory* (*Legal Consequences cf the Construction of a Wall in the Occupied Palestinian Territory*, Advisory Opinion, I. C. J. Reports 2004), para. 155; and *Legal Consequences of the Separation of the Chagos Archipelago from Mauritius in 1965* (*Legal Consequences of the Separation of the Chagos Archipelago from Mauritius in 1965*, Advisory Opinion, I.C.J. Reports 2019), para. 182. Recently, in the ILC's Draft conclusions on identification and legal consequences of peremptory norms of general international law, it recognizes this obligation in its conclusion 19 referring to 'Particular consequences of serious breaches of peremptory norms of general international law (*jus cogens*)'. International Law Commission, 'Draft conclusions on identification and legal consequences of peremptory norms of general international law (*jus cogens*) 2022', in *Yearbook of the International Law Commission*, 2022, vol. II, Part Two.
79. *Goiburú et al. v. Paraguay*, IACtHR, Judgment of September 22, 2006 (Merits, Reparations and Costs), para 132; *The institution of asylum, and its recognition as a human right under the Inter-American System of Protection (interpretation and scope of Articles 5, 22(7) and 22 (8) in relation to Article 1(1) of the American Convention on Human Rights)*, IACtHR, Advisory Opinion OC-25/18 of May 30, 2018, para. 199; *Denunciation of the American Convention on Human Rights and the Charter of the Organization of American States and the consequences for State human rights obligations (interpretation and scope of articles 1, 2,*

27, 29, 30, 31, 32, 33 a 65 and 78 of the American Convention on Human Rights and 3(l), 17, 45, 53, 106 and 143 of the Charter of the Organization of American States), IACtHR, Advisory Opinion OC-26/20, November 9, 2020, para. 162.

80. Ibid., para. 153.
81. *Goiburú et al. v. Paraguay*, IACtHR, Judgment of September 22, 2006 (Merits, Reparations and Costs), para. 88.
82. For example, in the case of *Varnava et al. versus Turkey*, 2009, express mention has been made of the jurisprudence of the Inter-American Court in this matter, such as the judgments in matters such as Cases Blake Vs. Guatemala (1998) and Hermanas Serrano Cruz Vs. El Salvador (2005), among others. See *Varnava and Others V. Turkey*, ECtHR Grand Chamber, Judgment, 18 September 2009, para. 93–98.
83. See, for example, the development of *jus cogens* in the ECtHR in: William A. Schabas, 'Le droit coutumier, les normes impératives (jus cogens), et la Cour européenne des droits de l'homme', *Revue québécoise de droit international* 33 (2020): 681–704.
84. In some cases, like Margus, no definitive position is taken. At least this is what can be deduced from the following text: 'Even if it were to be accepted that amnesties are possible where there are some particular circumstances, such as a reconciliation process and/or a form of compensation to the victims, the amnesty granted to the applicant in the instant case would still not be acceptable since there is nothing to indicate that there were any such circumstances.' *Marguš v. Croatia*, ECtHR Grand Chamber, Judgment, 27 May 2014, para. 139.
85. *Barrios Altos v. Peru*, IACtHR, Judgment March 14, 2001 (Merits), para. 43.
86. *Herrera Espinoza et al. v. Ecuador*, IACtHR, Judgment of September 1, 2016 (Preliminary Objections, Merits, Reparations and Costs), para. 214. See, among others: Claudio Nash Rojas, *Las Reparaciones ante la Corte Interamericana de Derechos Humanos (1988 - 2007)*, (Universidad de Chile, Facultad de Derecho, Centro de Derechos Humanos, 2009); Dieter Cassel, 'El alcance e impacto cada vez mayores de las reparaciones ordenadas por la Corte Interamericana de Derechos Humanos', in *La justicia constitucional and su internacionalización: ¿hacia un ius constitucionale commune en América Latina?* (México: Universidad Nacional Autónoma de Mexico, 2010), 215–58; Fabián Novak, 'The System of Reparations in the Jurisprudence of the Interamerican Court of Human Rights', *Recueil des Cours de l'Académie de Droit International de La Haye* 392 (2018): 9–204.
87. See, for example: *Mendoza et al. v. Argentina*, IACtHR, Judgment of May 14, 2013 (Preliminary Objections, Merits and Reparations), para. 307; *Alvarado Espinoza et al. v. México*, IACtHR, Judgment of November 28, 2018 (Merits, Reparations and Costs), para. 286. In the doctrine see: Antônio Augusto Cançado Trindade, 'Reminiscencias de la Corte Interamericana de Derechos Humanos en cuanto a su jurisprudencia en materia de reparaciones', in *La Justicia constitucional y su internacionalización: ¿hacia un ius constitucionale commune en América Latina?* (México: Universidad Nacional Autónoma de México, 2010), 192.
88. See: Gerald L. Neuman, 'Subsidiarity', in *The Oxford Handbook of International Human Rights Law*, ed. Dinah Shelton (Oxford University Press, 2013).
89. See: Jorge Contesse, 'Contestation and deference in the Inter-American Human Rights System', *Law and Contemporary Problems* 79 (2016): 141 y ss.
90. In the European model, for example, the ECtHR reparations do not have the same scope. Although the reparations evolved to indicate to the State reparation modalities such as *restitutio in integrum* and the so-called 'pilot judgment' are extended, it does not reach the level of intensity and depth of the measures ordered by the Inter-American Court. In the European court, a criterion has prevailed in which the ECHR only allows the ECHR to 'declare' the violation of the right and consequently the forms or ways to comply with the obligation to make reparation is the responsibility of the State. See, for example: Dinah Shelton, *Remedies in International Human Rights Law* (Oxford University Press, 2015), 211 y ss.
91. See, for example: *Compulsory Membership in an Association Prescribed by Law for the Practice of Journalism (Arts. 13 and 29 American Convention on Human Rights)*, IACtHR, Advisory Opinion OC-5/85 of November 13, 1985, para. 44.

92. See: Jorge Contesse, 'Contestation and deference in the Inter-American Human Rights System', *Law and Contemporary Problems* 79 (2016): 141 y ss.
93. *Las Dos Erres Massacre v. Guatemala*, IACtHR, Judgment of November 24, 2009 (Preliminary Objection, Merits, Reparations and Costs), para. 226.
94. *Plan de Sánchez Massacre v. Guatemala*, IACtHR, Judgment of November 19, 2004 (Reparations), para. 77.
95. Ibid.
96. *Las Dos Erres Massacre v. Guatemala*, IACtHR, Judgment of November 24, 2009 (Preliminary Objection, Merits, Reparations and Costs), para. 226.
97. *Barrios Altos v. Peru*, IACtHR, Judgment of November 30, 2001 (Reparations and Costs), operative paragraphs 3, 4 and 5; *Mapiripán Massacre v. Colombia*, IACtHR, Judgment of September 15, 2005 (Merits, Reparations and Costs), para. 315; *Pueblo Bello Massacre v. Colombia*, IACtHR, Judgment of January 31, 2006 (Merits, Reparations and Costs), para. 278.
98. *Ituango Massacres v. Colombia*, IACtHR, Judgment of July 1, 2006 (Preliminary Objection, Merits, Reparations and Costs), para. 408.
99. *Plan de Sánchez Massacre v. Guatemala*, IACtHR, Judgment of November 19, 2004 (Reparations), para. 105.
100. Ibid., para. 110.
101. Ibid., párr. 110.
102. *Mapiripán Massacre v. Colombia*, IACtHR, Judgment of September 15, 2005 (Merits, Reparations and Costs), para. 306.
103. Ibid., para. 308.
104. Ibid., para. 316; *Ituango Massacres v. Colombia*, IACtHR, Judgment of July 1, 2006 (Preliminary Objection, Merits, Reparations and Costs), para 409.
105. See: *González et al. ('Cotton Field') v. Mexico*, IACtHR, Judgment of November 16, 2009 (Preliminary Objection, Merits, Reparations and Costs), para. 450.
106. It has normative support in articles 33, 62.1, 62.3 and 65 of the American Convention, 30 of its Statute and in article 69 of its Regulations.
107. See, for example: Pablo Saavedra Alessandri, '40 años cambiando realidades una mirada al impacto estructural de las decisiones de la Corte Interamericana de Derechos Humanos', in *Cumplimiento e impacto de las sentencias de la Corte Interamericana y el Tribunal Europeo de Derechos Humanos. Transformando realidades*, coord. Armin von Bogdandy, Eduardo Ferrer Mac-Gregor, Mariela Morales Antoniazzi, Pablo Saavedra Alessandri (México: Instituto Max Planck de Derecho Público Comparado y Derecho Internacional Público, Instituto de Estudios Constitucionales del Estado de Querétaro, Instituto de Investigaciones Jurídicas, Universidad Nacional Autónoma de México, 2019), 551–612.
108. Article 2.33, Rules of Procedure of the Inter-American Court of Human Rights, 2009.
109. Article 35.1: 'The case shall be presented to the Court through the submission of the report to which article 50 of the Convention refers, which must establish all the facts that allegedly give rise to a violation and identify the alleged victims.' Rules of Procedure of the Inter-American Court of Human Rights, 2009.
110. *Hacienda Brasil Verde Workers v. Brazil*, IACtHR, Judgment of October 20, 2016 (Preliminary Objections, Merits, Reparations and Costs), para. 45.
111. Article 35.2, Rules of Procedure of the Inter-American Court of Human Rights, 2009.
112. *Massacres of El Mozote and surrounding areas v. El Salvador*, IACtHR, Judgment of October 25, 2012 (Merits, Reparations and Costs), para. 51.
113. *Hacienda Brasil Verde Workers v. Brazil*, IACtHR, Judgment of October 20, 2016 (Preliminary Objections, Merits, Reparations and Costs), para. 47.

Disclosure statement

No potential conflict of interest was reported by the author(s).

ORCID

Harold Bertot Triana http://orcid.org/0000-0003-0737-4710
Elena C. Díaz Galán http://orcid.org/0000-0003-0914-8944

OPEN ACCESS

Access to justice for atrocities in the comparison of land-mark cases on state immunity in Brazil and Italy*

Marco Longobardo and Federica Violi

ABSTRACT
This article investigates differences and similarities in the approach of Italian and Brazilian domestic courts to the topic of access to justice for atrocities and the role of state immunity, taking particular note of the limited and select dialogue between the two judiciaries and reflecting on the potential for further developments of the customary international law rule on state immunity. To do so, the article first outlines the rule on state immunity and offers an overview of the articulated Italian case law on why state immunity cannot bar access to justice for atrocities, considering the judicial developments occurred after 2004. The paper moves on to describe the recent 2021 decision of the Brazilian Supremo Tribunal Federal, in which the Brazil judiciary seemingly joined the Italian trend against state immunity when atrocities are committed. The two different judicial trends are then compared and analysed, with a discussion on the limited explicit reference to Italian decisions by the Supremo Tribunal Federal. The article concludes the research by describing the likely impact of these judicial trends on future developments on the relationship between access to justice for atrocities and state immunity.

What jeopardizes or destabilizes the international legal order are the international crimes and not individual suits for reparation in the search of justice. In my perception, what troubles the international legal order, [sic] are the cover-up of such international crimes accompanied by the impunity of the perpetrators, and not the victims' search for justice.[1]

1. Introduction

This article explores the dialogue or absence of dialogue between national judges in Brazil and Italy on the topic of access to justice for atrocities and the role of state immunity, comparing the attitude taken by the Italian and Brazilian judiciary in concluding that state

*The article was finalized on 12th June 2024.

immunity cannot bar justice for atrocities.[2] State immunity is one of the rules of international law that is more directly influenced by the judicial activity of domestic courts since domestic courts are primarily tasked with its application.[3] In the absence of a universal treaty on state immunity in force,[4] domestic courts have developed national case laws on the circumstances in which state immunity applies, contributing to the emergence and development of customary international law in this field.[5] Particularly delicate are those cases in which domestic courts have to decide whether state immunity can bar access to justice for atrocities committed by a state: while scholars have suggested different legal solutions to this issue,[6] various domestic courts have in parallel provided different answers.

In light of the goals of the special issue hosting this research, this article investigates in particular the solutions offered by two domestic judicial systems: Italy and Brazil. The choice of Italy is determined by the fact that, since 2004, Italian courts have denied that state immunity can be invoked to bar access to justice when certain violations of fundamental rights occur. As it is known, the International Court of Justice (ICJ) addressed this subject in the 2012 *Jurisdictional Immunities* case, rejecting the Italian argument that sovereign immunity can be disregarded in order to adjudicate reparations claims for international crimes.[7] Nonetheless, as detailed below, the Italian judiciary keeps denying the subsistence of state immunity vis-à-vis certain violations of fundamental rights, departing from the decision of the ICJ. The choice of Brazil as the second case study is due to the fact that the Brazilian Supreme Court (Supremo Tribunal Federal, henceforth STF) in 2021 declared that no state immunity can be invoked when human rights are violated.[8] Subsequently, in 2022, the Brazilian Supreme Court confirmed these findings, clarifying that these apply for violations occurring on Brazilian territory only.[9]

These two domestic jurisprudential trends share some similarities and, at the same time, present some differences in the outcomes and in the legal reasoning advanced. This article explores these convergences and divergences, taking particular note of the limited and select judicial dialogue between the Brazilian and the Italian case laws. With the wider perspective of national judicial dialogue in international law matters in the background,[10] the article explores the significance of the Italian and Brazilian case laws in further developments of the customary international law on state immunity. In light of the goals of the special issue where this article appears and of the boundaries of the analysis that focuses on Italian and Brazilian case law, particular – but not exclusive – attention is given to scholarship authored by Italian and Brazilian commentators.

This study is structured as follows: section 2 outlines briefly the rule on state immunity and offers an overview of the articulated Italian case law on why state immunity cannot bar access to justice for atrocities, taking in particular account judicial developments that occurred after 2004. Section 3 describes the recent 2021 decision of the Brazilian Supremo Tribunal Federal, in which the Brazil judiciary apparently joined the Italian trend against state immunity when atrocities are committed, taking into account subsequent 2022 developments as well. The two different judicial trends are compared and analysed in section 4, where the limited explicit reference to Italian decisions by the Supremo Tribunal Federal is discussed. Section 5 concludes the research by describing the likely impact of these judicial trends on future developments on the relationship between access to justice for atrocities and state immunity.

2. State immunity, access to justice for atrocities, and the Italian Case Law

2.1. State immunity in a nutshell

The rule on state immunity posits that 'no state can claim jurisdiction over another' on the basis of the principle of equality of states.[11] Accordingly, a state, as such, cannot be convened before the courts of another states, except in cases in which the former has consented to the exercise of jurisdiction by the latter.[12]

State immunity emerged as a rule protecting states in relation to any kind of activity. Yet, already at the beginning of the XX century some domestic courts started distinguishing between acts covered by state immunity, i.e. those acts undertaken as manifestation of the state's sovereignty (*jure imperii*), and acts not covered by state immunity because they are undertaken by a state as if it acts as a commercial entity (*jure gestionis*). Although the contours of these two categories are not always easy to discern, this distinction is considered part of customary international law on state immunity.[13]

As mentioned afore, at the time of writing, there is no binding treaty on state immunity at universal level. The 2004 United Nations Convention on Jurisdictional Immunities of States and Their Property never entered into force due to a lack of ratifications.[14] Accordingly, at the international level, state immunity is mainly governed by customary international law.

2.2. A new hope: does jus cogens trumps state immunity?

Since 2004, Italian courts have started arguing that there is yet another exception to state immunity beyond the acts *jure imperii* / acts *jure gestionis* dichotomy: according to this view, usually labelled as humanitarian exception, state immunity cannot be used to deny access to justice to victims of atrocities. For the purposes of this article, the decision of the Italian Supreme Court (Corte di Cassazione) in the *Ferrini* case will be taken as the starting point of this story. It should be noted that before 2004 other national jurisdictions – e.g. in Greece – had reached similar results.[15] However, the stubbornness of Italian courts in denying state immunity to bar access to justice for atrocities, coupled with the perceived leading role of Italian courts in shifting from absolute to relative immunity, resulted in a recognisable Italian position on the issue at hand.

In the *Ferrini* decision of 11 March 2004, the Italian Supreme Court denied state immunity to Germany for some crimes committed by the Nazi army in the north of Italy during World War II.[16] In particular, the decision regarded illegal deportations and denials of the status of prisoners of war, which were prohibited under international humanitarian law even prior to the adoption of the 1949 Four Geneva Conventions. In the Supreme Court's view, these actions amount to international crimes and the protection of human rights against these crimes amounts to *jus cogens*. Accordingly, state immunity, which is not a rule of *jus cogens*, cannot bar the access to justice to rights which have *jus cogens* status.[17] As a result, Germany could not invoke state immunity to bar justice for international crimes.

The *Ferrini* decision sparked significant academic debate[18] and was followed by a series of other Italian decisions that applied the same rationale.[19] For the purposes of this study, suffice it to note that the Italian Supreme Court argued on the basis of international law *only*: the conclusion that Germany did not enjoy immunity was, according to the judges, a consequence of a hierarchy between different international law rules that existed at the international level, rather than the result of the application of Italian domestic law. What the Italian Supreme Court did was simply identifying this international law hierarchy, recognising its transposition into the Italian legal system, and using this hierarchy to solve an apparent normative conflict between the ban on international crimes and state immunity.[20] The soundness of this conclusion was tested very soon.

2.3. The empire strikes back: the ICJ and the rejection of the Italian rationale

Germany did not stay idle in front of the Italian case law and the danger to be asked to pay for reparations for the crimes committed by the Nazis during their occupation of northern Italy. Rather, Germany convened Italy in front of the ICJ, lamenting that the Italian judiciary had violated German state immunity.

In 2012, the ICJ passed its judgement in favour of Germany. The Court rejected the idea that Germany could not invoke state immunity before Italian courts when it barred access to justice for victims of atrocities, stating that 'under customary international law as it presently stands, a State is not deprived of immunity by reason of the fact that it is accused of serious violations of international human rights law or the international law of armed conflict'.[21] According to the ICJ, there is no normative conflict between the procedural rule on immunity and the rules that are relevant for the merits of a case pending before a domestic court.[22]

Although the ICJ's decision sparked an animated debate among scholars,[23] it was implemented diligently by Italy. A number of Italian judgments, both by the Supreme Court and by lesser tribunals, acknowledged the ICJ's decision and denied Italian jurisdiction over similar cases.[24] The Italian parliament also intervened, by adopting Law no. 5/2013,[25] with which Italy acceded to the United Nations Convention on Jurisdictional Immunities of States and Their Property. Article 3 of this Law stated that Italian judges had to comply with the ICJ judgment, denying their jurisdiction in similar cases.[26]

The ICJ's ruling on this matter also affected the development of case law on state immunity outside Italy, both at national level and before the European Court of Human Rights, resonating in a series of backward national and international judgments that confirmed the application of state immunity even when atrocities occurred.[27] In light of the influence of the ICJ's case law in matters of international law, some held that this was the final position on the relationship between state immunity and access to justice for atrocities.[28] However, a reaction by Italian courts was underway.

2.4. The return of the Jedi: the Italian Constitutional Court against German immunity

The Italian decision of implementing the ICJ's judgment did not end the state immunity saga because of the intervention of the Italian Constitutional Court in 2014. A different Italian judicial body was ready to offer its rationale on why, notwithstanding the ICJ's decision, state immunity could not have barred the access to justice for atrocities.

At the time of the writing of this article, Italy is *not* complying with the ICJ's decision because of its Constitutional Court decision no. 238 of 2014.[29] The Italian Constitutional Court held that as a matter of Italian domestic law, the right to access justice is a fundamental principle guaranteed by Articles 2 and 24 of the Italian Constitution, and as a such, it cannot be set aside in favour of state immunity when the latter shields war crimes and crimes against humanity, which breaches fundamental human rights.[30] In this regard, Articles 2 and 24 are considered to be 'counter-limits' to the application of customary international law on state immunity in the Italian legal order.[31] Consequently, the Italian Constitutional Court ordered the Italian government and judges to disregard the ICJ's decision and considered null and void the Italian legislation that implemented the judgment. As a result, reparation trials against Germany for atrocities committed by the Nazis resumed before Italian courts.[32]

The main difference between the positions of the Italian Supreme Court and the Italian Constitutional Court is that while the former tried to argue on the basis of international law (*jus cogens* argument), the latter employed Italian constitutional law as the basis of its reasoning. The Italian Constitutional Court openly acknowledged the primacy of the ICJ in interpreting international law, even if it regretted the conclusions reached in the 2012 decision.[33] However, the Italian Constitutional Court emphasised its role to guarantee the application (and prevalence) of the rights protected by the Italian Constitution, a field which is outside the remit of the ICJ. External observer may dislike the outcome of the Italian Constitutional Court's decision, but nobody could context its primacy in the interpretation of the Italian Constitution. Conversely, on matters purely based on international law, the authoritativeness of the ICJ is far more significant than that of the Italian Supreme Court, and thus the ICJ's judgment appears to be more authoritative of the *Ferrini* decision.

The decision of the Italian Constitutional Court received extensive coverage by commentators in and outside Italy,[34] even if Brazilian scholars have not been particularly active in analysing it. On the plan of the relationship between Italy and Germany, it resulted in a lack of Italian compliance with the ICJ 2012 decision. As predictable, Germany did not stay idle.

2.5. The (phantom) menace of a new ICJ case between Germany and Italy on immunity

Following the Italian Constitutional Court's decision no 238 of 2014, Italy has resumed its violation of German immunity and has violated the duty to implement ICJ's decisions under Article 94 of the UN Charter. As a result, and as foreseen by many observers, Germany brought Italy again before the ICJ in 2022.[35]

At this stage, there is little to add to this development. Originally, Germany asked for provisional measures against the enforcement of some Italian judgments.[36] The Italian government, in response, has adopted urgent legislative measures to paralyse the implementation of judgments against Germany.[37] Accordingly, Germany has withdrawn the request for provisional measures,[38] but the case is still pending before the ICJ.

In parallel, a case was launched before the Italian Constitutional Court on the lawfulness, under the Italian constitution, of the urgent legislative measures adopted to paralyse reparation cases against Germany, which provided that Italy would have been responsible to pay the compensation owed by Germany.[39] In 2023, with decision no. 159, the Italian Constitutional Court has concluded that these measures are not in conflict with the Italian Constitution since the victims are provided with reparations even if this is materially paid by Italy rather than Germany.[40]

In the meantime, international law scholars have already shown an interest these new developments involving Italy and Germany on State immunity.[41]

3. The recent Brazilian case law on state immunity when atrocities occur

Comparatively, Brazilian courts have not dealt as extensively with the doctrine of state immunity as Italian courts have. Traditionally, the Brazilian domestic judiciary would understand and apply state immunity from jurisdiction as absolute.[42] However, the entry into force of the 1988 Republican Constitution generated a momentum for courts to restrict state immunity, specifically in the context of labour (law) cases.[43] As of then, Brazilian case law has followed consistently the *acta iure imperii / acta iure gestionis* categorisation and applied the restrictive doctrine accordingly. Yet, up until very recently, no exception was identified by either Brazilian lower courts or the Brazilian Superior Court of Justice in cases of *acta iure imperii*, regardless of the alleged (il)legality of the foreign state's act, whether occurred on the territory of Brazil, and/or in absence of alternative means of redress.

This stance has taken a radical U-turn with the decision on *Changri-La* case of the Brazilian Supreme Court, adopted in August 2021,[44] whereby, as already mentioned, the STF decided – with a slight 6–5 majority – that immunity from jurisdiction does not apply in cases of foreign states' unlawful acts constituting human rights violations.[45] The case was heard following the extraordinary appeal procedure. This procedure is employed in those cases where the STF recognises that a case may have 'general repercussions' extending beyond the *petitum* of the case. These are to be examined by the Supreme Court in plenary to establish a thesis that becomes a precedent. This makes the *Changri-La* case particularly important.[46]

Two petitions were filed to 'clarify' and circumscribe the scope of the decision adopted by the STF. The first one by the *Ministero Publico Federal*, requesting the scope of the decision to be limited to international crimes implying grave violations of human rights in the territory of the state; the second one by the *Advocacia-Geral da União* to delimit the scope of the decision to war crimes as recognised by international tribunals. The STF partially accepted the first petition, explicating the territorial requirement, in line with the tort exception case-law,[47] while rejecting the limitation *ratione materiae* to international crimes. The Court rejected the second petition on war crimes in full.[48]

The case concerned the sinking of a fishing boat during WWII, the *Changri-La*, and the death of the ten fishermen aboard, along the coasts of Rio de Janeiro, in the Brazilian territorial waters. Around sixty years after the facts, new findings revealed that the boat was intentionally sunk by a German submarine. This allowed the *Tribunal Maritimo* in 2001 to establish the facts and suggest that Brazil extended moral or monetary compensation to the victims.[49] This took the form of a symbolic public ceremony officially including the name of the victims in the Brazilian World War II memorial. This notwithstanding, in 2007, the descendants of one of the victims decided to start a judicial proceeding against Germany and sought compensation before Brazilian courts for the material and non-pecuniary damages incurred. The STF decision is the last step of a long judicial journey.

The following analysis reflects the order of the arguments articulated by the STF.

The Court constructed its decision starting from the characterisation of the sinking of the boat and consequent death of the crew. The STF framed the act as a war crime, and a violation of both the laws of armed conflict and human rights.[50] The Court spilled admittedly – while not fully convincingly – a lot of ink in trying to frame the relevant act as a violation of either international humanitarian law or human rights law. From an international humanitarian law perspective, it did so by relying first on Article 46 of the Regulations Annexed to the Convention (IV) respecting the Laws and Customs of War on Land[51] and the Convention (XI) relative to certain Restrictions with regard to the Exercise of the Right of Capture in Naval War.[52] The latter reference seems more fitting in relation to immunity of non-military vessels in naval war (and possibly, by extension, a prohibition of killing civilians aboard as non-military targets). Yet, the reference to the Hague Regulations is quite inaccurate, not only because it was adopted to govern war on *land*, but particularly because its Article 46 applies only to occupied territory; leaving aside the debate on whether certain maritime zones can be occupied,[53] nothing suggests that that portion of Brazilian territorial waters was under occupation at the time of the sinking of the boat.[54] Equally puzzling, albeit for different reasons, is the reference to the prohibition to kill persons at sea in the Statute of the Nuremberg Tribunal[55] as a war crime and the violation of the right to life as codified under Article 6 of the ICCPR. Here, the STF avoided engaging in the highly relevant question of intertemporality and hence validity of the two provisions mentioned above for the facts of the case, which occurred before the two instruments entered into force.[56] This line of arguments was of course necessary and instrumental for the STF to reach the conclusion it did.

Yet, what also emerges from this characterisation is that the judgement does not circumscribe the exception to the gravity of the violations – thus seemingly opening the door for a limitation to states' immunity for *acta iure imperii* to *any* violations of human rights, albeit committed in the territory of the state. Admittedly, this significantly expands the exception already formulated by other domestic courts, whether based on international or constitutional law.[57] Yet, the arguments advanced by the STF in relation to the humanitarian exception mostly engage with doctrine and case law related to *serious* violations. As mentioned above, the *Ministero Publico Federal* had asked the Court to circumscribe the decision to *international crimes* implying grave violations. The STF has rejected this delimitation in its latest decision, albeit due to the alleged unintelligibility of the category of international crimes. According to Cavalcanti, the STF failed to circumscribe the decision to gross violations, due to a wrongly conflation of the *jus cogens* category with the broader concept of human rights.[58]

The STF's analysis of both case law and legal instruments moves along the territorial tort exception (and specifically on Article 12 on the UN Convention on state immunity and national legislation across continents) and the humanitarian exception, with the Court relying on the Italian, Greek and South-Korean jurisprudence. As already noted in the literature,[59] the Tribunal did engage in a (comparative) analysis of both national and international instruments and case-law, albeit dismissing easily domestic and international case law moving in an opposite direction. It remains however surprising that the judges did not derive any prescriptive or operative conclusion from this analysis, somewhat undermining the dialogic nature of these references. The STF merely indicated that this plethora of evidence shows that exceptions to the rule of state immunity are conceivable and that the rule is neither static, nor insurmountable.[60] In doing so it also took a specific position towards the ICJ decision of 2012, relying both on Article 59 of the ICJ Statute and trying to distinguish the context of the present case from the Italian case, as will be explained further below.[61] In fact, most interaction with the *Jurisdictional*

Immunities decision occurred with extensive passages of the late Judge Cançado Trindade's dissenting opinion and the arguments formulated in the Italian counter-memorial.

How did then the Court come to exclude state immunity in the case at hand? The STF moved forward to focus on the right of access to justice and the right to truth. Specifically, it indicated that refusing to grant access to court to the claimants in Brazil would create an anomy, a state of exception, a 'zone of indifference of law within law', *à la* Agamben, whereby the victims would be left without justice.[62] The right of access to judicial review is identified both at a constitutional level (Article 5(XXXV)) and internationally, as provided in Articles 8, 10, and 14 of the ICCPR.

More interestingly perhaps, the decision of the STF is the only one so far establishing the inconsistency of state immunity with the full realisation of the right to truth.[63] This is not particularly surprising, given the regional context.[64] For historical reasons, Latin American countries have a solid tradition on the concept of both individual and collective truth, and the Inter-American Commission of Human Rights has been a forerunner in that regard. [65] While the reliance of the STF on the right to truth is not exceptional, the way the Court constructed its argument in the specific case is somewhat dubious. The judges relied on Article 32 of the 1977 Additional Protocol I, concerning the (fate of) the missing and the death. Yet, as already noted by commentators,[66] that specific provision does not integrate an individual human right *per se*. It rather entails a due diligence obligation on the parties to the conflict which, however, does *not* apply to its own nationals. Regardless of the (mis)interpretation of the Court concerning Article 32, the decision further enlarges the scope of friction between the doctrine of state immunity and the quest for justice.

For victims of violations of human rights or humanitarian law and their family members, the right to truth would imply an obligation for the perpetrator state to provide specific information on the circumstances of the violation and the fate of the victim. This 'procedural' dimension[67] of truth reflects the remedial evolution of individual human rights violations, which implies a jurisdictional or quasi-judicial assessment of the specific case, geared towards reparation. It has been argued that the right to truth is endowed with the character of inderogability. The non-derogable nature of this right would be an immediate reflection of its material scope (in matters of serious violations of international humanitarian or human rights law) and, as such, preclusive of any derogation.[68] The argument is that denial to (judicial) fact-finding could turn into acts of psychological torture, or the detriment of other rights related to, for example, private and family life, if such conduct prevents from seeking and knowing the truth about the fate of their loved ones. In this context, while taking the form of an autonomous rule, the right to truth becomes instrumental to the assertion and protection of other substantive rights and, among them, the right to an effective remedy.[69]

The STF concludes its reasoning with a (seemingly) constitutionally based decision: state immunity shall be delimited in cases of human rights violations. According to Article 4(II) of the Brazilian Constitution,[70] its domestic legal order cannot tolerate such a zone of indifference, as the article gives prevalence to human rights as a principle that guides Brazil in its international relations. As such, in the case at hand, the right to life, truth and access shall prevail over the immunity of Germany. According to the STF,

Article 4 of the Constitution instates a new normative paradigm whereby state sovereignty is no longer preponderant.[71]

As further elaborated below,[72] this reconstruction is particularly interesting, since the STF produces a singular hybrid in trying to reconstruct both the relevant normative provisions and violations through an overlapping (and not always rigorous) series of arguments based both on international and domestic law. This leaves the readers wondering first whether the violations have already occurred as a result of the German unlawful act or whether these would materialise in case state immunity is recognised, thus denying the claimants access to justice.[73] More relevantly, though, is the question of the *site*, more specifically of where the violation materialised. At an international level? At a constitutional level? Both? The answer to these questions reverberates also on how these parallel violations interact with state immunity.

4. Dialogues and encounters between Italian and Brazilian decisions

4.1. Mutual references to Italian and Brazilian case law, practice, and scholarship in Italian and Brazilian decisions on lack of state immunity

The Italian case law on the lack of state immunity when atrocities are at stake does not engage with Brazilian decisions. Notwithstanding a rich survey of relevant national and international case law,[74] the *Ferrini* decision by the Italian Supreme Court does not refer to any Brazilian case on state immunity. Similarly, the Italian Constitutional Court does not refer to any Brazilian precedent in its decision no 238 of 2014. This is unsurprising since the 2021 and 2022 Brazilian decisions discussed in this article are the first Brazilian cases dealing with state immunity when atrocities occur. More regrettable is that the 2022 order by the Tribunal of Rome referring the Italian legislation to the Italian Constitutional Court and the subsequent 2023 decision no. 159 by the Italian Constitutional Court do not take into account the Brazilian decisions. As a matter of doctrine, since the two Italian courts are not permitted to cite scholars in their decisions,[75] no reference to Brazilian authors (or any other) can be found in the text of the judgments.

Conversely, the 2021 *Changri-La* decision discusses in detail Italian case law and scholarship. The majority focuses its attention on the *Ferrini* case,[76] which is cited alongside with the subsequent *Milde* case.[77] A long portion of the *Ferrini* decision is quoted with approval, with reference both to its English and Portuguese translations. The *Ferrini* decision is considered by the majority as a portion of a wider customary international law patchwork comprising domestic legislation from US, UK, Australia, and Argentina, as well as domestic judgments from Greece, US, and South Korea.[78] In this, the majority in the *Changri-La* decision employs the *Ferrini* judgment to suggest, albeit not conclusively, that customary international law includes elements of flexibility when dealing with state immunity and atrocities. Moreover, the majority in the *Changri-La* decision quotes with approval the Italian official position presented before the ICJ in defence of the approaches taken in the *Ferrini* judgment.[79] The majority of the STF further quotes the opinion of the Brazilian General-Prosecutor, which incorporates references to scholarly criticisms against the 2012 ICJ's decision, including to three articles by Italian scholars (written in English).[80]

The dissenting opinions in the *Changri-La* case engages less with Italian case law and scholarship. The dissenting opinion by Gilmar Mendes assesses some domestic legislations on state immunity: domestic legislations from US, UK, Singapore, South Africa, Pakistan, Canada Australia, and Argentina are mentioned without significant elaboration, whereas Italian legislation is ignored.[81] The *Ferrini* decision is discussed in a long quote summarising the opinion of the Brazilian General-Prosecutor, with the aim of demonstrating that state immunity is applicable to atrocities as per the 2012 ICJ's decision.[82]

The dissenting opinion by Marco Aurélio Mello refers to the 2012 ICJ decision as 'o caso *Ferrini*'.[83] The judge goes on to describe in wide brushstrokes the context of the ICJ's proceedings, with reference to the Italian Supreme Court's judgement,[84] concluding that state immunity should apply. No direct reference to Italian case law, practice, or scholarship is provided by the dissenting opinion by Alexandre de Moraes.[85]

Overall, the *Ferrini* decision by the Italian Supreme Court and, to a lesser extent, the Italian position before the ICJ, the *Milde* decision, and Italian scholarship (in English) are taken into account in the *Changri-La* case, chiefly by the majority. This is not surprising from the perspective of the outcome reached by the majority, that is, the fact that state immunity cannot shield access to justice for atrocities. On the other end, the absence of any reference to the Italian Constitutional Court's decision no 238 of 2014 is striking, especially in light of the role played by Brazilian constitutional law in concluding that state immunity was inapplicable.

4.2. A comparison between the Italian and Brazilian approaches to the relationship between national and international law in the context of state immunity

There are two main aspects of comparison that are worth highlighting between the Italian and Brazilian case-law on state immunity. First, the role of existing alternatives to *judicial* remedies for victims; second, and perhaps most importantly, the relationship between international and constitutional law in cases involving state immunity.

As to the first aspect, it is worth recalling that the Italo-German situation in relation to reparations for the victims of World War II Nazi crimes is a particularly complex one. The 1961 Bonn Agreement between Germany and Italy concerning Settlement of Certain Property-Related, Economic and Financial Questions has represented a significant bone of contention in the immunity saga, both at a political and judicial level. Generally speaking, the Italian position[86] – at least until 2022[87] – was that the 1961 Agreement did in fact *not* settle the reparation issues for Italian victims of Nazi crimes, with the two states fundamentally disagreeing on the extent of the treaty and its scope of application. Italian claimants have also unsuccessfully seized German domestic courts to obtain reparations for the same acts.[88] This *impasse* has, in turn, given shape – albeit with different formulations and argumentations – to the 'last resort' argument, with the Constitutional Court insisting in particular in judgement no. 238 of 2014 on a *judicial* remedy being necessary for the victims to obtain justice, based on the lack of meaningful and effective judicial and non-judicial alternatives.[89] The STF does also sketch this argument, albeit with much less emphasis and 'merely' to distinguish *Changri-La* from the ICJ case.[90] More specifically, the Tribunal employs the argument of the absence of any compensatory schemes between Germany and Brazil for Nazi crimes merely to differentiate the Italian precedent from the Brazilian situation. The rather incidental nature of the consideration makes it difficult to discern whether this element has played a role for the STF in excluding the application of state immunity in the case at hand. Similarly, one can only find a very brief passage on the possibility for the victims to turn to German courts, when the STF states that: '... requiring the victims to turn to foreign jurisdiction would imply reserving the victims [a situation of] anomy ...'.[91] While we can imply that this short line dismisses the effectiveness of recourse to German courts, there is no engagement as to the parameters of effectiveness and feasibility of a different *judicial* remedy and – again – no clarity as to whether the STF considers that state immunity should succumb only in cases where no alternative judicial or non-judicial remedies are available to the victims. The arguments used by STF seem to work rather *ad adiuvandum* and not as part of the core reasoning of the decision. In the Italian case-law, instead, the absence of other effective and meaningful means of redress comes rather across as a *constitutive* element of the exception to state immunity in the cases of serious violations, both from an international and constitutional perspective.

The most interesting difference, however, between the Italian and Brazilian judicial attitude to state immunity is the way the difference courts approach(ed) the relationship between international and domestic law in shaping the exception to or non-applicability of the rule. As already mentioned in the previous paragraphs, *Ferrini* and decision no. 238 of 2014 concretely obtained the same result. Yet, the two Italian Courts elaborated their reasonings in diametrically opposed ways. While in *Ferrini*, the Italian Supreme Court based its reasoning in international law, identifying a humanitarian exception to the rule on state immunity already in the international legal framework, decision no. 238 of 2014 employed the counter-limits doctrine. It is worth recalling that this doctrine allowed the Constitutional Court to argue that a rule on state immunity that extends to *acta iure imperii* constituting serious violations of human rights of international humanitarian law cannot 'enter' the Italian legal order, by virtue of the inviolable right enunciated in Articles 2 and 24 of the Constitution, the right of access to justice for the victims. The Constitutional Court thus based its conclusions on constitutional law. These constitutional law-international law iterations across (civil) domestic courts and the Italian Constitutional Court have been extensively explored. [92]

The STF entertains instead a peculiar hybrid of difficult framing that requires closer analysis. First, it considers that the relevant German actions are crimes and violations of both human rights and humanitarian law under *international law*. In its operative part, it shifts focus on the remedial dimension of these rights, reasoning around the right to truth and access to justice as human rights protected both at *international* and *domestic* (constitutional) levels, without any further mention of the right to life. It then concludes that by virtue of Article 4(II) of the Constitution the right to life, truth and access to justice shall be given prevalence over the rule on state immunity. Seemingly, the relevant violations have occurred (or *might* occur)[93] both at domestic and international level, at least for the right to truth and access to justice. For the right to life, the reasoning seems to be limited to Article 6 ICCPR, without any further reference to domestic law.

This strange blend of international and domestic levels opens up two possible scenarios of interpretations as to where the *site* of conflict between human rights and the rule on state immunity might be located according to the STF. It also blurs the similarity that other commentators have identified between decision no. 238 of 2014 and the STF decision.[94]

The first possible way to read the judgement is as a starkly dualist decision. The STF does refer to (international) human rights in its line of argument. Yet, if we take on this dualist interpretation, these rights are relevant insofar as they have been transposed from international to *domestic* law. Accordingly, the reasoning of the STF would be firmly embedded entirely in constitutional law.[95] The STF establishes the prevalence of substantive and procedural human rights *as transposed* in the Brazilian domestic constitutional order. These *constitutional* fundamental rights are in conflict with the rule on state immunity,[96] and the latter shall thus succumb pursuant to Article 4(II). In this dualist scenario, the conflict with the rule on state immunity is *constitutional* in nature and can go two ways. Either as a conflict between two domestic norms, constitutional fundamental rights on one side and the rule on state immunity on the other side, as equally transposed into the Brazilian legal system. Or as the protection of the integrity of the Brazilian constitutional legal order against the international rule on state immunity that cannot enter the domestic 'fence' – *à la* decision no. 238 of 2014. In the context of this dualist interpretation, the hypothesis of the conflict between two domestic sets of norms, constitutional fundamental rights and state immunity as both transposed in domestic law, seems slightly more in line with a literal reading of the judgement for essentially two reasons. First, the STF does not explicitly theorise a counter-limits doctrine. Second, the STF indicates that the Constitution codifies an explicit normative option for a new paradigm where human rights prevail on the sovereignty of states in the international relations of Brazil,[97] whereby equality of states is cited in the very same article at paragraph V.[98]

The second scenario of interpretation is a rather monist one, whereby international and national law are considered together as part of one single permeable system. And it is this permeability that determines the outcome of the decision. If we take this monist reading of the judgement, the *site* of conflict differs from the dualist scenario. The relevant human rights (and international humanitarian law) violations have occurred (or *might* occur) at the level of international law, including the ones on the right to truth and access to justice. As such, the relevant provisions would also be identified as a matter of international law. This means that the conflict between human rights and international humanitarian law rules and the rule on state immunity would occur at an *international* level, an antinomy between two sets of *international* norms – *à la* Ferrini. Yet, the *prevalence* of human rights over state immunity is constitutional in nature as it is dictated by Article 4(II), which obliges Brazilian courts to forego the international rule on state immunity. This means that in this monist scenario, while the conflict is international in nature, the prevalence that determines the decision is constitutional. The reasoning of the Supreme Court thus has elements of both international and constitutional law.[99] Such a monist reading would give way to a rather fluid and dynamic understanding of the relationship between international and national law and perhaps better stand the criticism to STF of 'not sufficiently' engaging with or disregarding international law.[100]

The difficulty in locating the site of conflict – and perhaps the reticence of the STF itself in situating it – might be due to the seemingly unsettled debate over the monist or dualist nature of the Brazilian legal order.[101] While mostly focused on the incorporation of treaties, and more recently human rights treaties, the debate has significant bearing on the role of customary international law in the Brazilian domestic order.

Depending on one's standing on the matter, this also influences the understanding and resolution of the normative conflict under analysis. When it comes to the position of human rights (treaties), Brazilian scholarship appears to oscillate among several variations of either *moderate* dualism or *moderate* monism.[102] The 'moderate' characterisation is mainly linked to the addition of Constitutional Amendment 45/2004 (henceforth CA 45/04) to Article 5(3) of the Brazilian Constitution, which explicitly accords constitutional status to international human rights treaties adopted with a 3/5 majority. CA 45/04 was possibly prompted by an understanding in case law,[103] which would (already) recognise infra-constitutional value to human rights treaties adopted with simple majority. CA 45/04 'enhanced' the constitutional nature of those agreements adopted with the 'aggravated' procedure. The progressive prominence gained by human rights in the Brazilian constitutional architecture could be traced back to the proposal of late judge Cançado Trindade to include paragraph 2 to Article 5 of the Constitution.[104] This provision clarifies that rights and guarantees included in the Constitution do not exclude those deriving from international treaties ratified by Brazil, giving way to the so called 'dialogic internationalist monism' doctrine. In virtue of the direct applicability clause at Article 5(1), rightsholders would become beneficiary of the most favourable human right norm, regardless of its source, either constitutional or conventional.[105] The apparatus sketched above clearly indicates a constitutional tendency to place human rights at a higher hierarchical level. Any normative conflict with human rights norms should thus be assessed through a contextual interpretation of the Constitution that properly considers this prominence.

Where does this leave the incorporation of customary international law? So far, scholars seem to either exclude questions around the incorporation of customary international law from the analysis[106] or tend to solve it rather straightforwardly.[107] Mostly, the position seems to be that customary international law enters the Brazilian domestic legal order without any act of incorporation necessary and shall be immediately applied by the judiciary. The question was rarely entertained by courts and only arose before Brazilian courts in relation to the customary rule on state immunity from jurisdiction.[108] As mentioned already, judges relied then on the status of the rule under international law when endorsing either the absolute or restrictive approach. In his international law handbook, Husek purports that judges cannot deviate from customary international law, which – as he writes – cannot be 'contradicted'. Yet, this postulation is based on the idea that customary international law is in any event constitutionally-conform since it is (generally) reflected in the principles Brazil maintains in international relations pursuant to Article 4.[109] Quite relevantly to our purposes, this provision includes *inter alia* equality among states, which conceptually operates as the basis for sovereign immunity from jurisdiction.

While earlier restrictions on state immunity were solidly grounded in international law, the latest decision of the STF appears to move instead into a (new?) terrain of hybridity. Paradoxically, extending the debate to the *Changri-la* case, a dualist understanding of the conflict between human rights and the state immunity at the *constitutional law* level would seem more 'fitting' to explain the decision of the court. Sovereign immunity might be considered as enshrined in Article 4 of the Constitution via equality of states, and thus a 'domestic' rule. As such, it conflicts with a set of human rights also incorporated in the very same provision. The outcome reached by the STF is not surprising then, considering the contextual preference the Constitution shows for human rights. Yet, one could also consider the decision to reflect somehow the dialogic internationalist monist doctrine, by which the constitutional prevalence of human rights is due to the identification of the most favourable 'regime' for rightsholders. In other terms, if the interaction between sovereign immunity and human rights at the *international law* level leaves a protection gap for individuals, the constitutional human rights prevalence clause will be triggered and require the most beneficial rule to apply (whatever the origin thereof).[110]

5. Conclusions

The analysis conducted so far has possibly tried to build a bridge, rather than conduct a strict comparison, between the Italian and Brazilian judicial attitude towards possible limitations of the rule on state immunity from jurisdiction in cases of atrocities. The judicial bodies of both countries have found their own ways to deal with this vexed question. This article has attempted to identify the points of similarity and divergence as to how they have constructed the limitations on one hand, and searched for judicial dialogue to reinforce their arguments, on the other. Of course, both judiciaries have produced decisions that are 'rich' in considerations of principles and 'grand' statements, particularly the two Constitutional Courts. And of course, their decisions can be subject to criticism on lack of rigour or poor sensitivity for potential future implications.

The Italian Constitutional Court has sought 'refuge' in constitutional law, seemingly without contradicting the ICJ's reconstruction of the rule on state immunity and the purported absence of a humanitarian exception. In other terms, per decision 238/2014, access to justice comes from *within* the Italian domestic legal system, leaving – at least formally – the international rule on state immunity untouched. As such, the two legal orders are – at present at least – walking decisively parallel to each other, with the Italian legal system taking on a 'reactive' rather than 'proactive' stance towards international law. That is, until the international rule on state immunity will not develop to the point of *not* triggering constitutional counter limits and, as such, become 'tolerable'. The Brazilian decision lends itself to two alternative implications qua development of international law. The first dualist scenario would rather be a reasoning on the (non)interaction between international and domestic law. As such it would seemingly respect the 'authority' of the ICJ as ultimate interpreter of the current status of the conflict between human rights and the rule on state immunity at an international level. The monist reading, instead, would be a reasoning on hierarchy and prevalence which, albeit dictated by Brazilian constitutional law, operates at the level of (and decides on) the conflict between two international norms. Both scenarios seem plausible, possibly including even further variants. The second (more monist) scenario would of course contribute more significantly – and directly – to the evolution of the rule of state immunity at an international level, rather than aligning with the trend of relying on constitutional law as a barricade to protect fundamental human rights.

If one takes the monist reading in the Brazilian decision, it becomes apparent how the two Courts operate at different levels, with the Italian Constitutional Court showcasing no relevant state practice for the development of customary international law, with the Brazilian Court providing instead an example to the contrary. Yet, what these impulses show is that judges sit uncomfortably in a situation where formalism would erase with a brush, and at a very early procedural stage, the possibility for victims of atrocities to obtain justice. Domestic courts are progressively moving target in an attempt to circumscribe the rule of state immunity even further, in line with a parallel movement pushing human rights at the forefront of international law, be it relying on constitutional or international law, or a hybrid between the two. There is no reason to treat ICJ precedents as sacred and set in stone. And judicial courts are creatively dancing around them.

Notes

1. *Jurisdictional Immunities of the State (Germany v. Italy: Greece intervening)*, Judgment, 3 February 2012, ICJ Reports (2012) 99, Dissenting Opinion of Judge Cançado Trindade, 228, para 129.
2. For practical reasons, the expressions 'jurisdictional immunities', 'state immunity', and 'sovereign immunity' are used as synonyms. Similarly, 'executive' and 'government' are used interchangeably.
3. On the role of the domestic jurisprudence in the application and reconstruction of international law, see E. Benvenisti, 'Judicial Misgivings Regarding the Application of International Law: An Analysis of Attitudes of National Courts', *European Journal of International Law* 4 (1993): 159; Conforti, 'Preliminary Report on the Activities of National Judges and the International Relations of their State', *Yearbook of the Institute of International Law* 65, no. 1 (1993): 371; A. Roberts, 'Comparative International Law? The Role of National Courts in Creating and Enforcing International Law', *International and Comparative Law Quarterly* 60 (2011): 57; A. Nollkaemper, Y. Shany, and A. Tzanakopoulos, eds, *The Engagement of Domestic Courts with International Law: Comparative Perspectives* (New York: Oxford University Press, 2024).
4. The 1976 European Convention on State Immunity (1495 UNTS 181) is the only multilateral treaty in force and binds only 8 European States. The 2004 United Nations Convention on Jurisdictional Immunities of States and Their Property (2 December 2004, A/RES/59/3) is not in force because it has not gained the required minimum number of ratifications (30 ratifications are required; only 23 States are parties at the time of the writing of this article).
5. *Jurisdictional Immunities*, Judgment, para. 55. See, e.g. the excursus of judicial decisions in ILC, Draft articles on Jurisdictional Immunities of States and Their Property, with commentaries (1991), 36–38, paras 14–18.
6. See, generally, J. Bröhmer, *State Immunity and the Violation of Human Rights* (The Hague/Boston/London, Martinus Nijhoff Publishers 1997); M. Gavouneli, *State Immunity and the Rule of Law* (Athens: Ant. N. Sakkoulas Publishers, 2001); F. De Vittor, 'Immunità degli Stati dalla giurisdizione e tutela dei diritti umani fondamentali', *Rivista di Diritto Internazionale* 85 (2002), 573; C. Espósito Massicci, *Inmunidad del Estado y derechos humanos* (Cizur: Editorial Aranzadi, 2007); A. Bianchi, 'Human Rights and the Magic of Jus Cogens', *European Journal of International Law* 19 (2009): 491; C. Vicenci Fernandes, 'Violações aos Direitos Humanos e a Imunidade de Jurisdição do Estado Estrangeiro: Novas Tendências Jurisprudenciais em Relação à Proteção dos Indivíduos', *Revista Estudos Jurídicos UNESP* 14 (2010): 141; E. Cannizzaro and B. I. Bonafè, 'Of Rights and Remedies: Sovereign Immunity and Fundamental Human Rights', in *From Bilateralism to Community Interest: Essays in Honour of Bruno Simma*, ed. Ulrich Fastenrath et al. (2011), 825.
7. *Jurisdictional Immunities*, Judgment, para. 93.
8. Supremo Tribunal Federal, Recurso Extraordinario Com Agravo 954.858 Rio de Janeiro, Plenario (*Changri-La* case), 23 August 2021.
9. Supremo Tribunal Federal, Emb.Decl. No Recurso Extraordinário Com Agravo 954.858 Rio De Janeiro, 23 May 2022.
10. See, e.g. L. C. Martins de Araújo, 'O diálogo institucional entre Cortes Constitucionais: Uma nova racionalidade argumentativa da jurisdição constitucional justificada pelos diálogos

institucionais transnacionais', *Revista da AGU* 13 (2014): 226; L. C. Martins de Araujo and P. E. Vauthier Borges De Macedo, 'O Diálogo Institucional Entre Cortes Constitucionais: A Jurisdição Constitucional Justificada Pelos Diálogos Transnacionais', in *Teoria Constitucional*, ed. P. R. Barbosa Ramos and M. Mont'alverne Barreto Lima (2015), 328; A. Ridolfi, 'Giurisdizione costituzionale, corti sovranazionali e giudici comuni: considerazioni a proposito del dialogo tra corti', *Rivista AIC* 3 (2016): 1, www.rivistaaic.it/images/rivista/pdf/3_2016_Ridolfi.pdf. See also the Introduction to this Special Issue for a further articulation on judicial dialogue.

11. R. Jennings and A. Watts, eds., *Oppenheim's International Law*, 9th ed. (Oxford: Oxford University Press, 1992), Vol. I, 341.
12. With specific reference to the Brazilian and Italian traditions, see, among others, R. Luzzatto, *Stati stranieri e giurisdizione nazionale* (Milan: Giuffre, 1972); N. Ronzitti and G. Venturini, eds., *Le immunità giurisdizionali degli stati e degli altri enti internazionali* (Padua: Cedam, 2008); L. de Oliveira Moll, *Imunidades Internacionais: Tribunais Nacionais ante a Realidade das Organizações Internacionais*, 2ª edição, (Brasilia: FUNAG2011); C. Tiburcio, *Extensâo e limites da jurisdiçâo brasileira: Competência Internacional e Imunidade de Jurisdiçâo* (Salvador: JusPODIVM, originally published in 2016), 285–311; R. Nigro, *Le immunità giurisdizionali dello stato e dei suoi organi e l'evoluzione della sovranità nel diritto internazionale* (Padua: Cedam, 2018), 226–354. Outside Italy and Brazil, see e.g. H. Fox and P. Webb, *The Law of State Immunity*, 3rd ed. (Oxford: Oxford University Press, 2013); E. Chukwuemeke Okeke, *Jurisdictional Immunities of States and International Organizations* (Oxford: Oxford University Press, 2018), 21–230. See also the essays collected in A. Orakhelashvili, ed., *Research Handbook on Jurisdiction and Immunities in International Law* (Cheltenham: Edward Elgar, 2015); A. Peters et al., eds, *Immunities in the Age of Global Constitutionalism* (Leiden: Brill Nijhof, 2015); T. Ruys and N. Angelet, eds., *The Cambridge Handbook of Immunities and International Law* (Cambridge: Cambridge University Press, 2019).
13. *Jurisdictional Immunities*, Judgment, paras 59–61. See also the overview on state practice and opinio juris in ILC, *supra* note 5, 33–40.
14. Relevant data are available at https://treaties.un.org/Pages/ViewDetails.aspx?src=IND&mtdsg_no=III-13&chapter=3&clang=_en.
15. See, e.g. Greece, Court of Cassation, '*Prefecture of Voiotia v Federal Republic of Germany* (*Distomo Massacre* case), case no 11/2000, 4 May 2000', 129 ILR 513.
16. Corte di Cassazione [Italian Supreme Court], Judgment no 5044/04, *Ferrini c Repubblica Federale di Germania*, 11 March 2004, para. 9, reprinted in *Rivista di diritto internazionale* 87 (2004): 539.
17. Ibid., para. 9.
18. See, e.g. A. Gianelli, 'Crimini internazionali ed immunità degli Stati dalla giurisdizione nella Sentenza *Ferrini*', *Rivista di diritto internazionale* 87 (2004): 643; A. Bianchi, 'Ferrini v. Federal Republic of Germany', *American Journal of International Law* 99 (2005): 242; P. De Sena and F. De Vittor, 'State Immunity and Human Rights: The Italian Supreme Court Decision on the *Ferrini* Case', *European Journal of International Law* 16 (2005): 89; A. Gattini, 'War Crimes and State Immunity in the *Ferrini* Decision', *Journal of International Criminal Justice* 3 (2005): 224; M. Teixeira Thomé and Y. da Silva Felix, 'Imunidade de jurisdição e a efetividade dos direitos humanos sociais', *Revista de Direito Brasileira* 18 (2017): 173; E. Romeiro Fernandes Golin, *Imunidade de Jurisdição dos Estados e Direitos Humanos: Uma crítica ao Caso Ferrini* (São Paulo: Dialética, 2021).
19. See F. Marongiu Buonaiuti, 'Azioni risarcitorie per la commissione di crimini internazionali ed immunità degli Stati dalla giurisdizione: la controversia tra la Germania e l'Italia innanzi alla Corte internazionale di giustizia', *Diritti Umani e Diritto Internazionale* 5 (2011): 232; E. Sciso, 'Italian Judges' Point of View on Foreign States' Immunity', *Vanderbilt Journal of Transnational Law* 44 (2011): 1201.
20. N. Ronzitti, 'L'adattamento dell'ordinamento italiano alle norme imperative del diritto internazionale', in *Studi di diritto internazionale in onore di Gaetano Arangio-Ruiz*, ed. Andrea Giardina and Flavia Lattanzi (Naples: Editoriale Scientifica, 2004), Vol. I, 633.

21. *Jurisdictional Immunities*, Judgment, para, 91.
22. Ibid., at para. 93.
23. See, e.g. A. Ciampi, 'The International Court of Justice between «Reason of State» and Demands for Justice by Victims of Serious International Crimes', *Rivista di diritto Internazionale* 95 (2012): 374; R. Pisillo Mazzeschi, 'Il rapporto fra norme di *ius cogens* e la regola sull'immunità degli Stati: alcune osservazioni critiche sulla sentenza della Corte internazionale di giustizia del 3 febbraio 2012', *Diritti Umani e Diritto Internazionale* 6 (2012): 310; P. Wojcikiewicz Almeida, 'O Caso Imunidades Jurisdicionais do Estado (*Alemanha c. Itália*): A Corte Internacional de Justiça Na Contramão da Evolução do Direito Internacional', *Revista do Instituto Brasileiro de Direitos Humanos* 13 (2013): 371; D. Valadares Vasconcelos Neto, 'O Caso sobre Imunidades de Jurisdição do Estado Perante a Corte Internacional de Justiça', *Revista do Instituto Brasileiro de Direitos Humanos* 13 (2013): 327; L. N. Caldeira Brant and B. de Oliveira Biazatti, 'A Imunidade de Jurisdição dos Estados à luz da Jurisprudência da Corte Europeia de Direitos Humanos e da Corte Internacional de Justiça', *Anuário Brasileiro de Direito Internacional* 20 (2016): 100. See also Talmon, 'Jus Cogens after Germany v. Italy: Substantive and Procedural Rules Distinguished', *Leiden Journal of International Law* 25 (2012): 979; Moser, 'Non-Recognition of State Immunity as a Judicial Countermeasure to Jus Cogens Violations: The Human Rights Answer to the ICJ Decision on the Ferrini Case', *Gottingen Journal of International Law* 4 (2012): 809; Trapp and Mills, 'Smooth Runs the Water Where the Brook is Deep: The Obscured Complexities of Germany v. Italy', *Cambridge Journal of International and Comparative Law* 1 (2012): 153; Linderfalk, 'Jurisdictional Immunities of the State (Germany v. Italy): The Concept of a Normative Conflict Revisited', in *Essays in Honour of Michael Bogdan*, ed. P. Lindskoug, U. Maunsbach and G. Millqvist Juristförl (Visby: Juristförlaget i Lund, 2013), 243.
24. For a survey, see G. Nesi, 'The Quest for a "Full" Execution of the ICJ Judgment in *Germany v. Italy*', *Journal of International Criminal Justice* 11 (2013): 185.
25. Law 14 January 2013, no. 5, Adesione della Repubblica italiana alla Convenzione delle Nazioni Unite sulle immunità giurisdizionali degli Stati e dei loro beni, fatta a New York il 2 dicembre 2004, nonchè norme di adeguamento all'ordinamento interno published in *Gazzetta Ufficiale*, Serie Generale no. 24, 29 January 2013.
26. See F. Maria Palombino, 'Italy's Compliance with ICJ Decisions vs. Constitutional Guarantees: Does the "Counter-Limits" Doctrine Matters?', *The Italian Yearbook of International Law* 22 (2012): 195.
27. See, e.g. ECtHR, *Jones and Others v. The United Kingdom*, applications 34356/06 and 40528/06, Judgment, 14 January 2014. On previous case law on state immunity before the European Court of Human Rights, see Marcella Distefano, 'Immunità degli Stati e art 6 della Convenzione europea dei diritti dell'uomo: coerenza sistemica e garanzie di non impunità' in *Le immunità nel diritto internazionale: Temi scelti*, ed. Alessandra Lanciotti and Attila Tanzi (Turin: Giappichelli, 2007), 117; Alessandra Lanciotti and Antonio Panetta, 'L'immunità dello Stato straniero dalla giurisdizione e il diritto dell'individuo di accesso alla giustizia per violazione dei suoi diritti fondamentali', in *Diritti, principi e garanzie sotto la lente dei giudici di Strasburgo*, ed. Luisa Cassetti (Naples: Jovene, 2012) 335.
28. See A. Bianchi, 'Il tempio e i suoi sacerdoti. Considerazioni su retorica e diritto a margine del caso *Germania c. Italia*', *Diritti umani e diritto internazionale* 6 (2012): 293, 307; Id., 'On Certainty', *EJIL:Talk!*, 16 February 2012, www.ejiltalk.org/on-certainty/.
29. Text in *Rivista di diritto Internazionale*, no. 96 (2015): 23 (unofficial English translation at https://itdpp.files.wordpress.com/2014/11/judgment-238-eng-alessio-gracisnr.pdf).
30. Ibid.
31. See, generally, Palombino, 'Italy's Compliance with ICJ Decisions'.
32. See, generally, C. Focarelli, 'State Immunity and Serious Violations of Human Rights: Judgment No. 238 of 2014 of the Italian Constitutional Court Seven Years On', *The Italian Review of International and Comparative Law* 1 (2021): 29.
33. Italian Constitutional Court, decision no. 238, 2014, para. 3.4.

34. See, e.g. R. Kolb, 'The Relationship between the International and Municipal Legal Order: Reflections on the Decision No 238/2014 of the Italian Constitutional Court' [2014] Questions of International Law, Zoom Out II, 5, http://www.qil-qdi.org/wp-content/uploads/2014/12/02_Constitutional-Court-238-2014_KOLB.pdf; E. Cannizzaro, 'Jurisdictional Immunities and Judicial Protection: The Decision of the Italian Constitutional Court No. 238 of 2014', *Rivista di diritto Internazionale* 96 (2015): 126; M. Longobardo, 'The Italian Constitutional Court's Ruling against State Immunity when International Crimes Occur: Thoughts on Decision no 238 of 2014', *Melbourne Journal of International Law* 16 (2015): 255; A. Tanzi, 'Un difficile dialogo tra Corte internazionale di giustizia e Corte costituzionale', *La Comunità Internazionale* 70 (2015): 13; M. Iovane, 'The Italian Constitutional Court Judgment No. 238 and the Myth of the "Constitutionalization" of International Law', *Journal of International Criminal Justice* 14 (2016): 595; Oellers-Frahm, 'A Never-Ending Story: The International Court of Justice – The Italian Constitutional Court – Italian Tribunals and the Question of Immunity', *Zeitschrift für ausländisches öffentliches Recht und Völkerrecht* 76 (2016): 193; V. Volpe, A. Peters and S. Battini, eds., *Remedies against Immunity? Reconciling International and Domestic Law after the Italian Constitutional Court's Sentenza 238/2014* (Heidelberg: Springer, 2021).
35. *Questions of Jurisdictional Immunities of the State and Measures of Constraint against State-Owned Property (Germany v. Italy)*, Application instituting proceedings and request for the indication of provisional measures, 29 April 2022.
36. Ibid.
37. Decree-Law No 36 of 30 April 2022, converted into law by Law No 79 of 29 June 2022, published in *Gazzetta Ufficiale*, Serie Generale No 150, 29 June 2022.
38. *Questions of Jurisdictional Immunities*, *supra* note 35, Order of 10 May 2022.
39. Tribunale di Roma (Tribunal of Rome), *G. M.T. c. Repubblica Federale di Germania et als.*, order no. 154/22, 1 December 2022, www.sistemapenale.it/pdf_contenuti/1673820179_gazzettaufficiale-ord-nazisti-15422.pdf. For a comment, see P. Caroli, 'Sollevata la questione di costituzionalità della norma istitutiva di un Fondo (italiano) per le vittime dei crimini nazisti', *Sistema Penale*, January 23, 2023, www.sistemapenale.it/it/scheda/caroli-sollevata-qlc-norma-istitutiva-fondo-per-vittime-crimini-nazisti.
40. Italian Constitutional Court, decision no. 159 of 2023, text available at www.cortecostituzionale.it/actionSchedaPronuncia.do?param_ecli=ECLI:IT:COST:2023:159. For a comment, see A. M. Pelliconi, 'The Italian Constitutional Court's New Decision on State Immunity and the ICJ Germany vs Italy No. 2', *EJIL:Talk!* July 28, 2023, https://www.ejiltalk.org/the-italian-constitutional-courts-new-decision-on-state-immunity-and-the-icj-germany-vs-italy-no-2/.
41. See, e.g. K. Oellers-Frahm, 'Questions Relating to the Request for the Indication of Provisional Measures in the Case *Germany v Italy*', *Questions on International Law* 94 (2022): *Zoom-in* 5; R. Pavoni, 'Germany Versus Italy Reloaded: Whither a Human Rights Limitation to State Immunity?', *Questions on International Law* 94 (2022): *Zoom-in* 19.
42. On the evolution of the doctrine of state immunity in Brazil, see L. I. de Amorim Araújo, 'A imunidade de jurisdição trabalhista e o artigo 114 da Constituição', *Revista de Direito do Trabalho* 86 (1994): 37I; A. Cordeiro Pacheco, 'A justiça do trabalho e os entes de direito internacional público', *Revista dos Tribunais* 26 (2000): 211; M. L. Olivar and V. Raizer Borges, 'Las inmunidades de Estado Extranjero en la Pauta del Judiciário Brasileño', *Civil Procedure Review* 4 (2013): 99. Immunity from enforcement is still today considered as absolute.
43. *Changri-La* case, Majority Opinion, 1.
44. *Changri-La* case, Majority Opinion, 30.
45. The thesis (*Tema* 944) adopted by the Court dictates that 'unlawful acts committed by foreign States in violation of human rights do not enjoy immunity from national jurisdiction'. Note, however, that three judges – Mendes, Mello, and De Moraes – attached separate and dissenting opinions indicating that they consider immunity as absolute in cases of *acta jure imperii*.

46. See on the decision A.-T. Saliba and L. C. Lima, 'The Law of State Immunity Before the Brazilian Supreme Court: What is at Stake with the "Changri-La" Case?', *Revista de Direito Internacional* 18 (2021): 52; Id. 'The Immunity Saga Reaches Latin America: The *Changri-La* Case', *EJIL!Talk*, December 2, 2021, https://www.ejiltalk.org/the-immunity-saga-reaches-latin-america-the-changri-la-case/; E. Branca, 'Immunità degli stati e violazioni dei diritti umani. riflessioni a margine della sentenza "*Changri-la*" del Supremo Tribunal Federal brasiliano', *SIDIBlog*, January 24, 2022, http://www.sidiblog.org/2022/01/24/immunita-degli-stati-e-violazioni-dei-diritti-umani-riflessioni-a-margine-della-sentenza-changri-la-del-supremo-tribunal-federal-brasiliano/; V. Terzieva, 'State Immunity and Victims' Right to Access to Court, Reparation and the Truth', *International Criminal Law Review* 22 (2022): 780; Pavoni, 'Germany Versus Italy Reloaded', 34; J. A. Uriarte, 'Inmunidad de jurisdicción y derechos humanos: dos astillas no hacen fuego', *Revista Electrónica de Estudios Internacionales* 43 (2022): 1; S. T. Pereira Cançado Ribeiro, 'Novo caso das Imunidades na Corte Internacional de Justiça: Alemanha reage à Sentença N° 238', *International Law Agendas*, June 5, 2022, http://ila-brasil.org.br/blog/novo-caso-das-imunidades-na-corte-internacional-de-justica-alemanha-reage-a-sentenca-no-238/; E. Cavalcanti de Mello Filho, 'Karla Christina Azeredo Venâncio Da Costa and Others v. Federal Republic of Germany', *American Journal of International Law* 117 (2023): 309.
47. Supremo Tribunal Federal, Segundos Emb.Decl. No Recurso Extraordinário Com Agravo 954.858 Rio De Janeiro, 23 May 2022.
48. Ibid.
49. Processo No. 812/1943, Tribunal Marítimo, Acórdão de 31 de Julho 2001.
50. *Changri-La* case, Majority Opinion, 7–8.
51. Convention (IV) respecting the Laws and Customs of War on Land and its annex: Regulations concerning the Laws and Customs of War on Land. The Hague, 18 October 1907.
52. Convention (XI) relative to certain Restrictions with regard to the Exercise of the Right of Capture in Naval War, The Hague, 18 October 1907.
53. See generally T. Singer, 'Occupation of Sea Territory: Requirements for Military Authority and Comparison to Art. 43 of the Hague Convention IV', in *Operational Law in International Straits and Current Maritime Security Challenges*, ed. J. Schildknecht, R. Dickey, M. Fink and L. Ferris (Cham: Springer, 2018), 255; M. Longobardo, 'The Occupation of Maritime Territory under International Humanitarian Law', *International Law Studies* 95 (2019): 322.
54. The definition of occupied territory is embodied in Article 42 of The Hague Regulations.
55. Agreement for the Prosecution and Punishment of the Major War Criminals of the European Axis, and Charter of the International Military Tribunal. London, 8 August 1945.
56. On the specific issue of intertemporality in the context of the relationship between *jus cogens* and state immunity see F. Marongiu Buonaiuti, 'La sentenza della Corte internazionale di giustizia relativa al caso Germania c. Italia: profili di diritto intertemporale', *Diritti Umani e Diritto Internazionale* 2 (2012): 335; P. B. Stephan, 'The Political Economy of *Jus Cogens*', Public Law and Legal Theory Research Paper Series 2015–48 Law and Economics Research Paper Series 2015–23 (2015), http://ssrn.com/abstract=2623212. This point is also signaled by Branca, , 'Immunità degli stati e violazioni dei diritti umani'.
57. See on this Branca, , 'Immunità degli stati e violazioni dei diritti umani'; Uriarte, 'Inmunidad de jurisdicción y derechos humanos', 19.
58. Cavalcanti, , 'Karla Christina Azeredo Venâncio Da Costa', 313; See also the doubts raised by Saliba and Lima, 'The Immunity', *supra* note 46.
59. Saliba and Lima, 'The Immunity', *supra* note 46.
60. *Changri-La* case, Majority Opinion, 9, 24.
61. *Changri-La* case, Majority Opinion, 22–23. On this specific aspect, Saliba and Lima, 'The Immunity', *supra* note 46; Uriarte, 'Inmunidad de jurisdicción y derechos humanos', 19.
62. *Changri-La* case, Majority Opinion, 24–25.
63. Terzieva, 'State Immunity and Victims' Right to Access to Court', 788.
64. Yet, see below note 68 on the specific approach on the right to truth within the Brazilian domestic legal system.

65. See, e.g. Inter-American Commission on Human Rights Annual Report, 1985–86, AS Doc. No. OEA/Ser.L/V/II.68, Doc. 8 rev. 1, 26 September 1986. See also, *El-Masri v. the former Yugoslav Republic of Macedonia*, European Court of Human Rights, Judgement, 13 December 2012, para. 191: 'the great importance of the present case not only for the applicant and his family, but also for other victims of similar crimes and the general public, who had the right to know what had happened'.
66. In respect to the *Changri-La* case, this has already been noted by Terzieva, 'State Immunity and Victims' Right to Access to Court', 788, who refers to the ICRC Commentary on this matter, that is, C. Pilloud, J. Pictet, Y. Sandoz, and C. Swinarski, *Commentary on the Additional Protocols of 8 June 1977 to the Geneva Conventions of 12 August 1949* (Leiden: Martinus Nijhof Publishers, 1987), para. 1212
67. D. Orentlicher, 'Principle 4', OHCHR, Report Study on the Right to Truth, UN Doc.E/CN.4/2006/91, 8 February 2006. See also P. De Greiff, Report of the Special Rapporteur on the promotion of truth, justice, reparation and guarantees of non-recurrence, UN Doc., A/HRC/24/42, 28 August 2013, and lately UNGA, A/RES/68/165, 18 December 2013.
68. *Case of Ignacio Ellacriaetal v El Salvador*, Inter-American Commission, Report of 22 December 1999; *Kurt v. Turkey*, European Court of Human Rights, Judgment of 25 May 1998. It should be noted that the Brazilian approach to the right to truth is quite specific as it still does not extend to the determination of the criminal responsibility of the (alleged) authors of the relevant violations. In this sense, it is not absolute or inderogable within the Brazilian domestic legal system. See for an extensive analysis C. Osmo, 'Mobilization and Judicial Recognition of the Right to the Truth: The Inter-American Human Rights System and Brazil' in *Comparing Transitions to Democracy. Law and Justice in South America and Europe*, ed. C. Paixão and M. Meccarelli (Cham: Springer, 2021): 137. For a comparison of the IACtHR and the Brazilian judicial decisions on the matter, see also L. Ayres França, 'The Inter-American Court of Human Rights' *Gomes Lund Et Al. (Guerrilha Do Araguaia) V. Brazil* Judgment and the Brazilian Federal Supreme Court Judgment on the Constitutionality and Conventionality of the 1979 Amnesty Law', *Revista Interamericana y Europea de Derechos Humanos* 7, no. 1-2 (2014): 141. The right to truth, however, has been successfully mobilized in domestic civil courts, both as the right for individuals (and specifically family members) and society as a whole to know. As such, this seems in line with the findings of STF in this case as this relates to the right of access to justice, rather than a criminal indictment.
69. Y. Q. Naqvi, 'The Right to the Truth in International Law: Fact or Fiction?', *International Review of the Red Cross* 88 (2006): 245.
70. Art. 4(II) *The Federative Republic of Brazil governs its international relations by the following principles: [...] II – prevalence of human rights.* Constitution of the Federative Republic of Brazil. English Version, Supremo Tribunal Federal, Secretaria de Altos Estudos, Pesquisas e Gestão da Informação, 2022.
71. *Changri-La* case, Majority Opinion, 28, 30.
72. See *infra*, section 4.2.
73. Branca, , 'Immunità degli stati e violazioni dei diritti umani'.
74. *Ferrini* case *supra* note 16, paras. 6–11.
75. See Article 118(3), of the Disposizioni attuative del codice di procedura civile ('Implementig measures of the code of civil procedure').
76. *Changri-La* case, Majority Opinion, 1 March 2021, 12–13.
77. Italian Supreme Court, decision no 1072, 13 January 2009, text in *Rivista di diritto Internazionale* 90 (2009): 618. The *Milde* case is referred to in very generic terms in the Brazilian decision as a '2008' decision, but, in fact, although the case was discussed on 21 October 2008, the judgment was adopted in 2009.
78. *Changri-La* case, Majority Opinion, 12–17.
79. *Changri-La* case, Majority Opinion, 13–16 (with reference to *Jurisdictional Immunities*, Counter-Memorial of Italy, 22 December 2009, 65–67).
80. Ibid., 21–22 (referring to B. Conforti, 'The Judgment of the International Court of Justice on the Immunity of Foreign States: A Missed Opportunity', *Italian Yearbook of International*

Law 21 (2011): 135; De Sena and De Vittor, 'State Immunity and Human Rights'; R. Pavoni, 'An American Anomaly? On the ICJ's Reading of United States Practice in Jurisdictional Immunities of the State', *Italian Yearbook of International Law* 21 (2011): 143.

81. *Changri-La* case, dissenting opinion by O Senhor Ministro Gilmar Mendes, 9–10.
82. Ibid, 26–30.
83. *Changri-La* case, dissenting opinion by O Senhor Ministro Marco Aurélio, 3.
84. Ibid.
85. *Changri-La* case, dissenting opinion by O Senhor Ministro Alexandre de Moraes (who refers to the 2012 ICJ's decision in passing at 10).
86. *Jurisdictional Immunities*, Counter-Memorial of Italy, 22 December 2009, 16; *Milde* case, supra note 77, par. 8
87. On the recent development in the Italian domestic order, with particular reference to the extent and legitimacy of Italian Decree-Law no 36/2022 see Pavoni, , 'Germany Versus Italy Reloaded', 24.
88. As noted ibid., Italian claimants were not successful before German courts. The necessity identified in Italian case-law of *judicial* means of redress for Nazi crimes is thus not automatically generalisable and might be circumscribed to the specific case, allowing instead for non-judicial alternatives means of redress for future cases to satisfy the right to remedy.
89. The literature seems to be prone to acknowledge a right to a *judicial* remedy at an international level in cases of serious human rights violations, while serious international humanitarian law violations wouldn't entail the same right. See recently Terzieva, 'State Immunity and Victims' Right to Access to Court', 800–91.
90. *Changri-La* case, Majority Opinion, 23–24.
91. *Changri-La* case, Majority Opinion, free translation of the authors.
92. See *supra*, section 2.4.
93. See *supra*, section. 3.
94. Saliba and Lima, 'The Immunity', *supra* note 46; Branca, , 'Immunità degli stati e violazioni dei diritti umani', Uriarte, 'Inmunidad de jurisdicción y derechos humanos'.
95. This is the position taken by Uriarte, 'Inmunidad de jurisdicción y derechos humanos', 18.
96. It is interesting to note that a similar reasoning was conducted in the *Milde* case on Article 10 of the Italian Constitution and the constitutional relevance of fundamental human rights vis-à-vis international rules that would be in conflict with them.
97. *Changri-La* case, Majority Opinion, 28.
98. In his dissenting opinion, Judge Mendes criticised the balancing of the different principles in Article 4 of the Constitution, including 'equality among states' as arbitrary in tilting towards the prevalence of human rights.
99. Similarly, albeit somewhat more critical, Cavalcanti, , 'Karla Christina Azeredo Venâncio Da Costa', 314.
100. Saliba and Lima, *The Immunity*, *supra* note 46; Branca, 'Immunità degli stati e violazioni dei diritti umani'.
101. See amongst others G. Binenbojm, 'Monismo E Dualismo No Brasil: Uma Dicotomia Afinal Irrelevante', *Revista da EMERJ* 3 (2000): 180; A. Lipp Pinto Basto Lupi, 'O Brasil é dualista? Anotações sobre a vigência de normas internacionais no ordenamento brasileiro', *Revista de Informação Legislativa* 46 (2009): 29; B. Baía Magalhães, 'O sincretismo teórico na apropriação das teorias monista e dualista e sua questionável utilidade como critério para a classificação do modelo brasileiro de incorporação de normas internacionais', *Revista de Direito Internacional* 12 (2015): 78; A. C. Paulo Pereira and E. Silva Junior, 'Domestic Law an International Law in Brazil', *Panorama of Brazilian Law* 5–6 (2016): 197; A. Silva Oliveira, 'The Normative Hierarchy of Treaties in Brazilian Legal System', *Panorama of Brazilian Law* 9–10 (2018): 245.
102. See amongst others Binenbojm, 'Monismo E Dualismo No Brasil'; Magalhães, , 'O sincretismo teórico na apropriação das teorias'; M. Ariosi, *Conflitos entre tratados internacionais e leis internas: o judiciário brasileiro e a nova ordem internacional* (Rio de Janeiro: Renovar, 2000); N. Araujo and I. da Matta Andreiuolo, 'A Internalização dos Tratados no Brasil e os Direitos Humanos', in *Os Direitos Humanos e o Direito Internacional*, ed. C. Eduardo de

A. Boucault (Rio de Janeiro: Renovar, 1999), 82; H. Accioly, G.E. Nascimento e Silva, P. Borba Casella, *Manual de Direito Internacional Público*, 25th ed. (São Paulo: Saraiva Jur, 2021), chapter 2.4.

103. See e.g. ADI 1480 MC, Relator(a): Min. CELSO DE MELLO, Tribunal Pleno, julgado em 04/09/1997, DJ 18-05-2001 PP-00429 EMENT VOL-02031-02 PP-00213.
104. A. A. Cançado Trindade, 'Memorial em prol de uma nova mentalidade quanto à proteção dos direitos humanos nos planos internacional e nacional', *Boletim da Sociedade Brasileira de Direito Internacional* 113–118 (1998): 88–89. See Silva Oliveira, 'The Normative Hierarchy of Treaties in Brazilian Legal System', 254.
105. A. A. Cançado Trindade, *Tratado de Direito Internacional dos Direitos Humanos* (Porto Alegre: Fabris Editor, 2003), 403; V. de Oliveira Mazzuoli, *Curso de direito internacional público* (São Paulo: Editora Revista dos Tribunais, 2011), 90.
106. See e.g. Magalhães, 'O sincretismo teórico na apropriação das teorias', 78.
107. C. R. Husek, *Curso de Direito Internacional Público* (São Paulo: Imprenta, 2017), 67–68.
108. Lupi, 'O Brasil é dualista?' 34–35.
109. Husek, *Curso de Direito Internacional Público*, 68: – 'the practice [*of customary international law]* has no possibility to be contradicted' (free translation of the authors).
110. Many scholars consider the categorisation deprived of any analytical function by now and suggest letting the interpretation be guided by the most favourable rule doctrine (see Magalhães, 'O sincretismo teórico na apropriação das teorias', 92; Binenbojm, 'Monismo E Dualismo No Brasil'). In fact, in the context of the *Changri-la* case, recent literature opines that the decision goes beyond matters of mere dualism or conflict between constitutional and international law; '[t]he Brazilian Constitution provides for how the international legal order must be apprehended by organs in the Brazilian legal order—specifically by prioritizing human rights' (Cavalcanti, 'Karla Christina Azeredo Venâncio Da Costa', 311).

Acknowledgements

Thanks to Paula Wojcikiewicz Almeida and Lucas Carlos Lima for their feedback on previous drafts. Marco wishes to thank Lucas De Bragança Freixo for his help in understanding Italian-Brazilian dialogues and encounters. The usual disclaimer applies.

Disclosure statement

No potential conflict of interest was reported by the author(s).

OPEN ACCESS

Comparing universal jurisdiction in Europe and in Latin America: A vehicle for international justice or for colonial reckoning?

Alexandra Fowler

ABSTRACT

A particular concern in recent years has been the limited options for prosecutions of persons responsible for atrocities in States not amenable to ICC jurisdiction. The need for accountability for atrocities builds on long histories of human rights and humanitarian law practice, both treaty-based and customary in nature, which has been driven also by the work of the ECtHR and the IACtHR mechanisms. At the domestic level, ever since the Pinochet decision, universal jurisdiction (UJ) has been considered a promising way to fill the lacuna. Indeed, some commentators have observed a resurgence in the use of UJ in recent years based on a number of trials of ex-ISIS and Syrian regime members in European courts. Yet UJ as it has been practised has serious limitations. While there are exceptions, many European states are steadily turning the exercise of UJ into the application of extraterritorial jurisdiction based on active or passive personality, especially in relation to their former colonies. In Latin America too, there have been some recent examples of investigations and prosecutions on the basis of 'pure' UJ, but the vast majority of exercises of jurisdiction are in furtherance of extraditions, particularly at the behest of former colonial powers. This article compares the recent uptick in European and Latin American usages of UJ, concluding that to date both regions still exhibit little appetite for pursuing 'pure' UJ. It warns that significant colonialist pressures in both regions threaten to limit this crucial mechanism for international justice.

1. Introduction

International criminal law depends to a large degree on nation States being primarily responsible for carrying out justice for the most serious international crimes. The availability of universal jurisdiction ('UJ') is crucial in the fight against impunity, as the idea that war-torn States would or could hold independent and credible trials to international standards – even of the worst perpetrators – is often quite fantastical. Furthermore, international criminal tribunals often lack the capacity to bring defendants to justice and have significant jurisdictional limitations, putting those responsible for offences beyond their reach.

Although a number of European States have exercised UJ against foreign accused and the number of cases has been on the rise, the practice of UJ has not blossomed as expected. UJ is still overwhelmingly exercised by a minority within Europe, and despite promising advances in recent years in which a variety of States have relied on a form of UJ to bring charges against foreign accused, UJ has generally been exercised by former colonial powers when the victims have been their nationals. Further, when the accused is a national of the forum State, the State has focused on bringing charges other than for international crimes. In Latin America too, a small minority of States has been active in bringing UJ cases and the colonial link is also apparent, as Latin American States have overwhelmingly been concerned with bringing charges against accused from their former colonial powers for atrocities committed against their nationals.

This article argues that although 'UJ' – albeit in many cases more correctly forms of extraterritorial jurisdiction – is on the rise in both Europe and Latin America, it risks continuing to become a form of colonial score-settling unless all States embrace the opportunity it affords to become a mechanism for truly universal justice. Part 2 of the article gives an introductory overview of the nature of UJ, while Part 3 examines the exercise of UJ in Europe, from Belgium's flagship legislation through to recent colonial exercises of UJ. Part 4 examines Latin America's practice of UJ, particularly that of Argentina which has been most active. Part 5 looks at both regions' recent approach toward using UJ to address atrocities in Africa, highlighting again the risks of being seen to dispense justice infused with colonialism. Part 6 concludes that UJ in both Europe and Latin America need a reset to avoid being characterised more often than not as exercises of parochialism.

2. An overview of universal jurisdiction

UJ in its pure form allows a forum State to bring to trial accused persons who are not its nationals in circumstances where the victim is also not a national and the alleged crime did not occur in the forum. The international crimes subject to UJ include grave breaches of the *Geneva Conventions* (war crimes),[1] genocide (as per the *Genocide Convention*[2]), and torture (as per the *Torture Convention*[3]). The requirement to investigate and, if appropriate, prosecute or to extradite to another State willing and able to do so (*aut dedere aut judicare)* has also entered into customary international humanitarian law. Although crimes against humanity are not yet the object of a distinct convention, those States and academic writers who claim the right to act unilaterally to assert UJ over persons committing such acts invoke the concept of acting as 'agents for the international community'.[4] As further noted in the Separate Opinion of Judges Higgins, Kooijmans and Buergenthal in the *Arrest Warrant case*,

> '[w]hile no general rule of positive international law can as yet be asserted which gives to States the right to punish foreign nationals for crimes against humanity in the same way

> as they are, for instance, entitled to punish acts of piracy, there are clear indications pointing to the gradual evolution of a significant principle of international law to that effect'.[5]

At the base of UJ is international agreement that some crimes are so heinous that the entire international community has an interest in their suppression. The Separate Opinion also stated that although there was no duty to extend national jurisdiction to cases where the alleged crime occurred outside its territory and its nationals were not involved, States may choose to do so. That is,

> '[t]hat there is no established practice in which States exercise universal jurisdiction, properly so called, is undeniable. As we have seen, virtually all national legislation envisages links of some sort to the forum State; and no case law exists in which pure universal jurisdiction has formed the basis of jurisdiction. This does not necessarily indicate, however, that such an exercise would be unlawful'.[6]

Additionally, there was nothing in national case law which evidenced an *opinio juris* on the illegality of UJ. The PCIJ in the *Lotus Case* had earlier confirmed that international law allowed States 'a wide measure of discretion' to extend their jurisdiction as far as they wish, providing they do not fall foul of any prohibitive rule.[7]

Further, the Separate Opinion stated that no territorial presence is required for the exercise of jurisdiction where the offence violates the fundamental interests of the international community. States may exercise UJ as long as procedural safeguards for the defendant are respected, which include first offering the State of nationality the chance to prosecute, and ensuring there is independence of the prosecuting authority from the political arm of the State.[8] Much lies within the discretion of Public Prosecutors;

> '[i]n common law and civil law legal systems it is the responsibility of the Public Prosecutor to determine whether the prosecution of an international crime is pursued. The level of this discretionary power and the considerations to be taken into account in making the decision vary [considerably] from State to State'.[9]

In the UK, for example, the consent of the Director of Public Prosecutions is required in order for an arrest warrant to be issued against persons accused of having committed grave breaches of the *Geneva Conventions*.[10] The decision to launch a case thus depends *inter alia* on to what extent the Public Prosecutor is independent from his/her government, as well as naturally being influenced by bilateral or other political imperatives.[11]

While membership of the *Rome Statute of the International Criminal Court* has seen all European States adopt (in the cases of Denmark and Italy, be in the process of adopting) legislation defining war crimes, crimes against humanity and genocide,[12] there is some variation in the crimes provided for. Belgium, Switzerland and the Netherlands are well known as having enacted legislation enabling the prosecution of international crimes committed during non-international armed conflict, while other European States have not. In Latin America, many States have dictated provisions on UJ mostly on the basis of conventional obligations, and sometimes over crimes under customary law, such as piracy or the slave trade.[13] A couple of States in the European and Latin American spheres have provided for UJ for acts not yet widely regarded as international crimes, such as ecocide (Belarus and Colombia),[14] while Costa Rica's law allows UJ for terrorism and its financing as well as for international crimes.[15]

All that said, Principle 1 of the *Princeton Principles on Universal Jurisdiction* (2001)[16] makes clear that the person needs to be present before the competent judicial body. This clearly eschews cases of UJ *in absentia.* Indeed, many States do require at least a custodial nexus to exercise UJ. Yet even if the State has the accused in custody, this does not mean that a prosecution will go ahead. In some States it is possible for an individual or a group to initiate proceedings in respect of an extraterritorial crime; indeed, some of the most prominent early examples of UJ cases commenced in this manner. In fact in some (European) jurisdictions (Belgium and others) some of the most prominent examples of UJ were launched by individuals or victims' groups. Unfortunately, however, this mechanism has now for the most part been closed off under political pressure.

Regardless of the clear existence of the principle in both customary and conventional international law, it is up to each individual State as to whether it legislates for UJ, whether it covers crimes committed only during international conflict or also crimes committed in non-international conflicts, or only certain crimes. This of course reflects the fact that domestic implementation is not necessary under international law. Although technically UJ does not depend on the enactment of national legislation, Principle 3 of the *Princeton Principles* reminds States that their national judicial organs may rely on UJ even if their national legislation does not specifically provide for it.

That said, having laws on the books is crucial so that the domestic prosecution and trial process can go ahead smoothly. Following a major international survey in 2012 Amnesty International concluded that 163 countries allowed UJ over at least one crime under international law[17] – torture, war crimes, crimes against humanity, genocide (or the traditional one, piracy) – although this figure includes States which have had to enact implementing legislation in accordance with their membership of the *Rome Statute,* which does not equate to UJ *per se.*[18]

3. Defining UJ in Europe

3.1. Revision

Critics have cautioned that UJ may be applied, not in the pursuit of international justice, but to serve the interests of powerful Western States. For example, Kontorovich writes that 'far from being used as a tool of global policing, the UJ doctrine is, in practice, used to protect the parochial domestic interests of the prosecuting [S]tate'; this being because despite the promise of justice for international crimes in unconnected jurisdictions, in 'the overwhelming majority of cases' the forum State actually has a direct, differentiable, parochial connection with the offense.[19] So while the nominal purpose of UJ is to allow States to prosecute crimes without any nexus to the offense – to enforce a truly global legal order – in practice it has often been used by States in cases where a nexus (particularly a parochial – even colonial – one) exists.[20]

This criticism is well-founded. For example, Italy has been concerned with bringing the perpetrators of Latin American atrocities to justice in exercises of jurisdiction on the basis of passive personality. In late 1992 there was the discovery in a police station in Asunción of the 'Archives of Terror', which described the fate of tens of thousands of Latin Americans secretly kidnapped, tortured and murdered by the armed forces and the secret services of Chile, Argentina, Uruguay, Paraguay, Bolivia and Brazil during *Operation Condor* (the U.S. counterinsurgency strategy implemented in Latin America during the 1970s and 1980s). Italian prosecutors initiated a criminal investigation into the disappearance and murder of dozens of Italians who had been among the *Condor* victims,[21] and finally, in 2021 Italy's Supreme Court confirmed the conviction and life sentences of 14 former security officials and military personnel from Chile and Uruguay.[22]

Spain has also been active, but this has not been without a colonial context – it was Spain's own marginalisation of indigenous communities in pre-independence societies that laid the seeds for later political repression, thereby giving rise to future atrocities cases. Indeed, Guatemalan courts have reasoned that the extreme violence perpetrated on indigenous Mayans in Guatemala was the product of the racism that has marked relations with Guatemala's indigenous peoples dating from Spanish colonial times.[23] So while Spain is prominent in dispensing justice, this clearly suggests its responsibility at least in moral terms. To this extent, Spain prosecuting Latin American crimes could thus be viewed as an attempt to remedy in part its own past failings – or less charitably, to police those post-colonial governments.

Spain's liberal *Ley Orgánica del Poder Judicial* (LOPJ – Organic Law of the Judicial Power) was passed in 1985 and granted Spanish courts' jurisdiction over international crimes in *any* territory.[24] The first use of this law was the prosecution of Adolfo Scilingo – in 2007 the Spanish Supreme Court found Scilingo guilty of crimes against humanity and sentenced him to 1084 years in jail.[25] The case '… marked the first time in history a national court had processed and convicted an individual for crimes against humanity committed in another country'.[26] Following this case, Spain went on to successfully prosecute another Argentinian, Christian von Wernich, a former police chaplain, for his role in 'Dirty War' disappearances, torture and killings.[27] Victims groups then pushed for Spain to assert jurisdiction over General Augusto Pinochet for (*inter alia*) crimes against humanity against Peruvian indigenous communities during the 1960s and 1970s.[28]

Spain's UJ law has also been used for crimes in Guatemala. The early case of *Menchu Tum v Montt* (the *Guatemalan Genocide Case*) was brought in Spanish courts against former Guatemalan Head of State Efrain Rios Montt, for international crimes committed against the indigenous Mayan Ixil community. In contrast to the successful outcome in *Pinochet*, the Spanish Audiencia Nacional and Tribunal Superior construed the LOPJ to require a link to Spain,[29] butthis stance was reversed on appeal to the Spanish Constitutional Court[30], which fully endorsed the principle of 'pure' UJ, stating that international justice was 'a shared interest of all States'.[31]

Notwithstanding the Spanish Constitutional Court's endorsement of UJ, in 2014 Spain adopted legislation curtailing the LOPJ by excluding the possibility of conducting trials *in absentia*.[32] In 2020, Spain was able to extradite former El Salvadoran Army Colonel Inocente Montano Morale, formerly El Salvador's Deputy Minister for Public Security, from the US to stand trial for the 1989 killings of five Spanish Jesuit priests.[33] This prosecution proceeded with the accused in custody and on the basis of passive personality, which reflected the more parochial Spanish approach to jurisdiction in recent years.

The fate of Belgium's formerly very liberal UJ law is well-known,[34] but it should also be noted that other European States (such as Germany[35] and Sweden[36]) as well as the UK[37] also used to have expansive views on legal reach in their domestic laws.

However, in the years in the wake of the Belgian example they either saw no motivation to use them or found grounds to cut back on prosecutions by adopting measures such as requiring the suspect's presence in the forum, requiring government approval[38] or other conditions to be satisfied,[39] or deferring to foreign policy priorities.[40] As such, many European States have enacted or amended their law to only the minimum required by international law to meet the requirements of the *Geneva Conventions*, which requires the prosecution of crimes committed on its own territory or by its own nationals in foreign fora. Adanan asserts that '[t]hese legislative changes are the result of the deterioration in international relations with [S]tates whose nationals were the subject of [UJ] proceedings'[41] – this is clearly the case for some high-profile examples, but it should be noted that the central obligation of the *Ljubljana-The Hague Convention on International Cooperation in the Investigation and Prosecution of the Crime of Genocide, Crimes against Humanity, War Crimes and other International Crimes*, adopted in Slovenia in 2023, requires States to establish jurisdiction over defendants found on their territory (unless they extradite or surrender them to an international tribunal) – this is another indication that UJ is now only required in less than its 'pure' form.

For its part, the European Court of Human Rights (ECtHR) has assisted European states' application of their extraterritorial criminal laws. The main issue in contention in UJ cases in the ECtHR has been the principle of legality in Article 7 of the *European Convention on Human Rights and Fundamental Freedoms* (no retroactive application of criminal law, and criminal law and penalties are accessible and foreseeable), where the Court's rulings in such cases as *Kolk and Kislyiy v Estonia*[42] and *Kononov v Latvia*[43] have upheld the State's interpretation of its obligations. As far as genocide goes, in *Jorgic v Germany* the Court confirmed the State's position that it had the *erga omnes* obligation to punish genocide and could thus exercise its UJ on an extraterritorial basis and regardless of the nationality of the accused, thus confirming the position of other national and international courts.[44] This was a useful reaffirmation of the content of extraterritorial jurisdiction for genocide. Whilst many member States of the *Convention* now allow for UJ for genocide by foreigners of foreigners in foreign territory, at least if the accused is within the jurisdiction, only very few cases – such as those under Spain's previously liberal law (notably *Pinochet*) – have actually been brought.

Thus there is mounting evidence that over the first two decades of the twenty-first century the practice of UJ in Europe has evolved into a more conservative and limited form – one that has not taken advantage of the rich opportunity envisaged in the *Arrest Warrant Case*.

3.3. Resurgence?

In Europe there has however been a recent reversal of this apparent trend. Over the past 15 years Langer and Eason have noted that the geographical distribution of UJ complaints within Europe has shifted. They note that the number of complaints filed in Belgium and Spain has dropped sharply (this tallies with the introduction of legislation limiting the use of previously liberal laws in those two States). Interestingly however, Germany and France are now hosting significant numbers of cases, and the Nordic States –Denmark, Finland, Iceland, Norway and Sweden – have also quietly assumed a more significant role.[45]

Nearly all accused have been non-State actors, African figures (government and militia), and former Syrian government officials. In 2019 there were 22 countries of commission, 16 countries of prosecution and at least 207 persons under investigation. Eleven accused were on trial, and 16 had been convicted. These numbers represented an increase of 40% over the figures in 2018.[46] Just in relation to Syria, in 2020 there were 25 ongoing cases against former Syrian officials in Austria, France, Hungary, the Netherlands, Norway, Spain and Sweden, with four resulting in convictions and another three at the trial stage.[47] Overall, there has been an increase of roughly 500 cases in total between 2019 and 2022.[48] In 2023 trials or appeal hearings were to take place in Finland, France, Germany and Sweden for crimes allegedly committed in Rwanda, Sierra Leone, Sudan, and Syria.[49]

While these figures suggest a resurgence for UJ, the reality is more nuanced. For instance, many convictions in recent years in European courts, particularly those in Germany and France,[50] of suspects bearing the nationality of the forum State have in fact been for terrorism, not for international crimes.[51] For instance in Germany, it is reported that since 2015 there have been more than 32 convictions of female former ISIS members for terrorism, but only a tiny minority for international crimes of genocide or crimes against humanity.[52] Paulet gives a number of reasons for this:

> 'In many States [for instance the UK, Germany and Switzerland] the same units are in charge of prosecuting both types of crimes ... In the context of scarce resources, it is a zero-sum game: prosecutions for terrorism multiply at the expense of prosecutions for international crimes'. After all, prosecutions for international crimes are long and complex, requiring significant expertise and resources – 'more elements must be proved, and prosecutors are usually required to find and interview witnesses and survivors abroad, collect evidence in a context with which they are unfamiliar – and sometimes even conduct their investigations without seeing the crime scenes at all'.[53]

The same fact circumstances may be insufficient to prove international crimes but may lead to a conviction for terrorism-related offences. This makes sense, as many States have a much lower threshold for terrorism than for war crimes or crimes against humanity. Again, as noted by Paulet:

> 'States have increasingly prosecuted suspects under charges of terrorism rather than international crimes. [This is an] apparently reasonable choice: suspects appear faster in court, after shorter investigations requiring fewer resources. And yet ... terrorism and international crimes have fundamentally different legal bases and using the former to the detriment of the latter comes with significant drawbacks'.

The drawbacks are several – first, laws against terrorism do not cover atrocities committed by State agents. Similarly, charges of terrorism do not encompass the full scope of human rights violations entailed in international definitions of war crimes, crimes against humanity or genocide (for instance, the targeting of a particular ethnic group is not punished by terrorism charges *per se*). While obtaining terrorism convictions appears more attractive from a domestic political perspective, not prosecuting them *as international crimes* diminishes the importance of such crimes. Additionally, as terrorism is a threat to State security whereas international crimes often target individuals, this means a much-reduced role for victims (as initiators of prosecutions, and as providers of testimony) in the prosecution of such crimes, and less consideration of satisfaction and justice for those harmed.[54] The exception is where 'cumulative charging' has been employed – where charges for international crimes are added to the existing principal charge of terrorism. This has been employed in a minority of cases to date – most recently in the Islamic State-related *Jennifer W*,[55] *Nadine K*[56] and *Taha al-Jumailly*[57] cases – and there is much scope for an increase in this practice.

As far as prosecutions of non-nationals and non-residents go, Germany has also been active.[58] Germany's interest in flexing its prosecutorial muscle has been heightened with the entry into the country of nearly one million migrants from conflict zones, especially Syria. Among the arrivals have been witnesses and victims as well as some perpetrators, making it much easier to prosecute cases. The result has been a slew of low-level cases in German courts, such as that of Eyad al-Gharib[59] and that of Anwar Raslan.[60] These investigations have been assisted by the fact that since 2011 German authorities have maintained a 'structural investigation' into State-sponsored war crimes in Syria,[61] as well as into alleged crimes by Islamic State.

While the German law is liberal on the face of it, it has (like the revised Belgian law and the French, Swiss and Spanish laws) been fettered by the requirements that firstly, the case cannot proceed without the suspect's presence in Germany, and secondly, the Federal Prosecutor must agree to open any UJ case. Regarding the latter, to date there has been great reluctance on the part of the Federal Prosecutor to investigate or bring cases targeting high-ranking foreign officials, particularly if the case may involve 'extraordinary rendition'.[62] This is so even in cases where Germany has had a direct interest (on the basis of passive personality), such as against former U.S. Defence Secretary Donald Rumsfeld for the bungled 2003 kidnapping and 'enhanced interrogation' of German national Khaled el-Masri in Skopje, Macedonia, and in Afghanistan.[63] Bucking this trend is a rare case filed in March 2021 by Reporters Without Borders against Saudi Crown Prince Mohammed bin Salman for the murder of reporter Jamal Khashoggi and the detention of dozens of other journalists; clearly the Federal Prosecutor's agreement to proceed was due to a perception that Germany had 'safety in numbers' with other governments. (that said, the forum requirement must still be met, thus making the Crown Prince's actual prosecution unlikely).

Apart from cooperation with other European powers, France has hosted its own UJ litigation against a range of Syrian figures found in France, the latest being the *Nema* and *Chaban* cases in the Cour de Cassation.[64] Although French UJ law is confusing and contains a number of restrictive pre-conditions to the exercise of jurisdiction, the law has also been flexed in recent years in bringing a range of suspects in its former African colonies to justice. Most recently, in July 2022 a French court found a former Rwandan prefect guilty of complicity in genocide and crimes against humanity committed during the Rwandan genocide in 1994. This was followed in November 2022 by the conviction of the former Liberian commander of the ULIMO rebel group for crimes against humanity and torture committed during the first Liberian civil war (1989–1996).[65]

Overall, a renaissance for UJ in Europe in terms of numbers may be indicated,[66] but it is clear that European UJ in recent years has often been focused on other crimes, operates within limited circumstances, and plays it safe with prosecutions of persons from former colonies – assuming they can be found in the forum. This dovetails with Langer's observation of Europe's general move away from an interventionist 'global enforcer' model of

UJ in which States have a role in preventing and punishing the commission of core international crimes committed anywhere in the world, towards a 'no safe haven' model as resources are devoted almost exclusively to prosecutions involving defendants who are residents, asylum seekers or people otherwise present in their territories.[67] That is, the exercise of nationality or passive personality jurisdiction, not UJ as such.

4. Latin American perceptions and practice of UJ

4.1. Renewal?

In their 2019 paper Langer and Eason however documented 'a quiet expansion' in the use of UJ globally – that is, there have been setbacks for UJ in parts of Western Europe, but 'this same period has seen breakthroughs in the use of this practice elsewhere in the world as a growing number of States – in both the developed and developing world – have hosted or undertaken UJ litigation'.[68] Moreover, these are not just initial complaints and investigations, but formal prosecutions and even trials. Part of the reason for this is a search by victims and NGOs for new venues to bring cases, and an 'extraterritorial backfire effect' against certain European States, Spain in particular.[69]

As mentioned already, Latin America has laboured under a lengthy history of colonial oppression and exploitation (three centuries of Spanish and Portuguese rule), the deficits of which in many respects set its societies up for long-term social and political conflict, such as the anti-revolutionary military regimes and civil conflict of the 1970s and 1980s.[70] During this era, many countries suffered mass civilian casualties from gross human rights abuses (torture, disappearances, crackdowns on dissent), which were followed by a slew of generous amnesty provisions for senior and even junior junta officials alike which appeared to put accountability for any of these atrocities out of reach. Since the brutal 'State terrorism' of '*Operation Condor*',[71] most Latin American countries have made significant efforts to break with their autocratic pasts and are now firmly committed to democratic ideals and the protection of human rights.[72] Even so, making headway on justice, peace and reconciliation has been difficult due to a range of post-conflict intractabilities.[73]

One indication of this about-face is that many countries in the region are embracing the ICC's complementarity scheme (to promote, progress, and buttress existing domestic legal institutions in order to prosecute/prevent international crimes), as well as the norms of the Inter-American legal system in-order to realign themselves with the international community. For its part, the Inter-American Commission on Human Rights (IACHR) has noted that only the proper utilisation of the domestic judicial system to investigate, prosecute, and (if necessary) punish, will suffice to achieve full and comprehensive justice for the domestic population.[74] As such, countries previously unwilling to address past human rights violations have now committed themselves to the *Rome Statute of the ICC*[75] and to international justice.

With the signing of the Inter-American Democratic Charter on 11 September 2001 Organisation of American States (OAS) member States (including all of Latin America except for Cuba) committed not only to maintaining and strengthening democracy, but also to enshrining the essential elements of a democracy. Examples include the respect for human rights and fundamental freedoms, the exercise of power on the basis of the rule of law and popular will, and the transparency of government activities.[76] Additionally, the IACHR has been increasingly active (albeit from a low base) in support of human rights in the region, and the Inter-American Court of Human Rights (IACtHR) has reached a series of significant decisions on the State's obligations regarding fundamental human rights.[77]

This volume of activity has had an impact within individual States themselves, helping their own reckonings with the past and strengthening their internal justice and accountability systems. For example, the *Pinochet* trial in the UK was a significant external stimulus for Chile which, in the years since, has taken key steps toward accountability for crimes during the Pinochet era. Argentinian legislators have nullified their country's amnesty laws and judges have been emboldened to prosecute members of the former military junta, including those still serving. Delagrange notes that Chile and Argentina's monist constitutional structures (which allow international conventions to have constitutional weight and thus place a premium on international law) have assisted this process.[78] The discovery of the *Operation Condor* abuses has helped to catalyse a series of cases reckoning with the past, particularly in Chile and Argentina. In the IACtHR *Case of Goiburu et al v Paraguay* the State's acquiescence was considered as a 'positive contribution to these proceedings' which allowed the truth of the facts and merits of the case to be put on record, thus allowing a form of reparation and satisfaction for victims as well as a way of helping to prevent similar acts from occurring.[79]

Yet Latin America's nouveau internationalist motivation has often been accompanied by bureaucratic inefficiencies in particular and/or the caveat that the past be hidden behind a veil of immunity. Passing legislation that will effectively implement obligations regarding international crimes and requirements regarding privileges and immunities has been a difficult process for many Latin American States.[80] This is despite the fact that the IACtHR affirmed in *Goiburu* the *jus cogens* nature of full jurisdictional assistance in bringing such crimes to justice.[81] There are a number of issues inhibiting Latin American States' full adherence to the *Rome Statute*, among them issues regarding compatibility with domestic constitutions on issues such as life sentences, extradition of nationals, and of course, amnesty laws. Even Latin American States which have ratified the *Rome Statute* have been slow to adopt implementing legislation due to strong hegemonic pressure from the U.S., as well as internal pressure from domestic factions fearing prosecution.[82] Although UJ exists separately from ICC jurisdiction,[83] this has also been so for UJ cases in domestic courts. Mendez and Tinajero-Esquivel note this two-faced approach as follows:

> 'Many [Latin American] countries have proclaimed their adherence to international human rights treaties, and some have even included these principles in their constitutions. Many Latin American countries have taken other important steps toward taking their international human rights obligations seriously. Yet when ... Pinochet was arrested in London on October 16, 1998, Latin America rallied behind Chile in public opposition to any notion of extra-territorial criminal jurisdiction'.[84]

It is against this backdrop that a number of Latin American States have taken tentative steps forward with the passage of legislation allowing UJ over war crimes and crimes against humanity.[85] The clear standout is Argentina. Historically, Argentina has applied the territoriality principle of jurisdiction, even 'though it has long been party to treaties that include extraterritorial provisions.[86] Argentina was one of the 'like-minded' States that pressed for the creation of the ICC and it was one of the most active during the drafting and negotiation phase in Rome. Argentina signed and ratified the *Rome Statute* early and passed domestic implementing legislation, although it has had limited dealings with the ICC since.[87] Despite this internationalist bent, Argentina has no domestic legislation explicitly providing for UJ; rather, it relies on s118 of its Constitution which envisages trials for crimes 'committed outside the territory of the Nation against public international law' (*crímenes contra el derecho de gentes*), irrespective of where the crimes are committed.[88] Up until 2021, Argentina had conducted 96 investigations on the basis of UJ.

The first was when a group of victims of Franco-era crimes in Spain initiated proceedings before the Argentine courts. The first instance judge at the time closed the case on the basis of a lack of jurisdiction, but the Court of Appeal reversed that decision.[89] Accordingly, Rodolfo Martín Villa, Spain's Interior Minister from 1976-1979, was indicted on four counts of aggravated homicide. However, efforts since to have the accused detained in Madrid and extradited to Argentina have been fruitless due to Spain's amnesty law. It is reportedly unlikely that the case will proceed, which is a deeply disappointing outcome considering the 'hundreds' of Franco-era Spanish victims who had placed their hopes in this fledgling attempt at UJ[90] (even 'though the indictment was not for international crimes *per se*).

There have been other notable cases. In 2009 an Argentinian judge asked for Interpol arrest warrants to be issued for former Chinese President Jiang Zemin and former State Security chief Luo Gan for crimes against humanity in relation to the persecution of the Falun Gong movement.[91] China was of course critical of the move, and requested it be 'properly handled' in advance of the then upcoming visit of Argentina's President to China.[92] Indeed, it appears that the case has been dropped as there has been no progress since.

In late 2018 Human Rights Watch lodged a case with Argentinian authorities against Saudi Crown Prince Mohammed bin Salman for alleged war crimes in Yemen, for the torture of Saudi nationals and for the murder of reporter Jamal Khashoggi. The case was apparently motivated by the opportunity afforded by the Crown Prince's then imminent visit to Buenos Aires for the G20 summit.[93] However, while inquiries were being made of Turkey, Yemen and Saudi Arabia (among others) to ascertain whether investigations were taking place there, the Crown Prince left Argentina. Argentinian prosecuting authorities sent a rogatory commission to Turkey in September 2021, but there has been little further progress on the case.

The most recent Argentinian case has concerned the persecution of the Rohingya people in Myanmar. In 2019 the Burmese Rohingya Organisation UK (BROUK) filed a lawsuit before Argentinian courts against senior Myanmar officials (including former State Councillor Aung San Suu Kyi) for alleged genocide and crimes against humanity.[94] After initial uncertainties about overlap with the ICC investigation,[95] testimony has since been taken remotely from six survivors of sexual assault.[96] The Argentine investigation is proceeding in parallel with the ICC's work, which actualises the call by the UN Fact-Finding Mission on Myanmar for UN member States to exercise jurisdiction (including UJ) to investigate and prosecute serious international crimes as part of wider efforts to bring the Myanmar officials responsible to justice.[97]

It might be said that going after international crimes is a way of deflecting political attention from Argentina's own unfinished reckonings with the past. It may be a case of judges using liberal forum laws to go after low-hanging fruit. Perhaps it is a way of fulfilling justice and democratic longings, as expressed through Argentina's affiliation with ICC and IACHR ideals. Or perhaps it is about strengthening Argentina's own internal processes by using domestic processes to realise justice for atrocities elsewhere; as Roht-Arriaza has observed, '[t]ransnational prosecutions can catalyse domestic prosecutions'.[98] This may mean Argentina's usage of UJ could also benefit other Latin American States by helping to build a region intolerant of future abuse.

4.2. Reluctance

All that said, and perhaps reflecting its geopolitical position, Argentina's relatively regular flexing of its UJ muscles have not yet resulted in any substantive trials, much less convictions. Further, it is clear that there has not been any invocation of UJ by other Latin American States to anywhere near the same extent as has occurred in Argentina.

Chehtman notes that Latin American States have constantly had to face different forms of imperialistic influences and interventions – at first it was European conquest, then the threat of recolonisation. In the twentieth century there was an increasingly interventionist U.S. (the Monroe doctrine and the Roosevelt corollary, as well as direct and indirect interventions in Latin America during the Cold War, including *Operation Condor*), and in the twenty-first century the U.S. has made it its policy to thwart the ICC wherever it has attempted to grow roots.[99] This has been no more apparent than in the U.S.' approach toward Latin America and the OAS,[100] and despite the fact that past case law of the U.S. itself has on occasion invoked UJ.[101] At the same time, Latin American States have faced serious challenges from within their borders by radical dissident political groups and criminal organisations. All these influences have shaped Latin American States in similar ways, such as prompting them to be historically strong defenders of the principle of non-intervention in their internal affairs.[102]

While many Latin American States have introduced provisions on UJ into their Criminal Codes, mostly on the basis of treaty obligations and sometimes over crimes under customary law (such as piracy or the slave trade),[103] several of these extensions are connected (predictably) to U.S. policy such as its 'war on drugs', its 'war on terror', and its fight against corruption.[104] Indeed, there are a number of instances in recent years where the U.S. has managed to pressure different Latin American States to extradite defendants to stand trial in U.S. courts in pursuit of these agendas, although in many of these instances the relevant Latin American government has used the U.S.' hegemonic reach for its own interests (domestically to neutralise rival political influences or cover up scandals, or bilaterally to win favours such as trade agreements or economic aid).[105] There are also instances where Latin American States have managed to thwart U.S. efforts through 'covert blocking' (that is, utilising arguments which seek to minimise political confrontation with the U.S. administration, while not complying with US extradition requests).[106] Although Latin American States keenly reject outside pressure, their resistance to U.S. efforts 'seems largely based on the economic or political capital of individual defendants, rather than on some form of anti-imperialist or regionalist sensibilities'.[107]

Even so, on paper Latin American States appear to have embraced extraterritoriality (on the basis of active and passive personality) with 'remarkable enthusiasm', despite most States subjecting their extraterritorial reach to a number of different, self-imposed limitations.[108] This has led to a significant number of extraditions within the region as different States have attempted reckonings with their 'Dirty War' pasts.[109] Extradition has also occurred on occasion to and from former colonial powers on the basis of active or passive personality.[110] However, leaving aside extraditions (including those to or from Europe), the ambitious provisions on UJ throughout the region have rarely been invoked. Apart from Argentina (whose UJ investigations (above) have yet to bear any fruit), by 2021 there had only ever been five other investigations in the region initiated on the grounds of UJ *per se*.[111] This indicates that despite their tacit enthusiasm, Latin American [S]tates have generally 'followed a much more cautious, even indifferent approach towards exercising their normative powers abroad'.[112]

Moreover, it should be noted that the contribution of the Inter-American human rights system to UJ in the region has differed from the contribution of the European system to UJ in Europe. Whilst proceedings in the IACtHR have helped catalyse Latin American States' reckonings with the past, this has not been the case in the ECtHR where there have been few cases and far less evidence of the same effect on member States. Further, in the Inter-American system it is to be noted that access to justice issues more often than not have involved the claimants' attempt to access information about what happened to their relatives, whereas in the European Court access to justice has overwhelmingly been about whether the State has exceeded its power in charging and convicting, or approving the extradition of, the defendant. Whatever their differences however, many UJ cases tend to be characterised by long and complex arguments about whether national law and international law have both criminalised the conduct at issue in the same way, which goes to the concept of *nullum crimen nulla poena sine lege* (no crime, no punishment without law) – a fundamental tenet of both systems.

5. Comparing Europe and Latin America's UJ over crimes in Africa

Like their former colonies in Latin America, the concept of UJ has allowed European powers to target their former African colonies with investigations. France has been particularly proactive, with more than 14 investigations and/or trials currently on foot covering Liberia, the CAR, Sudan and in particular, Rwanda.[113] Its most recent conviction was of Claude Muhayimana in 2021, who received a 14-year sentence.[114] The African Union's Peace and Security Council (PSC)[115] has sharply criticised the application of UJ by European States across Africa.[116] It notes:

> '[the] need for international justice to be conducted in a transparent and fair manner, in line with the principles of international law, and ... the abuse of the principle of [UJ] poses a threat to the efforts aimed at promoting the rule of law and stability, as well as at building strong national and regional institutions'.[117]

As noted by Lee, '[v]ery few Western leaders are ever called to account for violating international law, while a steady stream of indictments have been issued by Western courts for nationals of other countries, predominantly Africans'.[118] These concerns are well-known.

The African Union and individual African States have argued that it does not allow African States to build their own responses to such crimes – rather, UJ has presented a 'threat to the efforts aimed at promoting the rule of law and stability, as well as at building strong national and regional institutions'.[119] In relation to Spain's 2015 exercise of UJ over former Rwandan Head of Intelligence Karenzi Karake, the PSC argued 'this abuse threatens to reverse the hard-won security and stability in Rwanda and in Africa as a whole'.[120]

Clearly in post-conflict societies such as Rwanda very difficult decisions have had to be made in the transitional justice process, and it is not often clear that there has been accountability at the most senior political and military levels to the satisfaction of the international community. In this light the large number of French prosecutions of persons in such societies assume a cogency they might otherwise lack.

Yet Langer and Eason note that even in those trials in Europe that have involved African defendants, most defendants had become citizens or residents of the prosecuting States prior to the initiation of proceedings against them. Given this, domestic European UJ trials have been far less concentrated on African defendants than the cases thus far pursued by the ICC.[121] This may suggest that African sensitivities over Europe's use of UJ (at least its active personality) to bring atrocities to account would be less in such circumstances.

Contrastingly, a colonial dimension is absent in Latin American discussions and practice on UJ with regard to Africa, perhaps suggesting there is the potential to expand its application in appropriate cases without attracting criticism that colonialism is at play. It is possible that Latin American States, with their experience in prosecutions of their own nationals for crimes committed during their 'Dirty Wars', and with the appropriate legislative and judicial framework in place and tested (including in human rights cases heard in the IACtHR), might be able to prosecute atrocities in Africa without the historical baggage many European States carry. Indeed, without further practice on UJ in other areas of the world, there is a 'risk of further entrenching Eurocentrism of international criminal justice resulting from the dominance of European domestic courts for the prosecution of international crimes under [UJ]'.[122] In this sense, Latin American prosecutions of African atrocities would be welcome. However, practice is scant to date.

Should former African leaders or senior security officials be arrested for trial in a Latin American court, some of the same general arguments regarding the use of UJ would remain. For instance, African States might again claim a 'clear violation of [their] sovereignty and territorial integrity' and an 'attempt to subordinate African legal systems to those of non-African States'.[123] Such criticism might be an unfortunate but unavoidable consequence of spreading the prosecution of UJ cases to non-African courts, but it is still likely to be less than the blowback from a European prosecution.

6. Conclusions

There is no doubt that some of the challenges regarding UJ afflict all States and are caused by a lack of legal clarity on its scope and definition, which opens the way for States to politicise its use. Despite the *Pinochet* ruling apparently clarifying officials' lack of functional immunity for the most serious international crimes,[124] there remain questions about the relationship between UJ and immunity for current heads of State and for diplomats. Domestic law on the matter differs between States, adding to the confusion.

UJ undoubtedly faces steep challenges. In just about every jurisdiction the decision to pursue a case depends on political will, meaning prosecutors and courts must be willing to take on the challenge of pursuing justice for crimes committed far afield. Further, States must be willing to allow prosecutions knowing that they could provoke a political backlash from the government on trial. Still, politics doesn't interfere with every UJ case; it is possible, after all, that a government's political goals align with those of the prosecution (for instance, there is considerable evidence that the *Pinochet* case only went forward because the Labour government in power in the UK at the time was not opposed).[125] The large number of investigations and prosecutions underway in 2021 is testament to this political confluence.

European States have however proven themselves to be hesitant to apply UJ principles broadly, apparently fearing that pursuit of anyone other than of low-level rank (and associated with terrorism) may endanger their foreign policy interests.[126] It is clear on the other hand that Europe has not held back in pursuing high-level Latin American defendants. Without a more global range of defendants, including at high levels, European exercises of UJ regarding Latin American States carry the risk of being seen in reductive terms as another form of imperialism.

Much remains to be done to bring Latin America's dictatorial/military regimes to account, and an external focus can assist that difficult reckoning with the past. However, to date the region's use of UJ laws is largely confined to extraditions, or for bringing charges against accused persons from former colonial powers for atrocities committed against their nationals. It is only Argentina which has begun to use its law more consistently with the universalist spirit underlying UJ; Argentina's activist flurry in recent years in investigating and prosecuting international crimes in its courts is commendable, but cases need to be driven forward more decisively. It remains to be seen what effect the election of the Milei government will be on the usages of Argentina's UJ law; given the new government's foreign policy priorities (particularly its affinity for U.S. norms),[127] it is possible that a new domestic scepticism toward UJ may supplant Argentina's recent activism. The availability of UJ as an avenue for justice where otherwise it may not be obtained would ill-suffer such a development – this is particularly because there is much room for Argentina's Latin American peers to share that activism, rather than their general preference to date to invoke (or agree to exercises of) jurisdiction for their own domestic political or economic gain.

The fight against impunity is a global one which requires the commitment of the whole international community, thus both Europe and Latin American States need to put their UJ promises and commitments to more robust use. If these regions will not do so, the practice of UJ risks being relegated further to an occasional politicised exception rather than a robust means for attaining justice that would otherwise be unattainable, and for dissuading future atrocities.

Notes

1. *Geneva Conventions I-IV*, adopted by the Diplomatic Conference of Geneva on August 12, 1949, with entry into force on October 21, 1950.

2. The *Convention on the Prevention and Punishment of the Crime of Genocide ('Genocide Convention')* was adopted by the UN General Assembly in Resolution 260 A (III) on December 9, 1948. It entered into force on January 12, 1951 after it had been ratified by 20 States.
3. The *Convention against Torture and Other Cruel, Inhuman or Degrading Treatment or Punishment* (the '*Torture Convention*') was adopted by the UN General Assembly in Resolution 39/46 on December 10, 1984. It entered into force on June 26, 1987 after it had been ratified by 20 States.
4. See the Joint Separate Opinion of Judges Higgins, Kooijmans and Buergenthal in *Case Concerning* the *Arrest Warrant* of 11 April 2000; Democratic Republic of the Congo v Belgium (2002) ICJ 1 ('*the Arrest Warrant Case*'), [51].
5. *Id*, [52], citing *Oppenheim's International Law,* 9th ed. 998.
6. See the Joint Separate Opinion of Judges Higgins, Kooijmans and Buergenthal in the *Arrest Warrant Case supra* (note 4), [45].
7. *Lotus Case*, P.C.I.J., Series A, No. 10, 18–9.
8. See the Joint Separate Opinion of Judges Higgins, Kooijmans and Buergenthal in the *Arrest Warrant Case supra* (note 4), [59].
9. A. Adanan, 'Emerging Voices: Domestic Regulation of Universal Jurisdiction – the Role of Domestic Prosecutors', *Opinio Juris*, http://opiniojuris.org/2016/08/29/emerging-voices-2/ (accessed August 29, 2016).
10. In accordance with the *Police Reform and Social Responsibility Act 2011* (UK) s153.
11. Adanan *supra* (note 9).
12. EUROJUST, 'At A Glance: Universal Jurisdiction in EU Member States' (2023), 2, https://www.eurojust.europa.eu/sites/default/files/assets/at-a-glance-universal-jurisdiction-in-eu-member-states.pdf.
13. Bolivia (CP, Art. 1(7)), Chile (Código Orgánico de Tribunales, Art. 6(7) and 6(8)), Costa Rica (CP, Art. 7), Cuba (CP, Art. 5(3)), Ecuador (CP, Art. 5(5)), El Salvador (CP, Art. 10), Honduras (CP, Art. 5(5)), Mexico (CP, Art. 2) Nicaragua (CP, Art. 16(3)(f)), Panama (CP, Art. 19), Paraguay (CP, Art. 8(1)(6) and 8(1)(7)), Venezuela (CP, Art. 4(9), 4(10)). See further See A. Chehtman, 'Strategic Approaches to Extraterritorial Jurisdiction in Latin America', Chapter 11 in A. Parrish and C. Ryngaert (eds.) *Extraterritoriality in International Law* (Edward Elgar, 2023).
14. *Ibid.* Re Colombia, see Act 2111/2021, Art. 333 (https://www.minambiente.gov.co/wp-content/uploads/2021/06/ley-2111-2021.pdf).
15. CP, Art. 7 (Costa Rica); see Chehtman *supra* (note 13).
16. *Princeton Principles on Universal Jurisdiction* 28 (2001), Princeton University Program in Law and Public Affairs, http://hrlibrary.umn.edu/instree/princeton.html.
17. Amnesty International, https://www.amnesty.org/en/what-we-do/international-justice/ (accessed December 13, 2023).
18. R. Goodman, 'Counting Universal Jurisdiction States: What's Wrong with Amnesty International's Numbers [updated]', *Just Security*, https://www.justsecurity.org/4581/amnesty-international-universal-jurisdiction-preliminary-survey-legislation-world/ (accessed December 13, 2013).
19. E. Kontorovich, 'The Parochial Uses of Universal Jurisdiction' 94 *Notre Dame Law Review* 1417 (2019), https://scholarship.law.nd.edu/ndlr/vol94/iss3/8/.
20. *Ibid.*
21. 'The Disappeared: Operation Condor Trial: 21 Former Top Officials Indicted in Rome', *la Repubblica*, https://www.repubblica.it/cronaca/2014/10/13/news/desaparecidos_rinvio_giudizio-97993047/ (accessed October 13, 2021).
22. 'Italy Confirms 14 Life Sentences for Operation Condor Killers', *TeleSUR*, https://www.telesurenglish.net/news/Italy-Confirms-14-Life-Sentences-for-Operation-Condor-Killers-20210709-0010.html (accessed July 9, 2021).
23. A. Walsh, 'The Indigenous People Genocide Case in Guatemala: Justice delayed, Justice Denied?', *Open Democracy*, https://www.opendemocracy.net/en/democraciaabierta/ixil-

indigenous-people-genocide-case-in-guatemala-justice-delayed-ju/ (accessed October 11, 2018).

24. P. Scott, 'The Guatemala Genocide Cases: Universal Jurisdiction and its Limits' 9 *Chi-Kent J. Int'l & Comp. L.* 100.
25. B. Garzon, 'Argentina: Scilingo Case', https://baltasargarzon.org/en/universal-jurisdiction/argentina-scilingo-case/.
26. M. M. Marquez Velasquez, 'The Argentinian Exercise of Universal Jurisdiction 12 Years After its Opening', *Opinio Juris*, https://opiniojuris.org/2022/02/04/the-argentinian-exercise-of-universal-jurisdiction-12-years-after-its-opening/ (accessed February 4, 2022).
27. Staff and agencies, ''Dirty War' Priest Sentenced to Life for Murder, Kidnapping and Torture', *The Guardian*, https://www.theguardian.com/world/2007/oct/10/argentina (accessed October 10, 2007).
28. UK courts eventually upheld the legal authority of Spain's arrest warrant which had relied on UJ; *R ex parte Pinochet v Bartle and ors (Appeal)*, (1999) UKHL 17.
29. N. Roht-Ariazza, '*Guatemala Genocide Case.* Judgment no. STC 237/2005', 100 *American Journal of International Law*, 209 (2006): 207–213.
30. Scott *supra* (note 24), 124. After a more than 10-year delay in getting a prosecution off the ground, in 2013 Rios Montt was tried and convicted for genocide and crimes against humanity and sentenced to 80 years in prison. A retrial was however ordered, but he died before the case could be concluded. See J.-M. Burt and P. Estrada, 'Court Finds Guatemalan Army Commits Genocide, but Acquits Military Intelligence Chief', *International Justice Monitor*, https://www.ijmonitor.org/2018/09/court-finds-guatemalan-army-committed-genocide-but-acquits-military-intelligence-chief/ (accessed September 28, 2018).; Walsh *supra* (note 23); 'Guatemala Recognises Mayan Ixil Genocide, but Absolves General', *TeleSUR*, https://www.telesurenglish.net/news/Guatemala-Recognizes-Mayan-Ixil-Genocide-But-Absolves-General-, 20180926-0031.html (accessed September 26, 2018).
31. Roht-Ariazza *supra* (note 29), 211; Scott *supra* (note 24), 120. Even so, this was not enough to prevent the Court rejecting the extradition request for Rios Montt and holding that Guatemala, not Spain, was responsible for prosecuting him given that his crimes were political offences. This was despite the fact that a UN Committee had already concluded that genocide and other crimes against humanity had taken place in Guatemala; Memory of Silence, Art. V, V.1.5.
32. LO1/2014 (Spain).
33. 'Justice Prevailed: Salvadoran ex-Colonel gets 133 Years for Priest Slayings', *Reuters*, https://www.reuters.com/article/us-spain-el-salvador-massacre-idUSKBN2621QP (accessed September 11, 2020).
34. M. Halberstam, 'Belgium's Universal Jurisdiction Law: Vindication of International Justice or Pursuit of Politics?' 25 *Cardozo Law Review* (2003): 247; 'Belgium Drops War Crimes Cases', *Deutsche Welle*, https://www.dw.com/en/belgium-drops-war-crimes-cases/a-978973 (accessed September 25, 2003).
35. See the *German Code of Crimes Against International Law*, which came into force in 2002.
36. Prop. 2013/14:146, 2, see Chapter 2 Section 3(6) Swedish Criminal Code.
37. J. Ku, 'Britain to Limit Arrest Warrants Under its Universal Jurisdiction Law', *Opinio Juris*, http://opiniojuris.org/2010/03/04/britain-to-limit-arrest-warrants-under-its-universal-jurisdiction-law/ (accessed March 4, 2010). See also S.A. Watts, ''Yes Prime Minister: Early Indications of the Impact of a Change in Policing Governance and the Introduction of Police and Crime Commissioners across England and Wales', University of Portsmouth (PhD thesis), https://researchportal.port.ac.uk/files/14319800/S.Watts_Thesis_Final_Mar_2019_1_.pdf (accessed February 2019).
38. For example France: Art. 689 of the *French Code of Criminal Procedure*, as discussed in Appeals No. 22-80.057 and 22-84.468, Cour de Cassation Plenary Assembly, https://www.courdecassation.fr/en/toutes-les-actualites/2023/05/12/press-release-universal-jurisdiction-french-justice-crimes.
39. EUROJUST *supra* (note 12), 3.

40. See also 'Belgium: Universal Jurisdiction Law Repealed' *Human Rights Watch* (August 1, 2003), https://www.hrw.org/news/2003/08/02/belgium-universal-jurisdiction-law-repealed (accessed January 2, 2023).
41. Adanan *supra* (note 9).
42. *Kolk and Kislyiy v Estonia (Judgement),* ECHR, Nos. 23052/04 and 24018/04, 2006-I.
43. *Kononov v Latvia (Judgement),* ECHR, May 17, 2010.
44. *Jorgic v Germany (Judgement (Merits)),* ECHR July 12, 2007, 50–51, 53–54.
45. M. Langer and M. Eason, 'The Quiet Expansion of Universal Jurisdiction', *European Journal of International Law* 30, no. 3 (2019): 799.
46. V. Paulet (TRIAL International), 'Universal Jurisdiction Annual Review 2020' (report in collaboration with REDRESS, and the European Centre for Constitutional and Human Rights), 13, https://trialinternational.org/wp-content/uploads/2020/03/TRIAL-International_UJAR-2020_DIGITAL.pdf.
47. TRIAL International, 'Applying Universal Jurisdiction to Prosecute International Crimes and the Implications for Syrian Victims', December 23, 2020.
48. This covers cases under investigation, closed, or newly opened; EUROJUST *supra* (note 12), 2.
49. Id, 4.
50. Paulet *supra* (note 46), 11.
51. Paulet *supra* (note 46), 6.
52. S. Koller, 'ISIS Women in Court: Monika K. – Crowdfunding for the Islamic State?', *Counter-Extremism Project* , https://www.counterextremism.com/blog/isis-women-court-monika-k-crowdfunding-islamic-state (accessed February 16, 2023).
53. *Ibid.*
54. See Paulet *supra* (note 46), 49.
55. R. Greenall, 'Jennifer Wenisch: German IS Woman Faces Tougher Sentence for Girl's Death', *BBC online*, https://www.bbc.com/news/world-europe-64901603 (accessed March 9, 2023).
56. UNITAD, 'UNITAD Welcomes German Court Conviction of ISIL Female Member for Aiding and Abetting Genocide Against Yazidis', *Relief Web*, https://reliefweb.int/report/iraq/unitad-welcomes-german-court-conviction-isil-female-member-aiding-and-abetting-genocide-against-yazidis-enar (accessed June 26, 2023).
57. See 'Yazidi Genocide: IS Member Found Guilty in German Landmark Trial', *BBC online*, https://www.bbc.co.uk/news/world-europe-59474616 (accessed November 30, 2021). Also see A. Clooney, 'Fifth Conviction of an ISIS Member in Germany for Crimes Against Humanity Against the Yazidis', *Doughty Street Chambers* (accessed October 25, 2021), https://www.doughtystreet.co.uk/news/fifth-conviction-isis-member-germany-crimes-against-humanity-committed-against-yazidis.
58. L. Morris, 'Why Germany is Becoming a Go-To Destination for Trials on the World's Crimes', *The Washington Post*, https://www.washingtonpost.com/world/europe/germany-war-crimes-justice/2021/03/05/b45372f4-7b78-11eb-8c5e-32e47b42b51b_story.html (accessed March 6, 2021).
59. See C. Otto *et al*, 'In World First, Germany Convicts Syrian Regime Officer of Crimes Against Humanity', *CNN online*, https://edition.cnn.com/2021/02/24/middleeast/syria-germany-officer-convicted-intl/index.html (accessed February 24, 2021). Also A. Vohra, 'Assad's Horrible War Crimes arc Finally Coming to Light under Oath', *Foreign Policy*, https://foreignpolicy.com/2020/10/16/assads-horrible-war-crimes-are-finally-coming-to-light/ (accessed October 16, 2020). Also R. Gladstone, 'An Old Doctrine that puts War Criminals in Reach of Justice', *New York Times online*, https://www.nytimes.com/2021/02/28/world/europe/universal-jurisdiction-war-crimes.html (accessed February 28, 2021).
60. Human Rights Watch, 'Seeking Justice for Syria: How an Alleged Syrian Intelligence Officer was Put on Trial in Germany', https://www.hrw.org/feature/2022/01/06/seeking-justice-for-syria/how-an-alleged-intelligence-officer-was-put-on-trial-in-germany (accessed January 6, 2022).

61. Vohra *supra* (note 59).
62. 'Factsheet: Universal Jurisdiction', Center [sic] for Constitutional Rights, https://ccrjustice.org/home/get-involved/tools-resources/fact-sheets-and-faqs/factsheet-universal-jurisdiction (accessed December 7, 2015).
63. See 'Guantanamos in Europe?', *der Spiegel International* (July 11, 2005, accessed January 9, 2023). The report 'CIA Secret Detention and Torture' by *opensocietyfoundations.org* claimed Germany was complicit in the CIA black site programme.
64. J. Remond Tiedrez, 'France's Highest Court Confirms Universal Jurisdiction', *EJIL Talk!*, https://www.ejiltalk.org/france-is-back-on-the-universal-jurisdiction-track/ (accessed June 1, 2023).
65. EUROJUST *supra* (note 12), 5.
66. K. Rapp, 'Universal Jurisdiction is making a Comeback', *World Politics Review*, https://www.worldpoliticsreview.com/universal-jurisdiction-offers-a-backstop-to-human-rights-tribunals/ (accessed July 27, 2021).
67. M. Langer, 'Universal Jurisdiction Is Not Disappearing: The Shift from 'Global Enforcer' to 'No Safe Haven' Universal Jurisdiction', *JICJ* 13 (2015): 245. See also W. Kaleck and A. Schuller, *Universal Jurisdiction Gains New Momentum* (FICHL Policy Brief Series No.96 (2019)).
68. Langer and Eason *supra* (note 45).
69. *Ibid.*
70. See T. Rosenberg (Council on Foreign Relations), 'Overcoming the Legacies of Dictatorship', *Foreign Affairs* (May/June 1995), https://www.foreignaffairs.com/articles/south-america/1995-05-01/overcoming-legacies-dictatorship.
71. See the *Case of Goiburú et al v Paraguay (Merits, Reparations and Costs),* Judgment of September 22, 2006, Series C No. 153, paras 66 and 72, https://www.refworld.org/jurisprudence/caselaw/iacrthr/2006/en/87619.
72. M. Delagrange, 'Latin America: The Next Frontier for the ICC?' (2009): 5 *University of Florida Law Review* 293.
73. *Id*, 296–304.
74. *Garay Hermosilla* et al *v Chile*, Case 10.843, Inter-Am. C.H.R., Report 36/96 (1996): 57; *Juan Aniceto Meneses Reyes* et al *v Chile*, Case 11.228, Inter-Am. C.H.R., Report 34/96 (1996): 56, 109; *Ignacio* Ellacuria et al *v El Salvador*, Case 10.488, Inter-Am. C.H.R., Report No. 136/99, 229–30.
75. Delagrange *supra* (note 72), 293–4.
76. Inter-American Democratic Charter, September 11, 2001, 40 I.L.M. 1289, 1291–92, reprinted in Organization of American States, Basic Documents Pertaining to Human Rights in the Inter-American System 149, no. 152 (2007), http://www.cidh.oas.org/Basicos/English/Basic. TOC.htm.
77. See for example *Myrna Mack Chang v Guatemala (Judgement),* IACtHR Series C, No. 101, 25 November 2003; *Caso Barrios Altos v Peru (Merits),* IACtHR Series C, No. 75, March 14, 2001.
78. Delagrange *supra* (note 72), 309–310 (see footnotes therein).
79. *Case of Goiburú et al v Paraguay supra* (note 71), 52–3.
80. Delagrange *supra* (note 72), 322.
81. *Case of Goiburú et al v Paraguay supra* (note 71), Separate Judgement of Judge Antonio Cancado Trindade, 66–8.
82. *Ibid.*
83. M. Cherif Bassiouni, 'The History of Universal Jurisdiction and its Place in International Law', in S. Macedo ed., Universal Jurisdiction: National Courts and the Prosecution of Serious Crimes under International Law (University of Pennsylvania Press, 2004), 39, 46.
84. *Ibid.*
85. See *supra* (note 5).
86. Such as the International Convention Against Torture, the Inter American Convention to Prevent and Punish Torture, and the Inter-American Convention on Forced Disappearance

of Persons; see A. E. Alvarez, 'The Implementation of the ICC Statute in Argentina' *Oxford Journal of International Criminal Justice* 480 (2007): 5.

87. The most recent dealings culminated in the conclusion of an enforcement agreement whereby persons convicted by the ICC may serve their sentences of imprisonment in Argentina upon a ruling by the Court and agreement by the Argentinian government – see ICC Press Release, 'ICC Signs Enforcement Agreement with Argentina', ICC-CPI-20170419-PR1297, https://www.icc-cpi.int/news/icc-signs-enforcement-agreement-argentina#:~:text=The%20International%20Criminal%20Court%20(ICC,Court%20and%20accepted%20by%20Argentina.
88. Constitution of the Argentine Nation, http://www.biblioteca.jus.gov.ar/Argentina-Constitution.pdf (accessed April 17, 2017).
89. It further mentioned Article 118 of the Argentine Constitution which provides tribunals with jurisdiction over crimes against the law of peoples (*crímenes contra el derecho de gentes*), irrespective of where they were perpetrated. See Paulet *supra* (note 46), 17–8.
90. 'Argentinian Judge Indicts Franco-Era Spanish Minister on Homicide Charges', *The Guardian online*, https://www.theguardian.com/world/2021/oct/16/argentine-judge-indicts-franco-era-spanish-minister-on-homicide-charges#:~:text=An%20Argentinian%20judge%20investigating%20cases,minister%20between%201976%20and%201979 (accessed October 17, 2021).
91. A Spanish judge also issued arrest warrants; see 'China Criticises Argentina for Arrest Request of Jiang Zemin, Falun Gong Support', *Voice of America – VoA*, https://www.voanews.com/a/china-criticizes-argentina-for-arrest-request-of-jiang-zemin-support-of-falun-gong--80053822/416662.html (December 24, 2009).
92. *Ibid.*
93. Paulet *supra* (note 46), 20. See also H. Smith, 'Argentina Urged to Arrest Saudi Prince MBS at G20 Summit Over Khashoggi Killing', *The Times*, https://www.thetimes.co.uk/article/argentina-urged-to-arrest-saudi-prince-mbs-at-g20-summit-over-khashoggi-killing-8h0m85s5v (accessed November 28, 2018).
94. 'Argentina Lawsuit Seeks to Hold Aung San Suu Kyi Accountable for Atrocities Against Rohingya', *Radio Free Asia online* , https://www.rfa.org/english/news/myanmar/argentina-lawsuit-11142019163937.html (accessed November 14, 2019).
95. Due to jurisdictional issues, the ICC is only investigating crimes which have been at least partially committed on Bangladeshi territory. See T. Khin and T. Ojea Quintana, 'Symposium on the Current Crisis in Myanmar: Inching Closer to a Historic Universal Jurisdiction Case in Argentina on the Rohingya Genocide', *Opinio Juris*, http://opiniojuris.org/2021/09/30/symposium-on-the-current-crisis-in-myanmar-inching-closer-to-a-historic-universal-jurisdiction-case-in-argentina-on-the-rohingya-genocide/ (September 30, 2021). Also BROUK, 'Argentinean Courts Urged to Prosecute Senior Myanmar Military and Government Officials for the Rohingya Genocide', https://www.brouk.org.uk/argentinean-courts-urged-to-prosecute-senior-myanmar-military-and-government-officials-for-the-rohingya-genocide/ (accessed November 13, 2019).
96. 'Argentina Court to Investigate Myanmar War Crimes Against Rohingya Muslims', *Agence France-Presse*, https://www.theguardian.com/world/2021/nov/29/argentina-court-myanmar-war-crimes-rohingya (accessed November 29, 2021); 'Argentina's Justice System to Probe Myanmar War Crimes Claims', Buenos Aires Times, https://www.batimes.-com.ar/news/argentina/argentinas-justice-system-to-probe-myanmar-war-crimes-claims.phtml (accessed November 30, 2021). Also 'The Buenos Aires Federal Chamber Ordered to Investigate the Complaint about Crimes Against Humanity in Myanmar', *fiscales.gob.ar*, https://www.fiscales.gob.ar/fiscalias/la-camara-federal-portena-ordeno-investigar-la-denuncia-sobre-crimenes-de-lesa-humanidad-en-myanmar/ (accessed November 29, 2021).
97. Report of the Detailed Findings of the Independent Fact-Finding Mission on Myanmar, Human Rights Council, A/HRC/39/CRP.2 (September 17, 2018), particularly para 1711 (430). Also, Compilation of all Recommendations made by the Independent International

Fact-Finding Mission on Myanmar, to the Government of Myanmar, armed organisations, the UN Security Council, Member States, UN agencies, the business community and others, A/HRC/42/CRP.6, Human Rights Council 42nd Session (September 9–27, 2019), 102 (15).

98. N. Roht-Arriaza, 'The Pinochet Precedent and Universal Jurisdiction' *New England Law Review* 35 (2001): 311, 315.
99. Chehtman *supra* (note 13).
100. See Delagrange *supra* (note 72), 312–4 and 317–20.
101. Considerations of passive personality have also been of key importance – such as in *Yunis* (1988), and *Bin Laden* (2000). See the *Arrest Warrant Case supra* (note 4), [24].
102. See A. Becker-Lorca, *Mestizo International Law. A Global Intellectual History 1842–1933* (CUP 2014). Indeed, the *Montevideo Convention on the Rights and Duties of States* (1933) with its defence of the principles of non-intervention, sovereign equality, and the 'objective' requirements for statehood is an apposite illustration of this sentiment.
103. Bolivia (Code Penale (CP), Art. 1(7)), Chile (Código Orgánico de Tribunales, Art. 6(7) and 6 (8)), Costa Rica (CP, Art. 7), Cuba (CP, Art. 5(3)), Ecuador (CP, Art. 5(5)), El Salvador (CP, Art. 10), Honduras (CP, Art. 5(5)), Mexico (CP, Art. 2) Nicaragua (CP, Art. 16(3)(f)), Panama (CP, Art. 19), Paraguay (CP, Art. 8(1)(6) and 8(1)(7)), Venezuela (CP, Art. 4(9), 4(10)). Costa Rica further provides for UJ for terrorism and its financing, as well as for other international crimes including genocide and crimes against human rights and international humanitarian law (CP, Art. 7). Colombia does not have a specific provision on UJ, but directly applies provisions in different treaties to which it is a party: see, for example, Colombia's Constitutional Court, C-621 (2001). Brazil has laws on UJ for genocide (where the defendant or victim is Brazilian) and torture (pursuant to treaty obligations) committed abroad; Statement of the Mission of Brazil to the UN General Assembly's Sixth Committee on UJ, https://www.un.org/en/ga/sixth/77/pdfs/statements/universal_jurisdiction/12mtg_brazil.pdf (accessed October 11, 2022).
104. K. Davis, *Between Impunity and Imperialism: The Regulation of Transnational Bribery* (OUP 2019).
105. Chehtman *supra* (note 13).
106. Such as double criminality, health issues, constitutional prohibition on the extradition of nationals; *ibid.*
107. Chehtman *supra* (note 13).
108. These include a requirement that the accused be found on their territory, that the conduct be criminalised in the [S]tate in which the offence was perpetrated, that the offender not be already convicted or exonerated by the relevant [S]tate or that the crime is not yet subject to statutes of limitations, and that the accused is not requested by the authorities of the State where the offence was committed or that the offence not be deemed political or connected with a political offence. See Chehtman *supra* (note 13).
109. One early case was the Brazilian Supreme Court's agreement in 1984 to the extradition to Argentina of Mario Eduardo Firmenich, the former head of Argentina's Montoneros guerrillas. See 'Mario Firmenich, a Former Guerilla Member from Argentina, on Daniel Ortega's Payroll', *connectas.org*, https://www.connectas.org/mario-firmenich-former-guerrilla-memeber-from-argentina-daniel-ortega/. More recently, in 2006 Peru was able to secure the extradition of former Peruvian President Alberto Fujimori from Chile to stand trial for extensive human rights abuses – see J. E. Mendez, 'Significance of the *Fujimori* Trial', *American University International Law Review* 25,no. 649, 650–2, https://www.corteidh.or.cr/tablas/r29316.pdf.
110. An example was the *Cavallo case* where a Mexican court agreed to the extradition of Cavallo to Spain for a ream of international crimes committed while a senior officer in Argentina's ESMA (Escuela de Mecanica de la Armada – a notorious detention centre on the outskirts of Buenos Aires run by the navy for the purpose of interrogating, torturing and disposing of political opponents); J. E. Méndez and S. Tinajero-Esquivel, 'The *Cavallo Case*: A New Test for Universal Jurisdiction.' *Human Rights Brief* 8, no. 3 (2001): 5–8. Spain ultimately extradited Cavallo back to Argentina.

111. Three in Chile, one in Brazil and one in Colombia.
112. Chehtman *supra* (note 13).
113. AFP, 'France Court Jails Rwanda Driver for 14 Years over Genocide', *justiceinfo.net*, https://www.justiceinfo.net/en/85656-france-court-jails-rwanda-driver-for-14-years-over-genocide.html (accessed 16 December 2021).
114. *Ibid.*
115. ISS PSC Report, 'The Strong Reaction of the PSC Following the Arrest of Rwanda's Intelligence Chief in London has Far-Reaching Implications', https://issafrica.org/pscreport/psc-insights/psc-stands-with-rwanda-on-universal-jurisdiction (accessed July 10, 2015).
116. Communique of the 519th PSC Meeting on Universal Jurisdiction, http://www.peaceau.org/en/article/communique-of-the-519th-psc-meeting-on-universal-jurisdiction-26-june-2015 (accessed June 26, 2015).
117. *Id.*
118. J. Lee, 'Opinion: Selective Justice', *ABC online* (March 16, 2009, updated February 5, 2020), https://www.abc.net.au/news/2009-03-17/30320.
119. Communique of the 519th PSC Meeting on Universal Jurisdiction, *supra* (note 116), 2.
120. *Id*, 5.
121. Langer and Eason *supra* (note 45), 783.
122. B. McGonigle Leyh, 'Using Strategic Litigation and Universal Jurisdiction to Advance Accountability for Serious International Crimes', *International Journal of Transitional Justice* 16, no. 3(2022), 363.
123. Communique of the 519th PSC Meeting on Universal Jurisdiction, *supra* (note 116), 6.
124. *Pinochet Appeal*, *supra* (note 28).
125. Margaret Thatcher was famously scathing in her opposition to the whole process; see C. Levey and M. Barcia, 'Why Thatcher's Shadow Still Hangs over Latin America', *Al Jazeera*, https://www.aljazeera.com/opinions/2013/4/15/why-thatchers-shadow-still-lingers-over-latin-america (accessed April 15, 2013).
126. Rapp *supra* (note 66).
127. L. Grinspan, 'Changing Course: How Javier Milei Will Transform Argentina's Foreign Policy', *Al Jazeera online*, https://www.aljazeera.com/news/2023/12/8/changing-course-how-javier-milei-will-transform-argentinas-foreign-policy (accessed December 8, 2023).

Disclosure statement

No potential conflict of interest was reported by the author(s).

The intercontinental dialogue on enforced disappearances: The case of massive disappearances during hostilities

Ioanna Pervou

ABSTRACT
This article discusses the intercontinental judicial dialogue on enforced disappearances. It first delves into the concept of enforced disappearances and explains through a historical perspective how the practice shaped the course of the two regions: Europe and Central and Latin America. It explores the key elements of the courts' jurisprudence and points to their differences. Then it goes in depth through the evolving dialogue between the two regional courts with regard to massive disappearance during hostilities. It elaborates on the functional term 'massacre' and examines how it is related to other legal terms, like extrajudicial executions. The article will point out the legal obstacles in characterising the widespread conduct of disappearances as a crime against humanity and will suggest how the non-legal term 'massacre' has assisted in such crimes' punishment. Finally, it analyses how justice is attributed in such cases and whether legal responses suffice.

1. Introduction: the intercontinental dialogue on disappearances

Latin American states have long suffered from enforced disappearances. The phenomenon's proliferation in the region during the second half of the twentieth century developed a catalytic role in the phenomenon's legal conceptualisation. The Latin American paradigm of enforced disappearances formed its archetypical understanding and shaped the phenomenon's legal capture (Dulitzky, 2019). In this context, the term 'enforced disappearances' became a synonym for the incessant use of military force to diminish opposition and ensure public order (Pervou, 2012). However, the phenomenon's contextual understanding and the international community's topical interest in disappearances at the Southern Cone, caused bewilderment. On particular occasions, the phenomenon's political aspect prevailed, and disappearances were deemed a result of authoritarian and totalitarian regimes' policies, attributing a political character to the phenomenon (Egeland, 1982).

Despite this conceptual entrapment in the Latin example, there is no doubt that the term's functional definition as well as the phenomenon's archetypical notion are inextricably linked to the Latin American region (Finucane, 2010). Its comprehensive understanding and legalisation is owed to the jurisprudence of the Inter-American Court of

Human Rights (IACtHR), alongside the struggles of human rights non-governmental organisations |(NGOs).[1] This functional term served as the prototype for all subsequent legal documents, including the UN Convention against Disappearances (CPED)[2] and the Inter-American Convention on Enforced Disappearance.[3]

As soon as disappearances occupied other regional courts and international bodies apart from the IACtHR, it became apparent that the phenomenon exceeded the Latin American paradigm. Although enforced disappearances in their archetypical understanding did not spiral in the European plane, the phenomenon occurred on several occasions. From hostilities against Kurds in southeastern Turkey,[4] to atrocities in the area of the Caucasus,[5] or the framework of atrocities in Cyprus and the former Yugoslavia,[6] disappearances have occupied the European legal order.

On this side of the Atlantic though, there have been significant inconsistencies in the phenomenon's legal reception (Taqi, 2000–2001). The European Court of Human Rights (ECtHR) initially avoided the already existing jurisprudence by the IACtHR and this caused inadequacies in the first wave of its judgments regarding disappearances.[7] The cases regarding the disappearance of Kurds in southeastern Turkey remain a black hole in ECtHR jurisprudence, primarily for three reasons. First, the ECtHR did not deviate at all from its admissibility criteria and did not accept the next of kin of the disappeared as indirect victims. Its interpretation of the European Convention on Human Rights' (ECHR) Arts 34 and 35 remained strict and this resulted in the inadmissibility of many cases which reached the ECtHR. The ECtHR did not recognise the victim's legal interest to make a claim regarding the whereabouts of the practice's direct victims and so it failed to legally observe their anguish and extreme pain.[8] Second, the ECtHR created an insurmountable barrier to applicants in terms of proof. The court maintained its high evidentiary threshold and required applicants to substantiate their claims regarding the state's complicity in the disappearance of their relative. It did not apply the legal construction according to which negligence to investigate allegations of disappearance constitutes a procedural breach of the victim's right to life and the prohibition of torture (Arts 2 and 3 respectively).[9]

This approach caused a *probatio diabolica* for the applicants (Scovazzi & Citroni, 2007), given that they had to provide information they could not possibly have, as states that perform disappearances conceal traces of the victims by definition. In this regard, the ECtHR could not establish proof 'beyond reasonable doubt', which also resulted in the dismissal of many cases (Sethi, 2001). Finally, the ECtHR did not find a deliberate state practice on behalf of the respondent state. It did not associate the collection of applications before it – its reflexes were weak in this sense – neither did it examine complaints jointly, nor speak of disappearances as the respondent state's designed strategy (Kurban, 2016).

These inadequacies in the ECtHR's first wave of disappearance cases emanates primarily from two major reasons. These are the belated start of a dialogue with the IACtHR and the absence of a distinct norm and a special international instrument forbidding disappearances before 2010.

Although the two courts have created distinct profiles, there have been several occasions when their rationale has proven the existence of a subtle or manifest judicial dialogue. The IACtHR is fairly considered a pioneer in the struggle against disappearances, while the ECtHR was for some time at the tail end of the developments. As far as disappearances are concerned, these interlocutions between the two judicial bodies followed the harsh criticism regarding the handling of the Kurdish disappearances. The course of the two courts is significantly different, and this partly justifies the discrepancy between their approaches. On the one hand, the IACtHR has built its jurisprudence on the practice of disappearances. The very first contentious cases before the IACtHR were related to disappearances and the first years of its jurisprudence were totally occupied with this state practice.[10] In contrast, the ECtHR had dealt with various applications before it encountered the phenomenon.

These discrepancies in addressing disappearances were not unreasonable. The starting point between the two regional judicial bodies was non-identical. Taking a closer look at the judicial course of the two, historically the ECtHR did not consider disappearances a distinct state practice in sheer violation of human rights.[11] It approached disappearances as a practice involving the victims' maltreatment which put their lives in danger. For the European continent, enforced disappearances have been considered a regional phenomenon which spiralled only in Latin America during the Cold War (Wright, 2000). This approach explains why it did not take advantage from the very beginning of the IACtHR's settled jurisprudence. Apart from that, the ECtHR did not take full account of the Human Rights Committee's response to personal communications to disappearance cases coming from other continents, such as Asia (Dimaranan, 1987).

The most important difficulty though, stems from the fact that there is no stipulation of a clear prohibition against disappearances in the general regional human rights treaties. Both the Inter-American Convention on Human Rights (IACHR) and the ECHR (as well as the International Covenant on Civil and Political Rights [ICCPR]) do not provide for a negative right against disappearances (Pervou, 2013). For this reason, regional jurisprudence did not progress straightforwardly, and it is characterised by suspended steps. Both courts wavered over which provisions of the IACHR and the ECHR were violated by a disappearance. The lack of a provision that would be a common focal point led to their dissimilar reading and interpretation of disappearances. The IACtHR unfolded its horizontal approach on the hierarchy of human rights. It considered that disappearances are a violation of people's right to access to justice and it further confirmed that the practice constitutes a *jus cogens* violation.[12] These two elements are perhaps the most crucial contribution of the IACtHR to the fight against disappearances. The IACtHR has underlined the most important element of disappearances, the victim's legal limbo and total dissociation from legal tools, thus a violation of the right to a fair trial. Deprivation of liberty and the cumulative concealment of their whereabouts turn victims into living ghosts whose access to legal assistance vanishes (Sadat, 2006). What is more, the IACtHR has moved one step further by affirming that their being cut off from the legal world forms a *jus cogens* violation, since their existence is fully dependent on the state organs. The inter-American jurisprudence has come to this conclusion without great reluctance or difficulty. The characterisation of enforced disappearances as a *jus cogens* violation has received negative comments. Criticism has focused mostly on the general reluctance of international judicial bodies to add another prohibition to the intrinsically short list of peremptory norms (Sarkin, 2012).

At the same time, the ECtHR considers the disappearances as a violation of ECHR Art. 3 and potentially a violation of Art. 2. The ECtHR has not placed emphasis on the victims' legal limbo and the flagrant violation of their access to justice. Therefore, the central tenets of their legal approach differ. This course of judicial thinking misses the complexity of disappearances and the perpetrating state's ultimate goal to render the disappeared legally invisible.[13] Taking into account the ECtHR's jurisprudential course over time and how legal positivism permeates its verdicts, it comes as no surprise that reference to peremptory norms is infrequent, or better, rare. As a result, the two courts' jurisprudence on disappearances is substantially different.

Throughout the years though, the dialogue between the IACtHR and the ECtHR has proved advantageous. The ECtHR has benefited from the Latin American experience and gradually taken a position in favour of the victims and their families, overcoming legal positivist barriers. Nevertheless, there are still aspects of the phenomenon which require attention in the European plane, such as victim status and the evidentiary threshold (Citroni & Scovazzi, 2009), as well as reparations, and the treatment of mass disappearances within the realm of atrocities. To the contrary, the IACtHR has a long way to go as far as unacknowledged administrative detentions and extraordinary renditions are concerned. These practices fall within the concept of disappearances according to the ECtHR, even though they do not follow the archetypical pattern of disappearances. This is perhaps the only point to have escaped the IACtHR's attention, giving rise to jurisprudential shortcomings (Pervou, 2012).

Overall, disappearance practices have been one of the domains generally mobilising dialogue between the two regional human rights courts. Yet, there are significant aspects which have not yet been fully addressed. First, how courts identify the existence of a pattern by the respondent state which verifies that disappearances are part of designed state practice. Second, if the existence of a certain disappearance pattern is synonymous with the 'widespread or systematic practice' required for the occurrence of a crime against humanity. Third, whether massive, enforced disappearances during hostilities fall under the same legal framework, and there is no difference in the legal treatment of disappeared and missing persons. Finally, if the jurisprudential affirmation of enforced disappearances requires the existence of a pattern and therefore the existence of some form of designed state practice, and therefore cases which are sporadic or isolated incidents are out of luck before regional human rights bodies. These questions are the major axes of this research article.

2. Widespread or systematic practice of enforced disappearance

One of the aspects which has not received much attention by the international community relates to the widespread or systematic practice of enforced disappearance, that constitutes a crime against humanity. According to the CPED's Art. 5 'the widespread or systematic practice of enforced disappearance constitutes a crime against humanity as defined in applicable international law and shall attract the consequences provided for under such applicable international law',[14] directly pointing to Art. 7(1)(i) of the International Criminal Court (ICC) statute which stipulates enforced disappearances as a crime against humanity.[15]

The provision of CPED's Art. 5 carries an inherent conundrum; that is, which are the features that transform disappearance from a human rights violation to a crime against humanity? Disappearances require, by definition, state complicity and the practice's complexity requires the involvement of state agents throughout every phase. As such, disappearances are almost always the result of deliberate state practice, even when they arise as a side-effect of another practice.[16] The involvement of multiple state authorities means that disappearances do not take place accidentally, rather they are predesigned. In these terms, the perpetration, in its archetypical form, is both widespread and systematic (Schabas, 2017).

Enforced disappearances in Latin America satisfied both of the elements a crime against humanity requires. Nevertheless, they were treated as human rights violations, and only on exceptional occasions did the IACtHR affirm the existence of a crime against humanity.[17] This is not irrational, keeping in mind the court's jurisdictional limits. The penal treatment of the perpetrators of a crime against humanity rests outside the IACtHR's competence. Nevertheless, the IACtHR took significant steps to guarantee that the convicted states would not allow those responsible to escape legal consequences and offered victims the highest attainable level of justice (Cassel, 2006–2007). This observation, though, points to the general deficit of the international legal regime regarding the available, or proper, fora to adjudicate cases in which a claim for a crime against humanity exists. Taking a close look at the inter-American jurisprudence, it follows that the IACtHR relied on the accumulation of innumerous individual appeals to reach the conclusion that disappearances were performed on a systemic basis by respondent states (Claude, 2010). Thus, the phenomenon was widespread, permeating state authorities, and practiced systematically. This approach was more than necessary for the establishment of states' responsibility for the commitment of disappearances, combined with the fact that no evidence was provided either to the victims or the IACtHR. Therefore, the repetitive occurrence of a particular pattern was the counterweight to the absence of evidence due to invocation of the state secrets doctrine.[18] However, the above underlines how the 'widespread or systematic' criminal law terminology is in practice applied by human rights bodies, stripped of all its doctrinal and theoretical elements. The functional use of the 'widespread or systematic' element comes out effortlessly in disappearances' jurisprudence (Pérrez Solla, 2006).

The very same observation applies to the European plane as well. The ECtHR has confronted disappearances as a repetitive human rights violation in particular regions. Except for in southeastern Turkey against the Kurds, the ECtHR identified patterns in the Caucasus as part of state policy to eliminate Chechen opposition (Chevalier-Watts, 2010). Yet, enforced disappearances were not practiced on a systemic or widespread basis by most member states of the Council of Europe. To the contrary, it was applied by a few states aiming at the obliteration of certain groups of people. These examples of enforced disappearances that came to the ECtHR's attention, although fewer, were also systematic and widespread. Yet again, the ECtHR avoided speaking of crimes against humanity, and it also did not speak of state patterns early enough (Andreu-Guzmán, 2001).

These examples are illuminating and demonstrate that human rights courts are naturally oriented to examine the existence of human rights violations, and with regard to disappearances, that it takes multiple individual complaints for judicial bodies to identify and establish a pattern (Barrett, 2009). At the same time, it is unlikely to verify that a state's practice constitutes a crime against humanity, even if the features of a systematic and widespread practice are proven.

This shortcoming is certainly not the fault of regional human rights courts, as it pertains to the definition of crimes against humanity *per se*. Legal scholars have so far expressed multiple opinions on the notions of 'systematic' and 'widespread' practice. The predominant view among international criminal lawyers is that the two prerequisites do not have a quantitative character (Robers, 2017). As such, a widespread or systematic practice is not necessarily repetitious, nor does it involve a large number of victims. Crimes against humanity may target a small group of people, or even a single person. In this sense, the two features refer only to state strategy and the intentional committing of acts which constitute international crimes (Giorgou, 2014).

If this interpretation is to be adopted, then archetypical disappearances in Latin America during the Cold War qualify as crimes against humanity, and the same applies in the cases of disappearances against Kurds and Chechens. All in all, this view is subtly disapproved of and international attestations of crimes against humanity cannot be fully dissociated from quantitative criteria. Although this does not form a solid line of argumentation, as it contravenes international theory, nonetheless it reflects current legal practice. After all, for an international crime to threaten the existence of the international community, strong disapproval and condemnation is needed. In most cases the latter are identical based on a crime's magnitude and the number of victims (Sadat, 2013).

Capitalising on the above remarks, three questions arise. First, whether the jurisprudential affirmation of disappearances can lean on the existence of a pattern. Second, if CPED's Art. 5 suffices to differentiate between a disappearance pattern and a crime against humanity. Third, if the two human rights courts' decisions have prompted a dialogue with the ICC's regime, alongside other criminal judicial bodies.[19]

The first two questions have already been addressed. Currently, the two courts' verdicts are not dependent on the existence of a pattern.[20] The commission of an enforced disappearance comes in many contexts and the accumulation of the CPED's constitutive elements is enough for the IACtHR and the ECtHR to reach a decision. This is both due to the courts' familiarisation with the phenomenon, as well as the success of the term's definition in the CPED's Art. 2. Regional human rights bodies rely on the cumulative existence of liberty deprivation, the concealment of the victim's fate or whereabouts and state involvement in both of these steps. These elements are clear and by now well-established in the international legal plane, and relevant jurisprudence that has ensued. Otherwise, neither the phenomenon's realisation, nor the progressive expansion of victim protection would be possible. With regard to the second point, the CPED incorporates the ordinary liaison between human rights and criminal justice in all human rights treaties. Reference to 'widespread or systematic' practices that formulate a crime against humanity is without further connotations in the conventional context. However, this very terminology blurs the line between state practice in violation of human rights prohibitions and a crime against humanity.[21]

Finally, the third point has not yet received sufficient responses. Although it is self-evident, on occasions, that governments have committed a crime against humanity by the repetitive practice of disappearances against certain groups, this link is not yet strong. This is predominantly due to the difficulty criminal justice faces in identifying the perpetrators' intent to commit such a crime. However, this intra-organisational dialogue is an ongoing process, with limited results so far (Nouwen, 2018).

Discussion on the widespread or systematic commission of enforced disappearances and the interplay between the CPED's Arts 2 and 5 still misses the humanitarian aspect. Although the convention's preamble refers to humanitarian law and respect to relevant provisions, there is no provision for massive disappearance during hostilities. There are two preliminary remarks at this point. First, that enforced disappearance as a state practice during hostilities can only be part of a well-designed strategy and people do not vanish for no reason. Otherwise, there are missing persons during warfare.[22] Therefore, they are systemic, and potentially widespread. Second, enforced disappearances take place on all occasions: they can be committed by legally elected governments in liberal democracies during peacetime, they can be the result of authoritarian regimes' policy, they may be the outcome of turbulence and upheaval in a state, or they can be practiced during armed conflicts, either international or non-international. Therefore, the absence of a reference for disappearances during wartime in the CPED is not due to omission; rather it is standard for human rights conventions not to touch upon humanitarian law, as it is *lex specialis* (Droege, 2008).

3. Massive disappearances during hostilities

Regional courts' jurisprudence cannot offer a definitive solution on the point which the widespread or systematic practice of disappearances qualifies for a crime against humanity. However, their contribution is of great value for massive disappearances during hostilities. Few cases have been examined before the IACtHR[23] and ECtHR on this subject. For this reason, the dialogue between the two bodies is not that vivid when massive disappearances are at stake. An in-depth elaboration of this topic includes three aspects: (a) which disappearance incidents qualify as massive, (b) whether the conduct of hostilities transforms the conduct of disappearances, and (c) how such incidents can effectively be addressed by juridical human rights bodies.

The term 'massive disappearances' does not appear in international legal documents and has mostly a descriptive value. In this sense, it depicts single incidents which have resulted in the simultaneous disappearance of many victims. As far as hostilities are concerned, the term is broad, and it incorporates any kind of intrastate or interstate conflict which involves two or more parties. As such, hostilities pertain to the entire set of humanitarian law rules. Thereat, massive disappearances during hostilities apply to any kind of conflict.

The final aspect reveals the discord between the IACtHR and the ECtHR on massive disappearances. The IACtHR has put forward the concept of 'massacre' to explain massive disappearances which have resulted, in most cases, in extrajudicial executions. Although this term does not carry a legal value, it accurately explains the concept of massive disappearance during hostilities, allowing the IACtHR to adjust the penalties respectively. More specifically, the inter-American jurisprudence encountered several incidents with dozens and hundreds of victims disappeared at once. Technically these incidents do not form disappearances, and they would be better conceived as massive extrajudicial executions. Yet, they took place as part of systematic and widespread strategies of enforced disappearances and the conducting states concealed the victims' fate, as they refused to reveal any information regarding their whereabouts and did not take responsibility over their deaths. What is more, massacres formed part of general state practices deployed by authoritarian regimes aiming at annihilating opposition or diminishing groups of people which they considered inferior (Nagle, 2008). For example, there are cases where massacres targeted rural populations which were considered perilous to the core principles and values for building a superior society.[24]

Recourse to the term 'massacre' has proven a brilliant juridical choice as it avails all difficulties to legally encapsulate such incidents. Massive disappearances (or extrajudicial executions) driven by racial, political or other similar motives may well establish genocidal claims,[25] or generally claims for crimes against humanity. However, the time and context of adjudication did not allow the IACtHR to investigate whether the *mens rea* of these crimes was fulfilled.[26] First, the IACtHR is not vested with the power to initiate criminal proceedings, and thus delve into the subjective part of international crimes. Second and most important, these incidents were significantly fewer than individual disappearances claims, and it was hard for the court to speak of a pattern. Massacre explains plainly what the claim is about without complex legal reasoning that would have to balance between human rights violations and crimes against humanity or demarcate enforced disappearances from genocide and extrajudicial executions. In this regard, the IACtHR touches upon systemic patterns of disappearances which ravaged member states for years, without delving into the establishment of individual criminal liability of the designers of these state practices. Nevertheless, despite its character as a human rights body, the IACtHR 'recognizes the limitations of monetary awards [...] and as a rule orders states to investigate and to punish those responsible' (Fulton, 2014), thus demonstrating interest in the criminal dimension of the practice.

On the contrary, the ECtHR has rejected this rationale when it has dealt with massive disappearances in the context of hostilities.[27] The most profound case before the ECtHR is *Cyprus v. Turkey*. This intrastate application is about the Turkish invasion of the northern part of Cyprus. The ECtHR could not speak of a massacre as the international community had already referred to the unaccounted victims of the Turkish invasion as 'missing persons'. More specifically, soon after the invasion took place the UN General Assembly voted in 1974 for a resolution entitled 'Assistance and co-operation in accounting for persons who are missing or dead in armed conflicts',[28] which exposed a legal gap in the 1949 Geneva Conventions which did not contain any provision for people who remained unaccounted for after the termination of an armed conflict. The term 'missing persons' prevailed for the unaccounted victims of the Turkish invasion. Although there is no substantial difference between missing and disappeared persons, for some years the former was preferred when referring to unaccounted victims in the context of armed conflicts, to signify someone missing as the result of warfare and not a deliberate practice of parties to the conflict.

In its decision, the ECtHR did not examine whether the perpetrating state deliberately formulated a strategy to conceal traces of the victims. The court's emphasis was on the fact that although there was strong presumption of the victims' death, since many years had passed after the conflict's termination, the victims had to be considered as disappeared since their corpses were not found and sufficient answers as to their fate and conditions of death were not provided. This reasoning adopted by the ECtHR came in alignment with the IACtHR's jurisprudence which held from the very beginning that even when the death of the disappeared victim is certain, their anguish and suffering persist when there is no specific information regarding the conditions of their disappearance. Thereat, the Court holds that clarifying the whereabouts or fate of the victim 'is of utmost importance for the relatives of the disappeared victim [...] since by doing so, the relatives would be relieved from the anguish and suffering'.[29]

In this sense, it could be argued that for the ECtHR, cases of enforced disappearances are treated in the same manner irrespective of the existence of an armed conflict. As such, all persons that would traditionally be treated as missing persons, are considered disappeared. This perspective was not only adopted for the Cyprus victims, but for the Katyn victims too.[30] This would be beneficial for victims, since the quantitative criterion leading to massive disappearance would suffice for the treatment of missing persons as victims of enforced disappearances. In addition, such a view entails that the existence of a pattern and evidence of designed state practice is not a prerequisite for the court to reach a verdict, given that such evidence cannot be easily gathered during hostilities. However, this is not the case for the ECtHR, according to its latest decision in the *Ukraine v. Russia* judgment. In that judgment, the ECtHR differentiates between missing persons and victims of disappearance, leading to the conclusion that the adjudication in the *Cyprus* and *Katyn* cases was based on the lapse of time between the incident and its judicial review, which meant that such victims did not go missing due to unrest, rather their disappearance was predetermined. More specifically, the ECtHR held that

> there had been 'sufficiently numerous' instances of abduction to amount to a pattern or system which was itself life-threatening to engage the applicability of Article 2 as regards that administrative practice, although most of those abducted had been released soon after they had gone missing.[31]

All in all, both courts take the stance that victims of massive atrocities during hostilities are to be considered disappeared, even if there is strong evidence that the victims were extrajudicially executed, or if their death is presumed.[32] This perspective is advantageous for two reasons: first, it takes into account that during hostilities the archetypical form of disappearances cannot easily take place. The conflicting parties aim at their strategic and military privilege over their opponent and do not benefit from enforced disappearances as they occurred once in Latin America. Second, the practice of disappearances offers better protection to the victims' next of kin, since the crime is continuous and because it is adjudicated that it creates great anxiety and anguish to the families of the disappeared. These elements are neglected if the victims were simply considered 'dead people' (after extrajudicial executions).

4. Conclusions

Intercontinental dialogue over enforced disappearances is vivid in judicial terms. The two regional bodies engage in a fruitful debate over the phenomenon's treatment. However, historical and geographical proximity of the IACtHR to regimes which rendered disappearances state strategy gives the court a clear lead in the relative jurisprudence. On the other hand, the ECtHR seems to have gradually comprehended the phenomenon, that is, the constitutive elements of the prohibition and the crime's multiple facets.

With regard to incidents of massive disappearances during atrocities, jurisprudence is rather limited, as mass lawsuits are fewer. The IACtHR has adopted a radical stance by employing the term 'massacre'. The term's extralegal character allows the court to sidestep legal barriers regarding the incidents' characterisation, the framework in which they took place, as well as the ensuing legal implications. This is not the first time the IACtHR has built its jurisprudence on functional definitions. The same path was followed with the definition of enforced disappearances: the IACtHR was primarily based on the functional/working definition provided by NGOs created by the victims' families. Thus, the IACtHR treats massive disappearances as massacres, irrespective of the context in which they have taken place, not differentiating its jurisprudence depending on whether there has been an interstate conflict, civil war, or mere unrest. The practice's human rights dimension is isolated and prioritised over potential considerations of humanitarian law. At the same time, the IACtHR recognises how massive disappearances entail individual criminal responsibility for those who designed and employed the practice, further obliging respondent states to deliver justice.

Respectively, the ECtHR tends to refer to missing persons when massive disappearances occur in the context of atrocities. This term has no significance compared to 'disappeared' as they both depict people unaccounted for. This marks the ECtHR's approach not to evade humanitarian law considerations. These subtle terminological differentiations play a pivotal role in its jurisprudence, resulting in a different course of reasoning. The ECtHR evaluates the context in which massive disappearances have occurred to reach a verdict. This approach, although anticipated and complete from a positivist perspective, examines the massive character of disappearances committed in relation to the conflict they were employed in. This position is consistent with the ECtHR's long jurisprudence regarding the application of human rights norms during conflict. In addition, the ECtHR has a limited approach to reparation forms compared to the inter-American system. Therefore, its jurisprudence offers fewer connections between human rights law and criminal liability.

All in all, both human rights bodies are relatively reluctant to make direct reference to crimes against humanity when massive disappearances are recorded and brought before them, and there is jurisprudential bewilderment on this point. Apart from the two courts' approach to massive disappearances cases, this puzzle between human rights, humanitarian and criminal law has rendered the CPED's Art. 5 a provision of limited significance, since there are no references to it by jurisdictional bodies, while it has received limited interpretation so far. It further gives rise to queries as to the cases where massive disappearances are not part of a widespread or systematic state practice. Overall, this dialogue is, so far, a privilege for both regional legal orders. It is high time the two courts paid extra attention to massive disappearance claims, whether they arise during hostilities, or not. The parallel application of human rights and humanitarian law norms is not a novelty, while its criminal law ramifications are a fact. Nevertheless, their relationship is not yet fully elaborated regarding enforced disappearance.

Notes

1. OHCHR, Enforced or Involuntary Disappearances, Fact Sheet No.6/Rev.4, https://www.ohchr.org/en/publications/fact-sheets/fact-sheet-no-6-rev-4-enforced-disappearances (accessed September 13, 2024); FEDEFAM, Fighting Against Enforced Disappearances in Latin America, http://www.desaparecidos.org/fedefam/eng.html (accessed September 13, 2024).
2. UN General Assembly, *International Convention for the Protection of All Persons from Enforced Disappearance*, 20 December 2006, UNTS 2716, p. 3.
3. Organization of American States (OAS), *Inter-American Convention on Forced Disappearance of Persons*, 9 June 1994.
4. *Çakici v. Turkey*, App. no. 23657/94 (ECtHR 8 July 1999); *Ismail Ertak v. Turkey*, App. no. 20764/92 (ECtHR 9 May 2000); *Taş v. Turkey*, App. no. 24396/94 (ECtHR 14 November 2000); *Ciçek v. Turkey*, App. no. 25704/94 (ECtHR 27 February 2001).
5. *Luluyev et al. v. Russia*, App. no. 69480/01 (ECtHR 9 November 2006); *Mikiyeva et al. v. Russia*, App. nos 61536/08 *et al.* (ECtHR 30 January 2014); *Z & Khatuyeva v. Russia*, App. nos 39436/06 & 40169/07 (ECtHR 30 January 2014); *Aslakhanova et al. v. Russia*, App. nos 2944/06 *et al.* (ECtHR 18 December 2012).
6. *Munira Muzkanović et al. v. Bosnia and Herzegovina*, App. no. 47063/08 *et al.* (ECtHR 3 June 2014).
7. European Commission, 'The ECHR and Human Rights Violations against Kurds in Turkey' (9 October 2018), https://projects.research-and-innovation.ec.europa.eu/en/projects/success-stories/all/echr-and-human-rights-violations-against-kurds-turkey (accessed September 13, 2024).
8. See *Skendžić & Krznarić v. Croatia*, where the ECtHR concluded that the compensation received by the relatives of the disappeared during civil procedures before domestic courts deprived them of victim status under Art. 3 of the ECtHR. *Skendžić & Krznarić v. Croatia*, App. no. 16212/08 (ECtHR 20 January 2011), para. 96.
9. *Mahmut Kaya v. Turkey*, App. no. 22535/93 (Report of the European Commission of Human Rights 23 October 1998), paras 342–3.
10. *Velásquez-Rodriguez v. Honduras (Merits)*, Inter-American Court of Human Rights, Series C, No. 4 (29 July 1988); *Velásquez-Rodriguez v. Honduras (Preliminary Objections)*, Inter-American Court of Human Rights, Series C No. 1 (26 June 1987).
11. PACE CoE, 'Enforced Disappearances', Res 1463 (3 October 2005), op. clause 2.
12. Trindade (2009); see also, Trindade (2011).
13. UNWGEID, 'General Comment on the right to recognition as a person before the law in the context of enforced disappearances', http://www.ohchr.org/Documents/Issues/Disappearances/GCRecognition.pdf (accessed September 13, 2024).
14. Article 5, CPED.
15. UN General Assembly, *Rome Statute of the International Criminal Court (last amended 2010)*, UN General Assembly, 17 July 1998, UNTS 2187, p. 3.
16. See for example, enforced disappearances as the result of pushbacks. Baranowska (2020).
17. *Barrios Altos v. Peru* (March 14, 2001) Series C, No. 75; *La Cantuta v. Peru*, Merits, Reparations and Costs, Series C No. 162 (29 November 2006), paras 167–9; *Almonacid Arellano et al. v. Chile*, Series C No. 154 (26 September 2006); cf *Goiburú et al. v. Paraguay*, Series C No. 153 (22 September 2006), para. 82.
18. *Flores Bedregal et al. v. Bolivia* (17 October 2022) Series C, No. 467.
19. *Prosecutor v. Ragevid & Todović*, Case No. X-KR/06/275, First Instance Verdict (28 February 2008); *Prosecutor v. Damjanović*, Case No. X-KR-05/51, First Instance Verdict (15 December 2006); *Prosecutor v. Simić*, Case No. X-KR-05/04, First Instance Verdict (11 July 2006).
20. *B.Y. v. Greece*, App. no. 60990/14 (ECtHR 26 April 2023).
21. ICC, *Situation in Burundi*, 'Public Redacted Version of "Decision Pursuant to Article 15 of the Rome Statute on the Authorization of an Investigation into the Situation in the Republic of Burundi", ICC-01/17-X-9-US-Exp, 25 October 2017', PTC-III (ICC-01/17-9-Red) (9

November 2017); ICC, *Prosecutor v. Katanga*, Minority Opinion of Judge Christine Van den Wyngaert, TCh-II (ICC-01/04-01/07-3436-AnxI_15(ENG) (7 March 2014); ICC, *Situation in Côte d'Ivoire*, Corrigendum to 'Decision Pursuant to Article 15 of the Rome Statute on the Authorisation of an Investigation into the Situation in the Republic of Côte d'Ivoire', PTC-III (ICC-02/11-14-Corr) (15 November 2011).

22. Human Rights Council, 'Study on best practices on the issue of missing persons, Interim report prepared by Prof. Latif Hüseynov, Rapporteur of the Drafting Group of the Human Rights Council Advisory Committee' (25 January 2010) UN Doc. A/HRC/AC/4/CRP.2/Rev.1.
23. *Jorge Vásquez Durand and family v. Ecuador* (23 March 2015) Series C, No. 11.458.
24. *Plan de Sánchez Massacre v. Guatemala*, para. 51.
25. Article II(b) of the Convention on the Prevention and Punishment of the Crime of Genocide stipulates that 'genocide means any of the following acts committed with intent to destroy, in whole or in part, a national, ethnical, racial or religious group, as such […] (b) causing serious bodily or mental harm to members of the group'.
26. UNWGEID, 'General comments on enforced disappearance as a crime against humanity' (21 December 2009) UN Doc. A/HRC/13/31, para. 39, op. clause 7. Yet, if perpetrators commit disappearances aimed at the destruction of a group, then their intent (*mens rea*) is genocidal (*dolus specialis*) and subsumes the intent to forcefully disappear the victims. In this framework, mass disappearances are not a crime against humanity, but part of the crime of genocide.
27. *Masacre de Mapiripán v. Colombia*, IACtHR, Series C No. 134 (15 September 2005); cf, *Cyprus v. Turkey*, ECtHR, App. no. 25781/94 (10 May 2001).
28. UNGA Res 3220 (XXIX) (6 November 1974).
29. *Ticona Estrada et al. v. Bolivia*, Inter-American Court of Human Rights Series C No. 191 (27 November 2008), para. 155.
30. *Janowiec et al. v. Russia*, App. no. 55508/07 & 29520/09 (ECtHR 21 October 2013).
31. *Ukraine v. Russia (re Crimea) [GC]*, App Nos 20958/14 & 38334/18 (ECtHR 26 June 2024).
32. *Varnava et al. v. Turkey*, App nos 16064/90, 16065/90, 16066/90, 16068/90, 16069/90, 16070/90, 16071/90, 16072/90 & 16073/90 (ECtHR 18 September 2009).

Disclosure statement

No potential conflict of interest was reported by the author(s).

References

Andreu-Guzmán, F. (2001). The draft international convention on the protection of all persons from forced disappearance. *ICJ Review – Impunity, Crimes Against Humanity and Forced Disappearance*, *73*(62–63), 80–81. https://www.icj.org/wp-content/uploads/2013/08/ICJ-Review-62-63-2001-eng.pdf

Baranowska, G. (2020). *Disappeared migrants and refugees: The relevance of the international convention on enforced disappearance in their search and protection*. German Institute for Human Rights.

Barrett, J. (2009). Chechnya's last hope – enforced disappearances and the European court of human rights. *Harvard Human Rights Journal*, *22*(1), 133.

Cassel, D. (2006–2007). The expanding scope and impact of reparations awarded by the Inter-American court of human rights. *Revista do Instituto Brasileiro de Direitos Humanos*, *7*(7), 91–107.

Chevalier-Watts, J. (2010). 'The phenomena of enforced disappearances in Turkey and Chechnya: Strasbourg's noble cause?'. *Human Rights Review*, *11*(4), 469–489. https://doi.org/10.1007/s12142-010-0156-9

Citroni, G., & Scovazzi, T. (2009). Recent developments in international law to combat enforced disappearances. *Revista Internationacional de Direito e Cidadania*, *3*(Feb), 89–111.

Claude, O. (2010). A comparative approach to enforced disappearances in the Inter-American court of human rights and the European court of human rights jurisprudence. *Intercultural Human Rights Law Review, 5*, 415. https://www.stu.edu/law/human-rights/ihrlr/past-issues/
Dimaranan, S. M. C. (1987). Increasing terror. In D. B. Schirmer & S. R. Shalom (Eds.), *The Philippines reader, A history of colonialism, neocolonialism, dictatorship and resistance* (pp. 318–320). South End Press.
Droege, C. (2008). Elective affinities? Human rights and humanitarian law. *International Review of the Red Cross, 90*(871), 509.
Dulitzky, A. E. (2019). The Latin-American flavor of enforced disappearances. *Chicago Journal of International Law, 19*(2), 447.
Egeland, J. (1982). Political 'disappearances' – A challenge for humanitarian law. *Nordic Journal of International Law, 51*(1), 189–199. https://doi.org/10.1163/157181082X00043
Finucane, B. (2010). Enforced disappearance as a crime under international law: A neglected origin in the laws of war. *Yale Journal of International Law, 35*(1) 176.
Fulton, S. (2014). Redress for enforced disappearance. *Journal of International Criminal Justice, 12*, 780.
Giorgou, I. (2014). State involvement in the perpetration of enforced disappearance and the Rome statute. *Journal of International Criminal Justice, 11*(5), 1012.
Kurban, D. (2016). Forsaking individual justice: The implications of the European court of human rights' pilot judgment procedure for victims of gross and systematic violations. *Human Rights Law Review, 16*(4), 731–769. https://doi.org/10.1093/hrlr/ngw032
Nagle, L. E. (2008). On armed conflict, human rights, and preserving the rule of law in Latin America. *Penn State International Law Review, 27*(1), 5.
Nouwen, S. M. H. (2018). Is there something missing in the proposed convention on crimes against humanity? A political question for states and a doctrinal one for the international law commission. *Journal of International Criminal Justice, 16*(4), 878.
Pérrez Solla, M. F. (2006). *Enforced disappearances in international human rights* (p. 206). McFarland & Company Inc. Publishers.
Pervou, I. (2012). The convention for the protection of all persons from enforced disappearance: Moving human rights protection ahead. *European Journal of Legal Studies, 5*(1), 165–166.
Pervou, I. (2012). Unacknowledged administrative detention: Another narrative of enforced disappearance. *Antigone, 7*(3), 124–128.
Pervou, I. (2013). The right not to be subject to enforced disappearance: Finding nemo in the international human rights regime. *Mediterranean Journal of Social Sciences, 4*(10), 104–113.
Robers, C. (2017). On the definition of crimes against humanity and other widespread or systematic human rights violations. *University of Pennsylvania Journal of Law and Social Sciences, 20*(1), 24.
Sadat, L. N. (2006). Ghost prisoners and black sites: Extraordinary rendition under international law. *Case Western Reserve Journal of International Law, 37*(2), 309.
Sadat, L. N. (2013). Crimes against humanity in the modern age. *American Journal of International Law, 107*(2), 334–377. https://doi.org/10.5305/amerjintelaw.107.2.0334
Sarkin, J. (2012). Why the prohibition of enforced disappearance has attained *Jus Cogens* status in international law. *Nordic Journal of International Law, 81*(4), 537–584. https://doi.org/10.1163/15718107-08104006
Schabas, W. A. (2017). Defining enforced disappearance as a crime against humanity. In M. Bidault, & others (Eds.), *Réciprocité et universalité: sources et régimes du droit international et des droits de l' homme: mélanges en l' honneur du Professeur Emmanuel Decaux* (p. 446). Pedone.
Scovazzi, T., & Citroni, G. (2007). *The struggle against enforced disappearance and the 2007 united nations convention* (p. 190). Martinus Nijhoff Publisher and VSP.
Sethi, G. S. (2001). The European court of human rights' jurisprudence on issues of forced disappearances. *Human Rights Brief, 8*(3), 30.
Taqi, I. (2000–2001). Adjudicating disappearance cases in Turkey: An argument for adopting the Inter-American court of human rights' approach. *Fordham International Law Journal, 24*(3), 966–967.

Trindade, A. A. C. (2009). *Jus Cogens*: The determination and the gradual expansion of its material content in contemporary international case-law. In *XXXV Curso de Derecho Internacional Organizado por el Comité Jurídico Interamericano - 2008* (pp. 3–29). General Secretariat of the OAS.

Trindade, A. A. C. (2011). The expansion of the material content of *Jus Cogens*: The contribution of the Inter-American court of human rights. In D. Spielmann, & others (Eds.), *La Convention Européenne des Droits de l' Homme, un instrument vivant – Mélanges en l'honneur de Chr.L. Rozakis* (pp. 27–47). Bruylant.

Wright, T. C. (2000). Human rights in Latin America: History and projections for the twenty-first century. *California Western International Law Journal, 30*(2), 304.

Index

FSC
www.fsc.org
MIX
Papier | Fördert gute Waldnutzung
FSC® C083411

Kolibri 360 GmbH
Ferdinand-Jühlke-Straße 7
99095 Erfurt, Deutschland
produktsicherheit@kolibri360.de